APR 1 6 2015

P9-DBT-215

THE
SELL

THE SELL

The Secrets of Selling Anything to Anyone

FREDRIK EKLUND
with Bruce Littlefield

AVERY

An imprint of Penguin Random House
375 Hudson Street
New York, New York 10014

Most Avery books are available at special quantity discounts for bulk purchase for sales promotions, premiums, fund-raising, and educational needs. Special books or book excerpts also can be created to fit specific needs. For details, write Special.Markets@us .penguingroup.com.

All photographs in the interior are courtesy of the author.

Library of Congress Cataloging-in-Publication Data

Eklund, Fredrik.
The sell : the secrets of selling anything to anyone / Fredrik Eklund,
with Bruce Littlefield.
pages cm
ISBN 978-1-592-40931-0 (hardback)
1. Success.   2. Success in business.   3. Selling—Psychological aspects.
I. Littlefield, Bruce (Bruce Duanne)   II. Title.
BF637.S8E37 2015
658.85—dc23
2014043824

Printed in the United States of America
1   3   5   7   9   10   8   6   4   2

Set in Adobe Caslon Pro
Designed by Spring Hoteling

For my brother, Sigge

CONTENTS

AN IMPORTANT MESSAGE FROM YOUR AUTHOR

My journey from small-town Sweden to the very top of the most competitive sales market in the world inspired me to write the book you're holding, and doing so has been an incredible experience. Within these pages I've included my tricks, gimmicks, aces up my sleeves, and sales secrets, but I feel it's important to <u>underline</u> something before you get started. Success takes hard work, research, knowledge, and commitment, but the real victory comes through honesty, transparency, and being true to your word. That's what makes a *truly* successful person.

The subtitle of this book is *The Secrets of Selling Anything to Anyone*, but I want to point out that some things in life are not for sale: your loved ones, your children, your pets, your values, your integrity, your beliefs, your spirituality. It's not only that they are priceless. They are *sacred*. As a super salesman, it's important to remind myself that not even I can sell certain things, especially my soul. Everything else is negotiable.

—Fredrik

FOREWORD

The first time I met Fredrik Eklund was poolside atop the SLS Hotel in Beverly Hills. I was in Hollywood shooting an episode of ABC's *Shark Tank*, and Fredrik was on the roof attracting attention. I can spot a great salesperson from across the street and certainly from across the pool. Fredrik has magnetism that's impossible to miss. At the time, I didn't know who he was (it was before *Million Dollar Listing New York*), but I did know one thing: He was a success. Fredrik Eklund has that killer instinct.

When I started my NYC real estate firm in 1973 with a $1,000 loan from a boyfriend, I had no experience in sales and no doubt that I'd be successful. Back then there weren't any female-owned real estate firms in the city. It was a business worked by women and *owned* by men. I wasn't welcome, but I certainly got noticed. From wearing my short skirts and bright colors to calling my sales team the "Power Brokers," I created my reality—that I was *the best seller in the city*. And what happened? In 1999, the Corcoran Group became the number one residential real estate company in New York City.

Fredrik, a Swede with no contacts and no real estate license, came to America, and, in less than a dozen years, leads the number one real estate sales team in the nation. Now that's the American dream. How'd he do it? He knew that perception creates reality, and he had the courage to spot and seize opportunity.

The number one trait I always looked for when I was hiring someone for my company and what I look for now when I'm investing in entrepreneurs on *Shark Tank* is passion, a *need* to succeed. Someone who'd rather die than not be the best. That's Fredrik, and after reading this book, that will be you, too.

Like any great salesperson, Fredrik is very persuasive. For example, bragging about him in this foreword wasn't enough. He even talked me into giving you my five personal beliefs about becoming a success, all of which are included in his secrets to selling anything:

1. **People want to do business with someone they like.** Don't ever be fooled into thinking that a job is only about the product. It's not. Business is all about the people. If people like you, they're going to want to work with you. And if they don't, you're going to have an almost insurmountable obstacle to overcome. Your job is to make them like you.

2. **Selling is nothing more than playing up the good and playing down the bad.** If knowing how to do this comes naturally to you, you've got a head start. If you don't, you can learn. When I worked in a diner, I was up against another

waitress to attract customers. All the men wanted to sit with her because she had big breasts. And, well, I *don't*. It was my mom who gave me my best sales (and life) advice. She told me to forget about what I didn't have, and use what I did have—a nice personality, a great smile, and the gift of gab— to get customers to want to sit in my section. I packed them in! Maximize the positive; minimize the negative.

3. **Every successful person knows how to fail well.** Successful people get knocked down like everyone else, but they take less time getting back up and back out there. Did you know the lowest rate of suicide is among commission salespeople? Why? Because they deal with so many rejections on a daily basis, they are more adept at handling life's hard knocks.

4. **Everybody wants what everybody wants.** This is the basic psychology of sales. Your task is to figure out how to make people think that what you've got to offer is the best thing since hot dogs and baseball. Two things to remember: More than one buyer creates urgency, and when people are told they can't have something, they want it all the more.

5. **The most successful people believe their success is only temporary.** Top producers end each year convinced they'll never have another year as good. Their own track record becomes their biggest competition. In great successes, fear breeds accomplishment.

For twenty-five years I managed New York's top sellers, and I know how hard successful people work to keep their trade secrets. So, why would you give it all away when you're number one? Why would you create thousands of new successful high-kickers? Let it be known: I think Fredrik is nuts for sharing his secrets, but I suppose a real success isn't afraid of competition. He thrives on it.

I leave you in good hands . . . and on the road to making millions.

—Barbara Corcoran
Bestselling author of
*Shark Tales: How I Turned $1,000
into a Billion Dollar Business*

INTRODUCTION

Make 'Em Want What You've Got

I became a salesman when I was seven years old. I was living in Stockholm, where I was born, and I signed up with a company I heard about through school to sell Christmas calendars and books. Those who sold the most each week would win a waterproof, yellow Sony Walkman. (Remember those?) I decided I didn't just want to sell a lot; I wanted to be the number one seller among the thousands of kids selling Christmas calendars in Sweden. I was going to sell more than *anyone*!

My goal made me obsessed. I went to bed every night, and, like a prisoner counting the days on his jail-cell wall, I charted on the wallpaper of my room a matrix-like plan to world-calendar-sales domination. When my dad came across my scribbles, he was *arg*! (That's Swedish for *angry*!) But it was too late! The writing was literally on the wall: I was on my way to becoming the biggest seller.

Every morning, I put on my favorite sweater my grandmother had hand-knitted for me, with two reindeers on the front, loaded all the catalogs on a sled, and went knocking door-to-door, schlepping my wares through the snow into Akalla, a suburb north of Stockholm. I knew the market because it was my neighborhood. A million homes were built there during the 1970s, and many retired people had moved in. The old ladies were my favorite targets, a captive audience for a friendly kid with a selling smile. I'd knock on their doors and take a step back so that when they answered, I'd be perfectly positioned to look up at them so they could notice my cute sweater. I'd say, "Hi. It's me, Fredrik. It's nice to see you again." Almost always, they'd invite me in. I became the grandson who was finally visiting. I sat with them and talked, talked, talked and sold, sold, sold. I made them *want* to buy a calendar from me.

The result? I drank a lot of green tea that winter, listened to more than my fair share of World War II stories, and broke all records for the calendar company. And I really mean *all* records. I even got a letter from the president of the company asking what my secret was. (But I kept the secrets for this book and am sending him a signed copy as my answer, exactly thirty years later!) I also won so many Walkmans that I sold them, too—to my classmates at school!

Today I use the same technique I used on the Swedish grannies when I'm showing million-dollar properties to Jennifer Lopez, Cameron Diaz, Leonardo DiCaprio, Justin Timberlake, Daniel Craig, or a family from the Upper West Side, and convincing them the time to buy is *now*—from *me*.

But you don't have to work on commission to benefit from my selling strategies. Because let me tell you something: You've been in sales your whole life, even if you haven't realized it. Have you been on a date where you dressed your best and turned on the charm? You were selling. Have you asked someone to take out the trash because you were tired and didn't want to? You were selling. Have you interviewed for a job? You were selling. That's why *The Sell* is for everyone. It describes all of the sales each of us make every day, even if our job title isn't "salesperson." Regardless of the industry you're in—Christmas calendars, Internet, real estate, baking, motherhood—understand this right here, right now: It's *all the same. If you know how to sell* you, *you know how to sell anything.* Whether you're selling medical equipment to a doctor or an early bedtime to your third grader, The Sell is a daily event in everyone's life.

What do sellers do? They persuade, influence, and convince someone to give them something in exchange for what they've got. How is that different from trying to convince your boss to support your idea? Or trying to talk your husband into going on a vacation to Tahiti when he'd rather go to Tokyo? Anytime we want someone to do something, we are putting The Sell into action. We sell a smile to get the better table in a restaurant, a kind remark to get our way with customer service, and sincerity to form long-lasting friendships. That is selling. Whether it is a car buyer's money, a coworker's help, your teenager's attention, or a best friend's guidance, realizing how to motivate someone into taking action is The Sell.

Are people buying what you're selling?

Are they buying *you*?

A decade ago, I moved to New York City from Sweden with a pair of sneakers and a dream: to make it to the top in the city that never sleeps. I didn't have a clue then as to how I'd actually make that happen or even what my career path would be, but I absolutely believed I would be the best. I believed in the only product I had: *me*. In my fairy tale, I knew that one day, regardless of the industry I chose, I'd be the king of New York. I visualized headlines, glamour, and a wallet stuffed with hundred-dollar bills. I knew it wasn't going to be easy in the most cutthroat city in the world, but I was ready for the battle.

My story began in the suburbs of Stockholm, Sweden. That's Sve*eee*den, wedged between Norway and Finland in Northern Europe and far away from big and glitzy Manhattan. Yes, it's very cold and dark in the winters, and, no, it is not Switzerland. (I've discovered a lot of Americans confuse the two.) And there are no ice bears (I'm told you call them polar bears) roaming around the streets, just a bunch of tall, blond people with blue eyes who love vodka, dancing the frog dance on Midsummer's Eve (intoxicated by the former), building safe cars, designing low-cost furniture that you put together yourself, rolling out stores with inexpensive clothes all over the world, and writing catchy pop music you love to hate (or hate to love).

We didn't have a lot of money when I was young, but my parents always made sure we got to travel. When I was ten years old, my father, Klas Eklund, a Swedish economist, unknowingly changed the course of my life. He had been invited to give a speech in New York City and exchanged the first-class ticket he had received for three economy tickets and brought my older brother, Sigge, and me with him.

Even as I am writing this, I still remember the yellow cab picking us up outside JFK Airport, the reggae music on the radio, the almost tropical heat as I rolled the window down in the backseat and dropped my head outside to see the approaching skyline.

I am sitting there again now, ten years old, and you are sitting next to me. Are you with me?

Feel the hot vinyl seat; roll down the window; smell that humid, sweet, and hopeful autumn air of 1987 New York. We are on this journey together, you and me.

The city's energy, excitement, and vertical living instantly hooked me. There was also a dark side to Gotham that I loved. I could smell the danger. At dusk, the cab took us through Times Square with its neon fireworks, and my jaw dropped. I could see the poor, the rich, and the gaps in between. The thousands of tourists with cameras signaled that *this* was the center of the universe. I believe there are certain impressions in life that are so strong they are etched into the neurons of your brain forever and actually change that chemical soup permanently. This was one of those moments. The second was my first commission check. The third was falling in love, and I hope seeing the face of my newborn daughter will someday be one, too.

My father, Sigge, and I climbed to the top of the Statue of Liberty, and I got to see her perspective of the glimmering city across the water, a beehive of excitement. There is a photo of me up in her crown, looking out, and you can see in my eyes how awestruck I was. I had the vision of my liberation. I decided right then and there that I would become one with the city. I would

I often think that until this moment, our family had been my little solar system. My brother and I were the planets orbiting the sun, our family home back in Stockholm. But suddenly the laws of gravitation were bent, perhaps because I saw another sun through the windows of the Statue of Liberty: New York. This sun symbolized a new goal: freedom, success, and the ultimate sell.

become very successful, but more important, someone who was following his dreams.

As we ferried back to shore, the rain came down hard and we had to run without cover from the boat in the Financial District just south of the Twin Towers to hide in a steakhouse with red leather seats and cigarette smoke. *Just like the movies*, I thought. *I will come back here. I will live here one day! I will create my own life.*

Fifteen years later, when I realized that dream and moved to Manhattan, I instantly felt at home and that anything was possible. New York was magical to me, and it still is. Just walking down Fifth Avenue in the heat of the summer makes my heart race with excitement. It is empowering to look up at the skyscrapers, watching them defy gravity and reaching—like all the dreamers in this city—higher and higher.

I moved with a few Swedish friends into a one-bedroom rental apartment on Thirty-Seventh Street in midtown across from Macy's. I didn't know anyone in New York, but we Swedes felt a certain companionship in our proud but naive attempt to leave Sweden and not look back. I did miss my family, but my drive to make it in my new hometown was stronger. I kept thinking that the only time to create my future self was now. Not tomorrow. Not next month or next year. *Now.*

I got a job selling panini outside the *Late Show with David Letterman* for forty dollars a day (plus one dry, but free, leftover panino for lunch), and I worked as a bartender for a grand total of three nights. I was pretty good at selling sandwiches, but it was hardly why I came to New York, and I hated bartending because I was lousy at it. That's when I started looking for a book like the one you have in your hand, an instruction manual for becoming successful, a book that could tell me how to recognize and cultivate my true talents. The books I found felt old or were written by someone I couldn't relate to. I wanted a modern handbook about reinventing myself and selling all I have to offer to the world.

I didn't find that book, but a friend did suggest my personality might be a good fit for selling residential real estate. So I took an accelerated real-estate-salesperson course at New York University and got my license in two weeks. I had no business contacts or a Rolodex of any New Yorkers' names. I didn't know Chinatown from Tribeca or Lexington Avenue from Madison, but I did know one thing: I had an insatiable hunger for success. I browsed the Internet and clicked on the city's most expensive apartments and read the bios of the salespeople that controlled them. I fantasized that one day I'd be one of them and find myself on top of the world—literally.

Today I am the number one real estate agent in New York City, the most competitive real estate market on the planet. I currently have $1 billion worth of residential property for sale on the market split between New York and Scandinavia, which is more than any other agent in the country. Last year, my teams in New York and Sweden earned a total of $20 million in commissions, and my New York team made $4 million last month alone (which I believe is a record in the history of the city).

In my ten years, I've closed on more than $3.5 billion in real estate—$1 billion in the first five years of business, another $1 billion in the following three, another $1 billion in the following two, and a bit more than $500 million in the last year alone. Several times this year I've sold more than $100 million in property in a single month. I compete with more than thirty thousand licensed real estate professionals on an island two miles wide and thirteen miles long, with more wealth concentrated in a small area than any other place in the world with the exception of London and Tokyo. I have sold out more than twenty-five buildings in new development and have a team of eleven people in NYC working for the largest real estate brokerage on the East Coast, Douglas Elliman, where my team is number one in the nation.

Out of one million real estate salespeople in the United States, and more than twenty million worldwide, I lead one of the top teams in the world, and I'm certainly the youngest among the top ten team leaders. I also have offices in Sweden and Norway with more than fifty employees working for my own brands there, Eklund Stockholm New York and Eklund Oslo New York, and have plans to open in Finland, Denmark, and the United Kingdom. Oh, and then there is the Emmy-nominated hit show on Bravo you might have heard of called *Million Dollar Listing New York*, which airs in more than 110 countries and follows me (and Ryan Serhant and Luis Ortiz) as we represent multimillion-dollar sellers in New York City, the real estate capital of the world. Movie site IMDb describes our show's premise as "follows some of Manhattan's most relentless Realtors as they close multimillion dollar deals faster than a yellow cab runs a red light." I couldn't have said it better myself.

I'm not telling you all this to brag. That will come later. This is to help you understand that if a kid off the shrimp boat from Sweden can make it big, you can, too. You, too, can be the best at what you do, whatever it is. *You are no different.* You probably even understand the language and know a few more people than I did. You have a leg up! Plus, you have this book in your hand. So, high-kick!

. . .

My story is evidence that anyone can sell what they've got, against all odds, and reach the very top. Whether you're offering the world terrific shoes; software; books; homes; legal, financial, or insurance services; massages; dentistry; airline tickets; tuna; or tamales—you name it—if you want to be successful, *The Sell* is essential reading. Yes, even if you are not going to work to sell every day, you still need this book. Any dreamer, anyone with a desire to excel in life, will find this book helpful.

I designed this book to make *you* the best you can be and to take you to the very top of whatever you can dream. I share everything I have learned and experienced in my life to become number one, all the ups and downs, my secret techniques, my failures, my many successes, and my unique way of looking at the world. I hope to make you laugh out loud, cry, take notes, and tell your friends about it. I want you to mark the pages, circle paragraphs, and underline sentences so that one day, when you run into me, we can discuss it.

But in the end, this book isn't about me. *The Sell* is about *you*.

You have the gift of The Sell inside you, and I am just here to activate it. It's like pushing a little button. Everyone's button is different, so finding that button within you is the first step. Once your engine is ignited, it cannot be stopped. Are you ready to locate that button? Are you scared of pushing it? Well, I'm not, and I cannot wait to get started. With you.

Let's make you a huge success.

There's a gold rush on—to your best selling self—and this book is your pickax. If you're not selling what you've got to offer every day, you're not making a better life for yourself and those you love. Young or old, The Sell never stops. Believe me, I may be selling multimillion-dollar penthouses now, but later I'll be selling those nurses in the old-age home on giving me that extra chocolate chip cookie.

But this isn't your granddad's sales book. This book won't tell you how to be slimy, pushy, or insincere. In the twenty-first century that old hunk of cheese won't work. The techniques of yesteryear are as antiquated as a cassette tape. The world has changed drastically in the last five years alone, so it's time to throw out all those old ideas and get with the program.

In the coming pages, I'm going to spill my secrets and share with you the tricks I've figured out to finding the real you and then making people love you and want what you've got. I say "secrets," because up to this day I have never shared them with anyone. Many have asked, and every time I have smiled and looked down in silence. I say "tricks" because in countless media interviews, reporters always want to know the "key" to my success, and my standard answer to all of them has been the same as it was to *The New York Times* a few years back: "to work harder than anyone else." There is some truth in that, but I was saving the real secrets for this book.

Each chapter of *The Sell* will help you be more effective in coming into your own, building relationships, establishing trust, and mastering the art of persuasion. I've broken down the book into three parts.

In part 1, you're going to learn how to

- embrace who you really are and share yourself with the world;

- identify your personal motivations and drive;
- get in the game;
- make yourself attractive;
- work out, eat right, and get your beauty sleep; and
- develop a sense of humor and charm.

Part 2 will provide you with step-by-step instructions on how to

- find people who want your services;
- craft the perfect message;
- negotiate the best deal; and
- make the sell and claim your reward.

Then, in part 3 I'm going to tell you how to

- get people to want to work with you;
- grab attention;
- grow your business;
- turn failures into victories; and
- enjoy your success!

For now, all you have to do is ask yourself, *Do I want to have more personal and professional success and lead a rich and fulfilling life?*

If your answer is yes, let's get started by making an important pact together: Someone has to be the best and living large, so why not you? Why not me? I think we both can agree: We deserve it!

PART
ONE

Whether you're selling cars or writing a blog, working in advertising or hawking hot dogs, *you* are your brand and your product. Never forget that. In order to be successful, you must learn to cultivate your brand and sell your wares through your personal strengths. When you know yourself and show people just who you are, you can accomplish absolutely anything. Being unaware of your strengths and weaknesses, likes and dislikes, abilities and inabilities is like trying to drive a car without gas. You can push the pedal, flash the lights, and spin the wheel all you want, but you're not going to get anywhere.

Each chapter of part 1 is designed to help you find *you*—the real you—and then help you figure out your biggest motivator, perfect your personal style, and make yourself more confident, enthusiastic, charming, and better prepared. The result is that we're going to get everyone to love you.

Now turn the page!

CHAPTER 1

BE *YOU*

Forget Selling—Begin by Finding Yourself

We're off! But first, I think an introduction is needed. I'm Fredrik. Nice to meet you! It's such a pleasure shaking your hand. Let's celebrate this moment. Look around. We are here, we are alive, and we are on our way to realizing our destiny. I congratulate you for being you. You are beautiful and are going to be everything you are meant to be. And if no one told you they love you today, I will—and I do.

How you connect with other people using your charm, intelligence, authenticity, humor (and looks) is a barometer for how well you persuade, inspire, and gain confidence. (And how much money you make.) It is also critical to how effective you'll be in promoting yourself whether you're pitching Donald Trump on a $2 billion development, or a fashion editor on your new design, or yourself via your profile on Match.com.

Every day—no matter what your station in life or your line of work—*you are selling yourself.* You. Are. Your. Brand. And. Your. Product. In business, it's important to know your product, but it's more important to know yourself and what you bring to the table. People trust what's genuine. You're not out to pull the wool over anyone's eyes. No amount of money or success is worth losing your good name.

SHOW PEOPLE JUST WHO YOU ARE

Let me tell you how being true to myself not only saved me, but made me, too.

After high school I applied to the Stockholm School of Economics, one of the premier business schools in Europe. Each year thousands of people apply and only three hundred are accepted—I was one of them. I knew I was one of the privileged, but it honestly didn't make me feel accomplished or right.

The Stockholm School of Economics was filled with young men and women, most from good families, all competitive, who dressed up for dinner parties and were destined to be bankers. At orientation on the first day, J. P. Morgan and Goldman Sachs brought sandwiches into the auditorium and presented a future I really wasn't interested in. The school was an institution, and as I walked down the marble-clad halls with cathedral ceilings, I felt I didn't have another four and a half years to give until graduation. I wanted to live right then and there, to get out in the sunshine and build something.

The final death to me was in statistics class my first semester, with its auditorium full of formulas and graphs. Everyone had to sit still for hours, taking notes, and all I could do was show up and tune out. I had a hard time sitting still, and to this day I still can't sit still for too long. I looked out the windows and imagined, *What if I could see the Empire State Building outside instead of the summer gardens dying in the crisp fall winds? How would that make me feel?*

As I was realizing the Stockholm School of Economics wasn't my thing, a friend introduced me to a girl named Maria who had an idea to build an Internet start-up offering customer-relationship-management software. Internet shopping was still in its infancy and hadn't really caught on with most consumers. Maria wanted to solve the missing human touch by giving online shoppers a virtual assistant, or avatar, to answer questions and help at checkout—Siri before Siri.

Maria needed a go-getter to help her find seed money. And she didn't have to ask me twice. That summer, Maria and I wrote the business plan in the computer room at my business school and went looking for investors willing to provide financial backing for a start-up, a.k.a. "angel investors." We bought student-discounted airline tickets for fifty dollars and flew to Paris to meet with potential venture capitalist types. We slept on the sofa of Maria's high school friend and came home with $1 million dollars, successfully selling 50 percent of the company before it really existed. And that's when I decided I wasn't going back to school.

I dropped out and (then) told my parents I was done with studying. My dad asked me to stay, telling me that an education is for *life*, something that no one could take away from me, ever. I said my *life* is my life, and no statistics professor can take it away from me, ever. My classmates thought I was crazy and told me I was making the biggest mistake of my life. I told them they would see, that I was going to prove them wrong. I hugged them good-bye and wished them well on their own journeys.

Big start-ups were hot, and Sweden was ahead of the curve. Mature, successful guys from the old business world were trying to find ways to climb aboard the new, faster economy. They knew they needed to get a horse in the tech race or be left behind, and they wanted to pair with young, smart tech types on the cutting edge. My father, a former speechwriter with the Swedish government, gave me the e-mail address of former Swedish prime minister Carl Bildt and several powerful, high-profile, and wealthy businessmen.

I sent an e-mail to Mr. Bildt and four or five other major names. I didn't worry if I was important enough. I took action before doubt could rear its ugly head. The e-mail simply said to show up at this address, at this time; we have an interesting Internet start-up, and we know you'll want to be a part of it. Maria and I set up a PowerPoint in a boardroom we'd rented for the day, complete with graphs of how much the company was going to be worth. They all came. Each saw the other familiar faces in the room and realized they couldn't (or shouldn't) say no. We offered each of them a small piece of the company in exchange for their names, experience, and faces. Attaching these power players, with their fifty or so years of political and business savvy, gave me—the twenty-year-old entrepreneur—huge street cred.

Two years later, we had more than forty employees and everything felt possible. According to the business plan, we were going to become the number one customer-relationship-management software company in the world. Our new company, Humany.com, was going to take on Oracle. I was the CEO and the youngest person in the company, and with Carl Bildt on the board, we landed on the front page of many Swedish magazines and even got a write-up in the *Financial Times*. The Internet was now on everyone's agenda. The new economy was on fire, and the Swedish media made me the IT whiz kid and placed me on the cover of our most popular magazine wearing a big smile and a Hawaiian shirt while standing in front of the former prime minister.

Working that hard, day and night, kept me sharply focused, and my outrageous dream to move to New York tamed. People said I was the perfect entrepreneur. The press called me a "risk taker," an "aggressive salesman," and a "tough negotiator" with a "strong sense of intuition." At first, I had to sell only an idea, then a company that didn't exist, and finally software that was still being programmed. By the time our software was finished (and didn't actually work), the Internet bubble was beginning to burst and so was my head. I was tired and confused. Most of these new start-ups were falling apart. Ours was, too, and our working relationship unraveled along with it. Maria and I began arguing about everything.

It was the turn of the new millennium, I was twenty-three years old, and it was still many years before Facebook and Twitter were founded. Things in the Internet bubble had to happen so quickly; the pressure to grow *and* be profitable at the same time was contradictory, and the investors and media pushed us to chase more money—or go bankrupt. I remember taking a cab home to the apartment Maria and I had bought together, going into my half of it, and crying by myself. I cried because I was exhausted, and I could see the inevitability of our business's collapse. I started to feel like a failure. It was too much at once. I had all these peoples' (and their families') futures in my hands, and I had no real experience in a world that was crumbling.

Failure was new to me, and I hadn't yet come to understand that failure is inevitable if you want to be wildly successful (more on that later). I briefly thought, as many do in similar situations, that there would never be another opportunity for me, that I'd never climb out of the mess I was in. I've now realized that we are all a combination of failure and success. Like experiencing joy and pain, without one, we'd never know the other.

As they say, I pulled myself up by my bootstraps, sold my shares in the company I had started just two years earlier, and got out. I made the very complicated decision to be true to my dreams and to leave the company, my family, and Sweden for New York . . . by myself.

Before I left, I decided there was one more thing I needed to do. I needed to tell my friends and family about the real me, to "come out." I broke up with my beautiful girlfriend, Simone, who was devastated, and I finally gathered the courage to tell my brother, my mother, and my friends that I was attracted to boys. A few months later, after I had fallen in love again, it was time to tell my father. My dad and I had a nice dinner at the new summer house he'd just bought, and before bed, he asked if I'd help him take the garbage up to the bin by the road. I was incredibly nervous, but it was pitch black out, and I couldn't see him, so that (and the wine at dinner) made it a little easier. I said, "Dad, I'm in love with someone." He asked me what her name was, and I said, "his name." He stopped. He was quiet. Then he said, "Fredrik, you are my son, and I will always love you. You can love whomever you want." My family and friends all proved supportive and assured me they loved me regardless.

Without being the true me—both personally and professionally—I'd never be writing this line right now. I acknowledge that as difficult as that six-month period was for me—quitting my company, coming out to my loved ones, and finally moving from Sweden—I had it easier than many others out there. But here's what occurs to me. Often the things we think are going to be hard are just hard to start. Once it's set in motion, it's liberating. I suppose it's sort of like jumping out of an airplane. The only real resistance is ourselves, our fear of the unknown. Whatever we need to do to live honestly and whatever transition we need to make in order to follow our dreams and be true to ourselves is the path we should take.

As excited as I was boarding my flight to New York, I was torn, and my head was a swirl of emotions. Had I made the right decision? Would I ever recover? How could I make it starting all over in a city where I didn't know a soul? I shook off my doubts and buckled up for the ride. I had no choice but to make it work. I wasn't going to come back with a broken tail between my legs. I was going to make everyone (and myself) proud. Because I had to.

YOU BEING YOU

I've learned the hard way that to be successful *and* happy in life we have to really be ourselves and showcase our true personalities. It's such a simple thing to say, but what a difficult thing to discover and carry out. Take note: The number one mistake you can make is watering down your true self because you're afraid others can't handle the 100-proof you. Don't fall for this. Failing to speak your truth and share yourself with the world in an open, honest way is a costly miscalculation. Many people go to great lengths to hide their true selves because they fear who they are is not the person they're supposed to be. Erase all that. *You are supposed to be you.*

Rather than reaching for the stars with everything they've got, many people let self-doubt and insecurity take over. Maybe you *are* inexperienced, but you can still be unique. Stop comparing yourself to others and realize that while you may not have the same things others have to offer, what you do have to offer—you—is enough. You just need to figure out who you are and play to your strengths.

Whether you're an actress from Springfield on her first Hollywood audition, an entrepreneur pitching his first start-up company to a venture capital firm, or, as I was just over a decade ago, an enthusiastic and ambitious (but also terrified!) young Swede trying to sell real estate in a foreign land with little relevant prior experience and no local contacts, your fundamental challenge is to establish other peoples' trust in you. And trust, after all, begins with one thing and one thing only: the truth.

If you want people to believe in you and in what you have to offer, you have to believe in yourself. So I say this: Step out into the world as boldly and confidently as you can. Be yourself and let people see exactly who you are. And, as people get to know you, share your personal story and allow your full personality to shine.

Now, let's hear about that story!

Look at yourself in the mirror. Take a good, long look. What makes you *you*? I need to know. The world needs to know. You *must* know. Why? That's your secret-power source.

What makes me *me*? *I have a European background, an impish sense of humor, deft social skills, and fun hobbies including cooking, photography, and taking care of my dogs.* Whatever your unique qualities and passions may be, they are your ammunition when you're with a customer, a client, your boss, a love interest, or whomever it is you're trying to sell your products, services, or self to. In the beginning of your career, as my story proves, sometimes personality is the only thing you've got.

We all make the same mistakes. We run scared of ourselves.

When I started, I was so nervous working in my first office that I often pretended to be somebody I wasn't. I thought making jokes would be inappropriate and that my signature, attention-getting high-kick—in which I raise one leg and scream, "Weeee!"—would get me fired. I thought I should hide my Swedish heritage and work on toning down my accent because I feared clients would think I had just gotten off the boat from Europe and knew nothing about New York real estate.

Other people can smell nervousness and insecurities like a shark smells blood. These things can be cute on a first date but never when you're asking people to trust you in business or with the largest financial decision of their lives. The first secret of this book is that the only way to conquer those nerves is by being your true self.

Break the ice, make some jokes, kick in the air, give your customer tickets to a Yankees or Dodgers or Cardinals game, compliment your client on her sparkly shoes, give your buyer a high five, or do what I have done at least once: Jump out into the middle of Fifth Avenue, stop traffic, and scream, "I love New York!"

Be loud, even weird. Tell the client a very personal story. Let your boss become a cocreator of your success by sharing your goals and dreams. Be anything but quiet and boring as long as you are yourself. Yes, I am telling you this: It is much better to be dumped by your client—or your coach or lover—for being too out there and memorable than for being too withdrawn and easily forgotten.

People will always forgive you—probably adore you—for being eccentric, but they will never forgive you (if they even notice you) for being boring. You've heard that cliché of thinking outside the box. I'm telling you to throw the box away. Forget the rules of normalcy. I'm not suggesting you join the freak show, but showcase your originality. Find your points of difference. You will rise to the top in your career by being a little unconventional. If you don't believe me, consider what happens in my industry. Hordes of newly licensed real estate professionals come out every year, and only a few become winners. The crazy and happy ones, not the normal and bitter ones, become the real superstars—the ones people will remember (and recommend) long after they do business with them.

No matter what job, endeavor, or industry you're in, the sooner you start being *you* and not some fabrication of what your mind thinks a successful robot from that world should act like, you will be on the road to big success. Why? People love being around someone who is comfortable and happy in his or her own skin. It is always a beautiful thing to watch, and it cuts through any resistance.

GETTING PAST NO

What's that? Yes. I know, I know. You've been beaten down. You've had pain. You've endured a lot of sh*t! People have told

I look after my miniature dachshunds, Mousey and Fritzy, and they look after me. When the world tells me no, their eyes always tell me yes.

you no so many times you want to get in bed, crawl under the covers with your favorite furries, like my Fritzy and Mousey, and never come out!

Well, since the world has told you no, let me take a moment to tell you *yes! Yes to you!*

Have you ever heard that life is 10 percent what happens to you and 90 percent how you respond to it? I couldn't agree more. Your response to any situation either moves you happily forward or holds you frustratingly back. It's time to move forward. Won't you please step inside Freud-rik's School of Psychodynamics, where we figure out the relationship between our inner life and the outside world?

I'm so glad you could come. Take a seat. We're going to talk to little you. You know, the little you at four years old. See that little self of you sitting there? You're sooooo cute! Where'd you get that darling outfit? You're bubbly, fun, and full of personality. You skip around the yard with a big smile on your face. You sing loudly in the tub. You love to giggle. Your teacher says you're an amazing artist. And you have the best lemonade stand in the neighborhood because you are the one standing behind it!

Now, what happened between that kid you were then and the *you* you are now? Did people call you names? Hurt your feelings? Were you abandoned by a loved one? Did your frenemies make you cry? Did your parents tell you to be a doctor instead of an artist? Did you give up on a dream and settle for less? It happened to all of us!

I've never told anyone this story, but I'll tell you now. I've always had really long eyelashes above my really blue eyes. When I was fourteen years old, the older guys in the schoolyard began making fun of me by saying I had "girly eyes." They would yell at me in their pubescent voices, "Look at him! He has girly eyes!" I died inside. I became so scared to pass those boys in the hall that one day I went home and used my mom's manicure scissors to cut off my eyelashes. My mom asked if I had burned myself, and I just nodded. I felt so ashamed I couldn't even tell my mom why I did it. I was trying to remedy a problem that I didn't even have.

But here's how the world works. Last week, I was out with Jennifer Lopez, showing her $20 million penthouses. We were standing on a terrace overlooking all of downtown Manhattan. She turned to me, took one step closer, as the sun must have been hitting my eyes, and said, "You have the bluest, most beautiful eyes. . . ." I thought of those boys back in Sweden and forgave them. My husband tells me that almost every day, but somehow I think J. Lo saying it makes a better ending to this story.

I'm telling you, we have to let it go. We don't want to spend any energy replaying the tape of those past hurts, holding on to past mistakes, failures, and sadness. You're safe now! You made it.

We are on a penthouse terrace together. Let's move on. Because the new you is actually the old you—the person you were before the world got you down.

Think of what Picasso said: "All children are artists. The problem is how to remain an artist once he grows up." I say don't grow up! As kids, we are amazing. We're colorful. We're eccentric. We're full of life. Then a lifetime of sniggers, side eyes, and naysayers encourages us to blend in, be like everyone else, be boring. Guess what? Boring is, well, *boring*!

I'm not saying you have to be loud or weird to be successful, but you do have to find what makes you special. You can be exciting and interesting, even if you're not an extrovert. Okay, fine. So you think you are boring. Let's talk about that, too. You didn't used to be boring, did you? Look back in your life. You had color; you had laughter; you had vision and dreams. Remember when you got so excited playing with your Transformers and Barbies, building sand castles, singing with your hairbrush microphone, or riding your bike? Let's go back there. Not to the activity itself, but to the *joy* you felt performing the activity. The key to success is going back there and finding that you. That's the real you, the exciting you, the happy you, the *you* others want to be around.

Someone very smart once said that happiness is temporary but that joy is eternal and love is recognizing that joy in others. I forgot who said it; maybe I just made it up? But I'm glad I did. Because when you are yourself and find joy in all you do and who you are, no one can take that away from you.

Need help getting there? Look at a child. Watch him play or eat an ice cream cone. It's like looking into the face of God. There's nothing wrong with a child having fun. In fact, we applaud it. But suddenly we get to be adults and the fun must die. We look at ourselves and wonder, *What is wrong with me?* It's a downward spiral into the vortex of the deadly uninteresting. You can make the decision to be sad for what you don't have or glad for what you do have.

I've got some good news. You can choose to start your day over again at any time. So, here at Freud-rik's School of Psychodynamics, we're going to pull out our erasers and wipe away all of those people who have put us down, the teacher who told us no, the bully who punished us for being different. If you want, write the names of the worst offenders on a piece of paper and literally erase them. Or if it makes you feel better, scratch them out! Scratch hard. They don't matter anymore. They are yesterday. This is *today*! We can start again.

Reidentify yourself! Spin around. Do the moonwalk. Skip around the room. Give yourself permission to be fun you again. All the great entrepreneurs I know are big kids. I certainly am. So find the playful kid in you and put him or her on your shoulder. That crazy kid is the first member of your new winning team. Bounce ideas off young you, push thoughts through that prism, and your work becomes more beautiful than it was before.

Do this and you're definitely on your way to improving your business! What's the worst that can happen? Um, let's see. . . . You start enjoying your life? If you can't be out there being the *you* you really are, you are wasting time (and your life)! Yes, you'll get by, working hard but making very little, and enjoying it even less. You'll become old, tired, and bitter, and, quite frankly, there are already too many old, bitter, underwhelming people in the world going to bed each night after pretending to be someone they aren't all day.

Finding that authentic, unique you is the secret to mastering the art of The Sell.

**STEPS FOR BURSTING OUT OF YOUR SHELL
AND BEING YOUR TRUE SELF**

Now, how do you do that? How do you find and express the real *you*? I know it sounds easy, but for a lot of people it isn't. Don't despair. You can do it in five easy steps:

1. **Look inside.** In today's society, with everyone on social media trying to prove how happy and accomplished we are, life can sometimes feel like a giant competition, but it's not. On some level it is a race, yes, but it's only a race against yourself. You are your own competition. We all start and end the race alone, which is a beautiful thing if you give it some thought. And one of the first rules of business is to know your competition, which in this case means knowing yourself.

   How do you describe yourself? Are you funny? Empathetic? Do you have an interesting talent? Do you juggle, read palms, know some sleight of hand? Are you an amazing cha-cha dancer? Do you play sports? Whatever that is, you're going to want to play that up. Capitalize on it. Don't be scared to bring out your box of tricks, make them stronger or louder. Show it off. It'll make others fall in love with you, the real you.

2. **Find your trademark.** Tarzan has his yell, Louboutin has his red sole, and I have my high-kick. They all were born out of a need to stand out. Let me tell you how the high-kick came about. I invented it around the age of fourteen. I had been

growing so fast, so quickly that I used to wake up in the middle of the night with extreme growing pains in my legs. I grew a foot in just two years, and it was borderline freaky. I was suddenly tall, but the weird thing about my body is that it was (and still is!) almost all legs. Every time I saw my grandmother, she literally didn't recognize me. So, I created a high-kick with my long legs to make my grandmother laugh and remember me. It worked. And now it makes everyone remember me.

What do you have? Do you have a signature? I used to try to get my business partner, John, to wear pink bow ties. He finally told me he hates bow ties, but he loves pink shirts. You must be comfortable with your trademark. Even if it's something small—a wacky broach, plaid socks, or a pocket square—find it and make it the billboard of *you*. You need it, it will make you memorable, and in the future that trademark will work for you even when you sleep—because others will copy it and spread *you* further into the world.

3. **Get over what other people think.** Let go of trying to please everyone or live up to anyone's expectations. It just doesn't work, and that's a proven fact. I always say to my team that you can fool everyone (for a while) but you can never fool yourself: When you go to bed at night, you know the truth, and that's the only thing that really matters. If you are not true to yourself and try to change yourself for others, you'll grow sad because no matter how much approval you gain from others, you will not approve of yourself. You are the one you need to make happy.

Be yourself; everyone else is already taken. Start with you and then others will be so comfortable around you, they'll have to love you. It might take a little time, but the wait will be worth it. I do know successful people who are hiding their true selves, and I know how empty their success feels because it isn't really theirs; it is someone else's they have copied or borrowed from. There's a great quote that everyone thinks is by Dr. Seuss (but is really by Bernard Baruch): "Be who you are and say what you feel because those that matter don't mind and those that mind don't matter." You were born to be you. Don't let anyone tell you otherwise. You are fabulous. And once you realize this, everyone else will, too, except the never-ending carousel of jealous naysayers (but more on their important function later)!

4. **Know what revs your engine.** What makes you smile? What makes you feel loved? Do you like a challenge? Do you enjoy working with people? Do you want your work to have an impact on your life and the lives of others? What do you dream of? Psychologists say the three biggest motivators are the need for *achievement*, the need for *affiliation*, and the need for *power*. Determine what combination of these things makes you the most excited to get up in the morning, and that will help shape your success. Mine is achievement, for sure. My entire life I've wanted to feel accomplished, as if I had achieved something, perhaps even something to be remembered for. Power, to me, is such a fleeting thing and not interesting unless you use it for good. Affiliation is probably the least interesting in my life, and I never felt any need to

belong to any clubs or associations, to be a member of something; if anything I was a loner who had always traveled by myself and loved to be in the minority of opinions. So what are yours? Let me hear them.

5. **Embrace failure.** In a competitive world, authenticity rises to the top. Accept your failures, as I have with my Internet disaster, just as you do your successes. That means admit your mistakes—we'll talk about some of mine later—as easily as you celebrate your triumphs. Take it one step further and really incorporate your failures into your successes, make them yin and yang. Wear your successes *and* your failures on your sleeve, with an open heart. Speak your truth and tell people your story, just as I have with you.

    If you're always 100 percent you, you'll be able to put your head down on the pillow at night and sleep well, and wake up again each morning ready to take on the world. This is something that being on television has really taught me: The more real I am, the more open I am about my failures and insecurities, the more love I've gotten. I once got completely humiliated on television, and after much resistance, I just gave in. I cried, and I let go. And it was the best thing for me. Not the character Fredrik that people love to watch on TV, but for me inside, my true self—to let my guard down and be okay with it.

Let me take this lesson of being *you* to the extreme by sharing another aspect of my experience living The Sell. When I am working with celebrities, I have learned that being myself is even more important. Celebrities have fame and money and don't care about titles, business cards, data, or reports. They have passed that stage or handed it over to their business manager. They assume you are the best at what you do because they've found their way to you or you to them—and since they are at the top of their game, you must be, too. They do want discretion, but more important, they want somebody real. All day, every day, they deal with people chasing them, telling them what they want to hear, and nodding at their every whim. Everyone is so damn nervous around celebrities. You need to act as their self-assured friend. You need to make them stop seeing you as an anxious, quivering wreck and instead start seeing you as the confident and charismatic person you are. Only then do they want to deal with you.

When a celebrity looks at me and thinks *I can actually have lunch with this guy*, that's when I have won them over. And everyone wants to have lunch with *you*, not you pretending to be someone else. I have shown apartments to Sarah Jessica Parker, Kim Kardashian, Jennifer Lopez, Mick Jagger, Justin Timberlake, Leonardo DiCaprio, Cameron Diaz, Jessica Alba, Hilary Swank, Sofia Coppola, Ben Stiller, the Olsen twins, Britney Spears, Daniel Craig, David Bowie, Iman, Marc Jacobs, P. Diddy, and so many more. I've met them all. And you know what? When I first meet a celebrity, I'm me. I high-kick in front of them, too.

Oh yes: I shook Leonardo's hand, and then right there, in front of his bodyguard, entourage, and even the sneaky paparazzi across the street, I kicked high up in the air and showed my colorful socks and pointy toes, and squealed, "Weeeee." I'm sure he was thinking, *This guy is insane*. But, more important, he thought, *With that confidence, he must have a lot of experience*. And,

I like him! After my high-kick, I retracted to a boring pose with both feet on the ground, corrected my suit and my hair, paused for a second, and said with a straight face, "I'm number one for a reason." And guess what? It worked. It works every time.

I always tell my team: No one wants to work with a dull, frightened, self-loathing person. I certainly don't. And in my business, every transaction involves a lot of money and is a super serious process. It's probably the biggest financial decision in the client's life, and if that client doesn't enjoy the company of his or her agent, he or she should move along. I know I would. I'd rather work on my own and do the search or selling myself than work with Mr. Hard Sell or Ms. Boring. The same is true whether I'm buying a car or a cup of coffee or getting my hair cut. We want to be around good people. When I'm purchasing something, I want the person in front of me to be 100 percent confident, fun, and real with his or her own special personality.

Find yourself. Be yourself. Sell yourself. Trying to do otherwise is a real waste of time. Embrace and celebrate all that you are. Be the best version of you and people will want to do business with you. Let me put it to you bluntly: Life itself is a people business. All the successful people in the world are highly attuned social beings.

We should be able to march confidently into a room, be ourselves, and at the same time really notice and take in all the people in that room. We should be able to detect and understand their behaviors and emotions, picking up on what they say and how they express themselves through body language. We should be able to appreciate and empathize with their most important needs, wants, and dreams. I'll give you some tricks on this in later chapters, because when you have these key social skills, you'll attend any meeting, event, or gathering and end up walking home with a slew of new friends and acquaintances (and potential clients or customers).

When you know who you truly are, you are able to listen and talk just the right amount, build trust, and be with people of all ages, sexes, cultural groups, and income levels. Just like it's supposed to be. It works like this: When you're you, you're remembered, talked about, and even bragged about. This has the effect of a stone thrown in water. The ripples go on and on. You'll reach the best destinations . . . by *being you*!

CHAPTER 2

KNOW WHAT FUELS YOUR FIRE
Clarify Your Drive for What Makes You Work

When friends suggested I try real estate, I could see how it agreed with my big personality, as well as with my people and business skills. I applied to NYU's real-estate-salesperson program and enrolled in the two-week accelerated class. After passing the school test and then the Department of State test, I searched Craigslist.org for anyone who would hire me. I found a small boutique firm in Chelsea called JC DeNiro, which was founded by Robert De Niro's uncle Jack. I went in and met with him and confidently assured him I was going to break the office sales records. He must have believed me. He gave me a desk.

The JC DeNiro office had a nice, downtown New York personality, but it was small. It couldn't have been more than seven hundred square feet, and every desk was different, as though they'd been found one at a time on sale or off the street. Every morning I walked to work in my ratty sneakers, wearing one of the few dress shirts I owned. (Selling panini for forty dollars a day hadn't allowed me to splurge on my wardrobe!) I was always the first to arrive. I'd settle into my desk, which was way too low and small for my long legs, and read listings—thousands of listings—and listen as the other four salespeople talked to their clients and negotiated deals. I'm not sure whether they looked at me as the tall guy with the weird accent or as competition, but one thing was certain: No one was really interested in helping me. We were all working on commissions, not salary, and that has a way of pitting people against one another, encouraging them to constantly focus on the sale.

I was eager. I memorized neighborhoods, streets, buildings, prices, and square footages. I discerned the basic but grand real estate equation: Location multiplied by square footage equals price, and in New York we factor in building amenities and views. (There are, of course, a lot of other nuances about pricing any product that complicate the equation, but that's the basic formula for New York real estate.) The bottom line from my early days is that I lost a lot of time trying to figure out the variables myself, but I definitely kept myself busy.

The storefront office had this heavy gate you had to roll up in the morning and roll down at night, and I seemed to always be the one doing it because I was the first to arrive and the last to leave. John, my business partner now more than a decade later, used to walk by the JC DeNiro real estate office back then and says he remembers the tall blond guy (funny how I am called a dark-haired guy in Sweden, but always blond in the United States) with the big blue eyes who was always there—early in the morning and late at night. Little did he know that five years later, he'd be working with me and we would become the number one sales team in America.

One afternoon, a few weeks into my job, I saw an older gentleman outside peering in the storefront window. He was in his late sixties, looking a little confused. In most retail real estate offices, as with other sales organizations like car dealerships, there's a system called "having the floor," which is a rotation for first dibs on walk-in clients. Each salesperson is allotted a time during which any walk-in becomes his customer.

Skit i det! I thought. *Screw the system! I need a client. I need to succeed.* My floor time wasn't until Sunday. So, I made the street my floor. The world was my floor. Outside the door that man didn't belong to anyone.

I opened the door and stepped onto the sidewalk. "Hi," I said. "What can I do for you?"

"Oh," he mumbled, "I, um . . ."

"Do you live in the neighborhood?" I asked, turning on my charm.

"Yes," he answered. "I live around the corner at West Twentieth Street, and I've been wondering how much my apartment might be—"

I leapt into action and finished the sentence for him. "Worth? I'll tell you. Let's go see it." My well-worn sneakers were already walking toward the corner. I turned back to look at him and gestured for him to follow me. He followed. It seems counterintuitive, but a good seller knows that people want to be told what to do, as long as you are smiling when you give them the orders. You have to be decisive for them: *I'll give you my opinion right now. You want my opinion.* I don't think he had ever really thought of selling. He was just fishing for potential pricing, or maybe taking a break perusing the listings in our window. I basically pushed myself into the apartment, like I did when I was a seven-year-old selling Christmas calendars.

Let me stop right here and share a lesson that has stayed with me from my childhood. There was a framed poster hanging on the wall of my parents' bedroom. It was of a beautiful duck, floating elegantly atop the surface of a placid lake. He was calmly swimming along, head held high in the air, almost smiling (if ducks can smile). Beneath the smooth surface of the water, though, his little feet were flapping furiously. A successful person in any industry or new life endeavor is like that duck: calm above the water but paddling feverishly underneath. Paddling because we are not always in control and because we always want to be moving *forward*. The frenzied paddling might be scary because you are in new waters, but that also makes it so exciting.

I am that duck. And you are, too. We are all ducks. Above the surface, I didn't tell Mr. Potential Seller I'd never sold real estate. I didn't let him see that I was nervous, paddling like crazy under the surface. I gave him no time to consider even momentarily that there might be other salespeople in New York. I concentrated on *me*: my energy, my great personality, and the way I carried myself and spoke. My *hunger* to win. I presented myself as his local broker with international panache. I was going to make his apartment so incredible he'd have a slew of people begging to buy it.

He took me upstairs to a tiny two-bedroom apartment of about 750 square feet. It was, in my mind, the perfect first product for me. It hadn't been touched, painted, or decorated for years, but it was in one of the hottest new neighborhoods—West Chelsea—and with a little elbow grease would be an easy commodity to move. I told him I'd make it great and get it ready for market.

We spent an hour talking in the living room. I told him about my journey to America, how passionate I was about real estate, how obsessive I was about selling (a word anyone interested in hiring you loves to hear), how the area was changing, prices were shooting up to record levels, but how I still felt New York City was underpriced compared to London and Monaco. I reminded myself to be myself, all while listening to him, too. My goal was for him to see me as a friend, not a real estate sales guy. And something happened to me there, in that sunny little living room with a view over Chelsea: I started to relax and gave up on trying to pretend to be someone I wasn't, a robot from realestateville. I wasn't dressed for the part, nor had I closed millions of dollars in sales, but I made him laugh and got him to share with me his life story, too.

When the discussion came to pricing his apartment, I told him I would get him the magic number in an hour. After all, I had no idea what the price was, and I had to go back to the office to run a comparable market analysis. I shook his hand firmly, looked deep into his eyes, and thanked him for his time.

And then outside, in the sunset on Ninth Avenue, I high-kicked and thanked the gods for giving me a chance. I've always seen my career, and life, as a long staircase to heaven, with literally thousands of little steps to climb. Every now and again, you just know—you can feel—that you are about to lift your little duck foot for the next step. It can be an opportunity that arises, a chance for you to shine, or it could be a difficult decision, like two paths dividing in the forest, and you kind of know one is short and easy but without scenic views and adventure, and the other is uphill, winding, and a tougher hike but so beautiful and worth the extra effort. Whenever you are about to get to the next minilevel, close your eyes and cherish lifting your foot, because life is all about recognizing our accomplishments, however small a step they may be. Standing outside my very first listing pitch, I closed my eyes and knew this was one of those steps.

The market was moving upward quickly at the time, so my strategy was—after consulting with my broker—to price it 10 percent higher per square foot than the average sale in the immediate area, which was as bold a move as it was to exit my office and greet a client on the street. It turned out to be a great play because West Chelsea, just like the Meatpacking District, was one of the most underpriced commercial areas but was turning more and more into a residential neighborhood and was going to see the highest price appreciation over the next decade. He was so happy—actually surprised—with the price I said I could get that he didn't even want to meet with anyone else. "If you can get me there," he said, "we have a deal!"

Before I listed it, I helped him move some things out and spruced up the space a bit by redistributing some furniture. I went to the hardware store, bought a couple of gallons of white paint, and spent a few nights painting it myself. I took the bus out to IKEA, purchased nice towels, candles, and flower vases, and returned with an armload of shopping bags to add a nice flair to my first client's tiny apartment . . . that I priced at $535,000.

I was late for my first open house. In Sweden, that's the rudest thing you can ever do, but I had planned it. I also had allowed *no* showings for two weeks before the first open house. Even the listing description online said, "First showing at the first open house, NO EXCEPTIONS." When I arrived, there was a line around the block. There must have been sixty couples there. My palms were sweaty, but quickly dried when I personally shook every single buyer's hand in line. It took a few minutes, and created a bit of a scene, which was my goal—to pull attention to the long line and make everyone notice I had arrived and that I was in control. The doorman's head was shaking at the crowd. He'd never seen anything like it. That's when my height—another advantage I have—came in handy. I announced to the crowd that I'd be taking people up in small groups in the building's tiny elevator and that buyers were welcome to run up the five flights of stairs instead—first come, first served.

It created a feeding frenzy. I handed out offer sheets I had printed, like I just assumed that every person there was going to bid right away or they knew they would lose the apartment. People did what I said, and several were putting in offers right in front of one another in the apartment and in the elevator on the way down, and one guy even wrote his on a napkin he had in his pocket. By the end of the open house, we had multiple offers, and I sold the apartment for $560,000, $25,000 above ask, a record for the building and attention-getting per square foot for the entire neighborhood.

My client loved me. My buyer loved me because I made her *very* aware she had won an intense bidding war with multiple backups wishing she would pull out. I even loved me. I felt New York loved me. And my date the night my first contract was signed loved me, too, because I took us to my favorite Mexican restaurant on Forty-Second Street (they gave unlimited free chips and salsa) to celebrate.

I will never forget that first commission check of $16,000. I thought to myself, *What an obscene amount of money for something this fun.* Right after the closing, I bought myself a fancy pair of shoes and took a leftover show sheet of my first sold apartment to a Chelsea frame shop and had it put in a cute brown frame as a trophy for my apartment wall.

But although my ship had set sail, it was small and the ocean of New York real estate knowledge seemed deep and endless. I had so much to learn, and I was honestly scared and alone. And my mom kept writing to say, "We miss you."

So, what kept me going? The answer takes me back to my childhood in Sweden.

Growing up, people told me I shouldn't think I was better than anyone else. It's the Swedish way to be. We call it *Jantelagen*, which means "humility and restraint." According to the Law of Jante, you are not supposed to think you're anything special. Individual success and achievement are considered unworthy and inappropriate. You're supposed to be average, like everyone else. "Den spik som sticker upp måste man hamra ner!" (*The nail that sticks up must be hammered down!*)

When I was eleven years old, my neighbor's dad bought a Volvo Turbo. The day he got it, I saw him in the driveway using a knife to scrape off the word *Turbo*. I asked him what he was doing. "Well, you know, Fredrik," he said, "the thieves." I could see the embarrassment flush across his face. It was a realization for me, a pivotal moment. It wasn't about thieves. He was worried about what people would think. He was defacing his beautiful car so that he wouldn't look anything but average. Bless his heart. Fortunately, my grandmother had an opinion about Jantelagen, too. She told me, "Skit i det!" (That's "Screw that!" in Swedish.)

In my later teens, I thought my ego was a curse, something I had to work on, to diffuse, in order to better myself. But I couldn't. I wanted to be the best. It wasn't enough to be in the school play; I had to get the lead role. It wasn't satisfying to just do well in school; I wanted to get the top grades. Over time I accepted my competitive spirit and need for attention as a part of who I am, and I realized that both were integral to my personality. They're what make me *me*. I could feel guilty and try to deny those parts of myself, or I could make them work for me. Fortunately, I listened to my grandmother and said, "Skit i det!" Today I am so thankful for this ambition and attribute my success to owning it, rather than trying to scrape it off with a knife.

Escaping the Jantelagen ideology was one of the driving forces behind my move to the United States, and from the moment I made my first deal, my goal was to become the best I could be, to climb to the very top, to be the nail that sticks up and not be hammered down. I want the "Turbo" proudly displayed in everything I do.

I wasn't going to wait for anyone's permission to succeed. My obsession to be the best was the wind behind my sails (and sales).

By the end of my first year in real estate, I had sold $50 million worth of property and was nominated for "Rookie of the Year" by the Real Estate Board of New York. I was wearing only the finest shoes and suits, and there were so many framed show sheets on my apartment wall, I'd run out of space.

NOW, LET'S FIGURE OUT WHAT MOTIVATES YOU TO SHINE AT WORK

There was a poster in my high school of a naked woman and naked man separated by a line between them. Beneath the image was the question "Which one are you looking at?" The campaign was designed to help teenagers figure out and be comfortable with their sexualities. Sweden is obviously a super liberal country, but the point is, life is short! You have to figure out what lights your fire quickly. If you don't know what you love and why you do something, you'll never figure out your passion and what you do best.

Why do we work? The old-school answer might have been to put food on the table, clothes on our backs, and shelter over our heads, but the twenty-first-century answer is a little more complex. Yes, we still work for the basic necessities of survival, but in addition, we now work toward something more—happiness and fulfillment.

I don't know about you, but I don't want to be one of those zombies working for fifty years so that I can *then* retire and enjoy my life. If retirement means enjoying what you're doing, I want to retire today. I want to love my life (and my work) and everyone in it *now*, not tomorrow or after it's over. I want the *world* to be my lover now, not only when I'm sixty-five years old sitting on a cruise ship. I want to experience all her beauty, the untouched and the already explored. If your work isn't something you enjoy, perhaps it's time to change jobs. Even if you're not in your dream career yet, you can figure out what about your current job brings you satisfaction and craft your future endeavors toward that.

There are plenty of reasons to work, but there is only one powerfully motivating reason to work—and that's to find fulfillment. My thought is that career fulfillment can be found two ways, and hopefully at the very same time: through the things you can do with the money you make or the glory your job brings you.

What makes you happiest about the money you earn? Is it

being able to make your family comfortable? Taking your sweet-heart on an extravagant vacation? Putting your kids through college? Driving a fancy car? Buying that big house or a penthouse from me in New York? Or is it simply having enough money so that you're not constantly worrying about it?

Maybe it's not about the money at all. Maybe your fuel comes from your feeling of self-worth. To have people say you're the best hairstylist in town or that you make the most delicious hamburger in the world. To hear your name praised at the sales meeting or be the number one person in your office. To win awards. To get press. To be famous.

When I discuss this subject with people, some say, "I'm not looking to be rich. I just want to be able to give back to those less fortunate." Or "I'm working to be satisfied creatively." Those are both great and worthy, but each still boils down to making enough money to be able to give back or having someone recognize your creative merit. As I have become more successful, money and notoriety have enabled me to do more. I've been able to give back to my family, my brother, and his kids, to help abused animals, and to aid the sick and homeless children in Africa. The money has allowed me to give more, and giving more has been rewarding to my personal self-worth.

I'm often asked where I get my drive. I've spent a great deal of time identifying what fuels my fire. I've analyzed it, questioned it, owned it, loved it, and then acted on it.

Ever since I was a little boy, I have liked being in the spotlight. When I was four years old, I set up my own little theater stage on the coffee table in our living room. I hand-drew invitations, put them under the doors of a dozen or so of our neighbors in the suburbs of Stockholm, and charged five kroners (about eighty cents) a head to come see me stand on my makeshift stage and pretend I was a witch wearing my pointy, black construction-paper hat. I basked in the applause. I now recognize that getting attention for my talents and efforts makes me feel fulfilled, much more so than money.

The spotlight, my need for attention, and my need to win drive me. Let's call it wanting to be *the best*! That makes me happy. Being ambitious with a healthy self-esteem and being a cocky, egotistical schmuck are different things. The things I'm good at please me, but I'm very aware of the distinction between being proud and thinking I'm God's gift to the world. Though I will admit that after the season one finale of *Million Dollar Listing*, Andy Cohen invited Ryan, Michael, and me onto his *Watch What Happens Live* on Bravo, and viewers voted on which of us three stars had the biggest ego. I won, of course, and it made me laugh at myself, but yes, I was also happy! High-kick!

Now to money. I realized when I was five years old that we all need money, so I built a "moneymaking machine." Modeled after an ATM, it was a cardboard box with a thin opening to deposit money into. Money I would keep. I was very proud of the box and encouraged people to put coins into it, even a bill or two. Being my personal ATM invention, there was no way to take cash out, except when I greedily opened the back of the box and emptied it each night! So, yes, I like money, but my ambition to be number one is what really drives me.

John Gomes, my business partner, is driven almost entirely by money. Of course, like me, he is happy when we are number one in sales, but not because of the big blue ribbon—because of the big *green* one! When the door opens to our office and the office manager's assistant comes in with those magical white envelopes holding our commission checks, angels sing. John jumps out of his chair and rushes up to her.

"Oh my God!" he screams. "*Cheeeeeeecks!*" His face gets red with excitement. Sometimes I see pearls of sweat on his tanned forehead. The clouds part and sunshine bathes him. I think he might be sexually aroused. He calms himself down, or at least pretends to calm himself down. He opens the envelope with his special silver letter opener that no one is allowed to touch but him. Then he gently pulls out the check. Depending on the size of the check he has a few different movements and sounds (small = eek, medium = squeal, large = whoop!), but the end result is always the same: He calls his bank and tells them to make room in the vault—*ASAP, darling*—because he is sending our assistant over to deposit his new fortune. When it's deposited, he logs in to his bank account and looks at all the numbers on the screen just to make sure it's real. More angels sing. Time has stopped for him, and he doesn't even know I am in the room. He is alone, in the clouds, high up somewhere in money heaven.

It's a beautiful thing to watch. And it makes me laugh.

"Okay, make fun of me," he says. "It's fine. I have no problem admitting I am obsessed with money." I love him for it. Because he is my business partner, and his obsession with money helps me, too.

"Everyone loves money," you might say. But the thing about John is that he doesn't just love money because it gives him power to buy material things or go on expensive vacations or wine and dine his friends. He loves to *make* the money itself. His real thrill comes from making it, not spending it. Making more is his favorite game. Do you recognize yourself in John? Does the money itself also excite you? If you do, stop for a moment and recognize this fact—and then be proud of it. There is nothing wrong with it. In fact, it will probably make you very, very successful.

Regardless of what you do for a living, if you want to be amazing at it, you need to know what inspires you to do it. As I've become more successful, I've come to lead more people and have had the opportunity to help them find their motivations. I've loved helping my team home in on what inspires them. I've found that you first find what you're passionate about and then set specific career goals that bring that passion to life.

Simply put, in order to be successful, you need a clear picture of what *fulfills* you. What high-kicks you into gear? What lights your fire? I want you to be able to answer that question in a split second. If I wake you up in the middle of the night and shake you, I want you to scream out precisely what drives you. What are you working hard for? That's what will ultimately make your life rich and happy.

KNOW YOUR OWN BIG DREAM!

Let me let you in on a secret. If you don't dream big, others will do it for you and you'll be helping them make their dreams come true. Fulfilling your own dreams is the way to live to your highest potential, and you owe it to yourself to make your time on this marble count. What does your big, most fulfilling dream look like? You should see it in great detail. You need to know it, feel it, be it. Why? Because you don't only have a goal; *you are your goal.* We grow by having a big dream of ourselves doing something great. What's that great dream of yours? A glamorous wedding? A house on a lake? Climbing Mount Everest? Don't be scared to dream bigger! Want to fly with me into space?

When I was in school, I wanted to be the host of a huge talent show, but there wasn't one. So, I created the show and made myself the host. It became a yearly event, and last I heard, it is still a popular school event. When I got my New York real estate license, my initial dream was to make my first deal, but my big dream was to become the number one agent in the city. Some people would say that's dreaming too big. But those people are thinking too small. After all, someone has to be number one. Why not me? Why not you? In my mind, New York is the capital of the world and the most competitive real estate market on the planet, which means, if I could achieve number one here, I'd arguably be number one in the world! Guess what? As I write this, *The Real Deal*, the real estate bible of New York, just named me the number one agent out of the thirty thousand agents in the city. (Since you asked, the next big goal I've set for myself is to have a number one bestselling book.)

How will your goal affect your life? If you achieve it—*when* you achieve it—what will you be able to do? How will it *feel*? Will you be rich? Adored? Let's say your dream is to make $1 million. What will you do with it? Will you buy yourself a big diamond, or be more charitable? Will you put away money for your daughter's education, or go on an African safari? Will you buy your mom a retirement house on the beach, or buy yourself that condo on the ski slopes?

Now, back out of that. Break it down into smaller steps to keep you motivated along the journey. What will you do with your first $100,000? Pay off your credit cards? Put 10 percent away for retirement? Or breaking it down further, how about taking money from your next paycheck and having a nice dinner out and a new pair of shoes? That's what I did with my first commission check! Those shoes were a symbol of the new me. Walking the city streets in them made me happy.

Big goals can't be accomplished overnight. What are the little steps you must take to get there? Which *action* can you take today that will move you toward your dream? Nothing is all that hard when broken down into small, achievable tasks. There are times, of course, along the way when I've considered giving up, when I've thought, *I can't go any further. I can't do any more. I've plateaued or reached my limit. The only way from here is down. I'm not going to make my goal.* I think we all have those moments in which the climb seems too hard, the clouds too dark, and we feel so disappointed in our circumstances we just want to go to bed and cry.

This is when it's important to keep the finish line in mind— to see it, or rather to see yourself running over it. The really successful people I know have moments of doubt along the way, but the secret is they know to just keep going. They don't even stop when they pass the finish line. The minute you think of giving up, or dropping out of the race, close your eyes and see yourself running across that finish line. See yourself achieving that big dream.

The night I finished my first class of real estate school, I went back to my tiny one-bedroom apartment on West Thirty-Seventh Street and plopped down on the bed, closed my eyes, and rather than dwell on the difficult and slow-moving present, I concentrated on the exciting photo finish. I could see myself walking down a beautiful path in Central Park, surrounded by an early-morning fog. My hair was slicked back, and I was wearing a long, expensive trench coat. I could feel the rich fabric of my coat, and I was no longer in my cramped apartment. I was walking through a city I not only lived in, but had conquered, too. I was the *number one seller in New York*. I stopped in the center of the park and pulled from the pocket of that coat an old photo taken of me in 1983 on my way to a dance party my kindergarten had arranged. I looked down at it. It was me in the small garden behind our apartment in the suburbs of Stockholm, little me with fat cheeks and giant sunglasses and no idea I would end up here.

That's how real my dream was.

As an exercise, make your most fulfilling dream real by writing this on a Post-it and sticking it on your bathroom mirror:

My dream is to _____

_____

_____

_____

_____

_____

_____.

Some people say I have always dreamed too big. I say they think too small.

If you post it on social media and tag me, I'll read it and cheer you on. The key to your dream is taking that first step. Take it now.

CHAPTER 3

SHADOW A WINNER

Get Ahead by Being a Protégé

After I began writing this book, I asked my social media followers what they wanted to see in *The Sell* and quickly received thousands of comments, questions, and ideas. The most popular question was what a normal day in my life looks like. How do I make it work, from early morning to late night? I thought this was a great idea because I remember how frustrating it was for me early on in my career when no one made the effort to show me the ropes. I spent a lot of time figuring out the basics, but I don't want you to waste a single second of your time. So let me pull back the curtain on my day to show you exactly what it takes for this high-kicker to sell $1 billion in real estate a year. Don't worry if real estate isn't your game (see chapter 2), you'll still learn a lot of tips that will help you be successful in whatever your dream career is.

I really have three different types of days in a week:

1. Monday–Friday: 5:30 A.M.–9:30 P.M. are my on hours.

2. Saturday and vacations—completely off!

3. Sunday 50 percent on / 50 percent off.

Before we go into the long Monday–Friday workday, let me comment on the importance of having one day in the week that's completely off. There's a reason God rested on the seventh day! *On* cannot exist without *off*. We need the yin-and-yang contrast within a week. It balances the soul. I deserve my day off because, as you'll see, I work nonstop during my days on. "Nine to five" is so last century. The modern workday is eye open to eye close. I need my day off like a flower needs rain. It makes me stronger, happier, and better. My day off is a refuge amid the chaos, and I spend it squeezing joy out of life, whether it's sitting in the park with my dogs or having brunch with friends. The day off gives me a break from the reality of all the things running through my head. Life moves so fast that if you don't grab moments to stop and admire it, you could miss it. So take your day off and relish it!

Now that we agree on that, let's get to work!

Pretend you're a fly on the wall (with a notebook!) watching me on a regular Tuesday in the active spring selling season while I am not filming *Million Dollar Listing New York*, traveling to Europe to run my offices there, or promoting this bestselling book. How does my regular "on" workday look like in New York?

Today is super important. I'm exchanging a day of my life for it!

Let's start from the moment I wake up. Are you with me?

Good morning! Fritzy and Mousey look so cute tucked in between my husband, Derek, and me that I always wake up with a smile.

Are you ready for this roller coaster? Do you see me there? In bed? Do you see me sleeping so nicely? (The deepest and best sleep is always, unfortunately, in the early-morning hours when it's time to wake up.)

5:30 A.M. Alarm goes off! *Noooooooooooooo! It's too early! It feels like I just went to sleep. I want to stay in this cozy bed with my love and our Fritzy and Mousey!*

Yes, I feel it, too. Everyone does. No one wants to get out of bed this early! None of us like it, not you, not me, not Madonna, not the president of the United States, *no one*. We all try to make excuses. We reason with ourselves as to why we deserve to stay in bed longer, and we negotiate with ourselves and the alarm clock: just five more minutes, just going to close my eyes.

And it is because you feel this way that you *must get up*. This is how your life will change. The moment when the alarm clock goes off is the moment of truth. This is the very second you become the new you, and leave others in your dust, including the unsuccessful old you. So, high-kicker, remember this: *If you stay in bed, you're JUST LIKE EVERYBODY ELSE!*

I assume you are reading this book because you *don't want* to be like everyone else. If you want to be *extraordinary*, you have to *get up early*. The early bird catches the worm. Treat these first thirty seconds of your early morning as the most important of your life. They chart the course of your future. Everything else comes after. Let's look at the clock together as the seconds tick after the alarm goes off:

:01 *Noooooooooooo!*

:03 *Ooooooh, it's dark.*

:05 *Oh, my bones hurt. . . . Please, let me . . .*

:08 *Why didn't I go to bed earlier, oh why?*

But listen to me, high-kicker: *Get yourself up! And do it now.*

:10 You hear that beat? If you don't, turn it up! I've programmed my phone to wake me up with Abba's "Money, Money, Money." There's nothing like a quartet of singing Swedes to start my day in the "rich man's world." If you don't have a wake-up call that motivates you—gets your blood pumping in the right direction—you need to find one that does.

Or try this: You hear your heartbeat? That's amazing! Because when you don't anymore, you will get your dear sleep . . . and plenty of it.

:11 As you sit up, be thankful you are alive. Say your little prayer *for* something good and *to* something bigger than yourself. Perhaps a prayer that today is the day you make The *ultimate* sell, the biggest moment of your career. Then make your way to the coffee or shower or sit-ups or yoga mat in any order you like!

You set the tone for your day, so you must set a positive intention. And for you competitive people out there, use this as your motivation to get going: *These are my dues; I'm paying them now. Everyone else is sleeping. It's dark outside. I might be alone now, but someone up there can see me, see me moving toward my dream, and no one can take that dream away from me. Yes, today I am going to appreciate what I have before the hands of time make me appreciate what I had; today is a beautiful battle I was given by God because I am His strongest soldier.*

Remember this, high-kicker: The future always depends on what we do in the present.

While I'm making coffee, I feed Fritzy and Mousey. And what do they do? Eat and run right back to bed. But that's the difference between them and me. I'm a human being who wants to be successful, and they're sweet dogs, the BFFs of someone successful.

5:45 A.M. I head to the gym. I'm in a hoodie, unshowered. I have not brushed my teeth. I'm unpolished and raw, shuffling my feet like a robot. New York City is silent for once, streets empty, lonely traffic lights, closed shops. The creatures of the night are crawling home and pay me no mind. I walk to the gym, which is two and a half minutes away. For those two and a half minutes I am off, enjoying the moment because as my day continues, and the insanity builds, these moments will become cherished. Being off is precious. I stand in the middle of Seventh Avenue looking south with my back toward the traffic that isn't there anyway. I turn my music on in the headphones as I walk down the sidewalk. I look straight up at the skyscrapers; I smell the morning New York air; I take it all in. I feel proud and happy. I did it. I overcame the impossible, which was getting out of bed and out of the apartment on my way to the gym.

I get to the gym. It's kind of empty. I generally take the few minutes before 6:00 A.M. to sit in the locker room and respond to e-mails from Scandinavia. Because of the time difference (they are six hours ahead of New York), I have hundreds of e-mails. Most e-mails, I've found, can be answered in a few words. One or two words will do it most times. *Agreed / Noted / Yes / No / K / Jordan [my assistant] will get back to you.* When I unwillingly switched from the BlackBerry to the iPhone a couple of years back, I was forced to use fewer words, and I haven't looked back.

6:00 A.M. Switching music, turning up the volume, my workout starts. Between my sets of weights, I get mental. I can, with machine-gun fire, return five hundred e-mails during the workout, between sets. Rat-a-tat-tat rat-a-tat-tat rat-a-tat-tat. It's a workout in itself. I might be exaggerating by a hundred or so, but my fingers can tap out *a lot* of e-mails in those forty-five-second breaks between sets! I feel electric, turbocharged, and productive. I lift heavier; my mind works faster. For me, that hour is the ultimate steroid for mind and body.

7:00–7:10 A.M. I walk home with a forty-gram protein shake in my hand, my first calorie intake of the day. The city is starting to wake up. Something can happen then: It must be a release of hormones, endorphins, and the sense that anything is possible. Whether I'm in neon sneakers in the summer, or deep inside a goose down parka in the winter, I look at my own reflection in the retail windows as I pass, and I think, *There you are, hi you, I'm proud of you*, and the reflection gets distorted like in the amusement park when the legs get long or the face blows up and becomes all one big chin, and I smile and think, *Life is all about perspective.*

7:10–7:35 A.M. I'm home on the sofa with Mousey (Fritzy is still in bed sleeping), continuing to return e-mails, review my calendar, and get my whole day structured. This is the window of time I have to take control of it all. I'm able to make any adjustments in time or request support for something. I finish the protein shake, perhaps have a little more coffee. I address last night's e-mails (the ones that came in after I shut my phone off at 9:30 P.M.). In these twenty-five minutes, there is a lot of communication with Jordan, my business partner, and my team members: who is going to be here, there, do this, that. We split the world between us and draw our plays like a coach in a locker room so we know where everyone should be moving.

7:35 A.M. I shower, shave, and take a moment to make sure I give my love some love. I pick out my perfect suit, special socks, and just the right shoes.

7:50 A.M. I start to feel rushed. Everyone else is beginning to wake up. I can feel that good things are going to happen. I see the fires I have to put out. The mood of my day has suddenly gone from classical piano to guitar. And a band begins to form. There is a faster beat now. It's getting harder to keep up with the day, and it hasn't even really started yet. Later, that band will be so loud (like Swedish death metal) that I think I'm going to start crying . . . but I will get to that in a few hours . . . and whenever that happens I'll need to snap myself back into *focus* and—

8:00 A.M. Ding! I'm in the elevator. It's going down, but I am feeling up. This is my Batman moment. Standing still, clenched fists. Like putting on my armor to conquer my day. For you, it might be pulling out of the driveway in your Batmobile. Or watching your kids take off in their yellow submarine. Whatever that moment your day really begins is, know it and savor it.

8-something A.M. I come out of my building, hair perfect except for that one small clump in the back of my head that I have never been able to tame and now call my "nerd antenna," shiny car waiting. Albert, my driver, opens the door, although I have told him that I can do it (after all, I've still got that Swedish Jantelagen in there somewhere). I feel really good. On the way to my first appointment, I stop at Starbucks and am in and out in no more than two minutes. If there is a line, I go to the next and grab a green tea Frappuccino and a little protein. (I love the chicken hummus box with thirty-three grams of protein, but some locations don't carry it. Starbucks, perk up, bitches! That should be in *all* locations!)

8:30 A.M. I'm finishing my snack and walking into an elevator somewhere in the city. I am in constant communication with the flight control tower: Jordan. Usually John's car is outside. He is negotiating in his backseat. Most of our meetings start around 8:30 A.M. and they run back-to-back throughout the day. There is no dead time. There can't be. Dead time is for Saturdays, vacation, and when I'm a grandpa. I am booked two weeks in advance, and I make sure of it. There's always something on my calendar. I always say to my team that we are never better than our last deal, and that deal gets cold quickly. A half-empty calendar is death to me, because it means two things: I don't have enough business to take care of, and I haven't been proactive enough to create new business. No one should ever have an empty calendar, unless it's your wedding day and your future spouse has thrown your phone in the water.

At any one time, I have a hundred active listings. I'm not just showing apartments; I'm also pitching to get new apartment listings. But the majority of my day I'm in standing weekly meetings with developers, done in fancy boardrooms, up in skyscraper offices. We arrive to these cathedral marble lobbies, go through security, and ride the elevator constantly checking e-mails. We enter the conference room where fifteen to twenty people are gathered:

architects, interior designers, developers, bankers, website designers, collateral material firms . . . and I make a lot of decisions with the team conceiving a new building, creating this vision together with hundreds of millions of dollars in sellout per project. It's high stakes and high pressure.

I notice the meeting is in a room with a view: floor-to-ceiling glass, and I stand as close to it as I can. I take a photo and post it on social media. I lose time for a moment; it's my off moment amid all this on. Instantly, a thousand likes within the first four minutes, and I feel connected and creative at the same time. Validation, but not vanity, and I turn back to the meeting.

I've learned that people like to observe an off moment in others. Everyone identifies with a special moment. They know it makes them feel alive. Or gives them something to remember. And talk about. No one wants to be or work with a robot. Anyway, for me, the moment I'm taking that picture is the time I'm off smelling the flowers. Sometimes it becomes a talking point in the meeting—Fredrik's social media—and these days it's part of every launch plan for every new listing and building. No other real estate broker in the country has more followers than I do, and I think I am helping to write the textbook on social media in real estate, and I turn around from the window and tell everyone that. And don't worry: I'll let you in on a few of my social media secrets later in this book ☺

Noon–2:00 P.M. This, for most people, is lunch hour. Lunch is a big waste of time, so I generally work right through it. Not that you shouldn't eat, but who wants to waste two and a half hours of their day doing it? Don't believe me that lunch hour is actually two and a half hours? Let's say thirty minutes to get there, an hour and a half sitting there eating waaaaay too much food and being tempted by that glass of rosé calling your name with a smooth pink voice. Then thirty minutes to get where you're going next, feeling bloated and lethargic! That's two and a half *hours*! Unless you're meeting with your publisher about your best-selling book or the president about your ideas to save the world (Call me! I have some thoughts!), business lunches are a complete waste of time. Better to eat something healthy on the go.

I eat efficiently. I'm not talking fast food. I've found that the longer you sit in front of food with a group of people, the unhealthier you eat. Also, because when I get bored, I turn to food and overeat to keep myself occupied. Organic/raw/fresh takes no time. Every town has a juice bar now. A lot of the time I have a liquid lunch, with three scoops of protein and lots of fiber and vitamins. It's healthy, very filling, and can be consumed in six minutes, usually while I take a little walk in the neighborhood I am in, usually negotiating at the same time. Is this daily juice purchase too expensive for your wallet? Then buy fresh fruits and vegetables and make your own. It takes all of five dollars and five minutes to be healthy and efficient.

If there is no time to even have a liquid lunch, or I'm just that hungry, I will bring food to my meeting. It's shocking to some; it's normal to me. I usually say to the person or people I'm with (whether in my car or in a meeting), "I'm back-to-back all day. Would you mind if I eat a little lunch?" Now, I wouldn't bring stinky stew into the car or sit in a conference room with a big bag of french fries, but using my chopsticks to perfectly put a piece of delicious, beautiful pink salmon sashimi in my mouth while recommending the sushi venue to the room? That can be excused. After I'm done, I say, "Thank you so much for giving me the time to eat. You have saved my day, really!"

I must be borderline hypoglycemic because if I don't get something to eat, I become a bitch. I'm a danger to other people and myself. So, my point here is don't forget lunch—just be smart about it, the calorie intake, what it contains, where you do it, and how long it takes. It is all related.

2:00–6:00 P.M. Long meetings. They happen in every industry, usually in the afternoon. I put an hour cap on all meetings (and a start and end time frame for all phone calls), simply because I need to go to the next. I always apologize as the meeting starts that I'll have to be out the door at X time. I've found that if you apologize in advance about something, people will excuse you for almost anything. Anytime I'm in a meeting with lots of people and their piles of agenda items, I conduct other important business with my iPhone on the chair between my legs. I close and open my thighs every seven or eight minutes and look down to scroll through e-mails. I take a bathroom break every thirty minutes and go into the stall to quickly address e-mails that I need to answer. Don't look at me like that! Yes, you can laugh if you think it's funny. But do you think you can sell a $1 billion worth of real estate a year and run multiple offices in other countries, have a television show and now a bestselling book, and take three-hour meetings without looking at your phone? No. And honestly, it makes those boring long meetings bearable. And when I have to go, I go. I stand up, excuse myself, and leave. Simple and straightforward, and regardless of how uncomfortable it is, it's always better than being late for the next meeting.

Before we continue this day, let's discuss a couple of things:

Working efficiently in real time. I work in the now, putting out the spark before it has a chance to burn down the forest. Remember, time kills all deals, and if the barn is on fire, I bring out the hose fast. When there's a problem, you have about two and a half minutes to grab the reins and solve it. Sometimes there are a dozen or more people on an e-mail, and if you don't respond to it quickly, it can turn into a giant tumor that explodes and can cause you a giant headache or, worse, kill the deal! That's why if you're shadowing me, you'll see me always keeping on top of my e-mails. (More on my ideas for dealing with e-mail later.)

Business cards. I don't want to be one of those players in a poker game passing out business cards at the end of a meeting. I want to be the dealer. I've never had a business card. I mean, they have been printed for me, but I have never kept them in my suit jacket to hand out. I throw them out. When someone asks for my card, I say, "I'll e-mail you," or "You'll find me," depending on who it is. Maybe it seems nonchalant, or even slightly rude, but it's very clever. Why? If I want their business, I will take *their* business cards, and I will e-mail them. In my e-mail, there's my signature line. It says so much more and gives many more options than anything that can be said on a few lines of a business card. My e-mail auto-signature gives a link to my listings, brags that I'm the number one broker in the nation, highlights my press hits, and provides a link to order a copy of this book. How can a business card do that?

Here is another secret of mine: When I want people's business, I e-mail them the minute I leave the meeting. Often I grab their business card, shake their hand, say good-bye, and then turn the corner where they can no longer see me, stop, and write them an e-mail. The key is that there is an e-mail from me *before* they have had a chance to look at their phone or computer. *Wow*, they think. *This guy is good.*

I come home every day with a pile of business cards. What's

remarkable about the stack is just how unremarkable it is. The information there is very limited. The paper is already looking dull and wrinkled. In the world of social media, what exactly about a one-by-two-inch piece of printed paper is going to get my attention? A bragging corporate title? A company logo? Oh, look! It's not paper; it's made out of plastic embossed with gold lettering. The only thing gold-embossed in my life is the cover of my bestselling book—a much more impressive business card, indeed.

Here's the thing. You could buy one of those business card scanners from the *SkyMall* catalog you used to find on an airplane in the seat pocket in front of you. (Do people actually buy those?!) Or you could right-click on someone's signature in an e-mail and *boom*, you've got the address in your contacts forever.

Unless you're a Japanese businessman and you've got the urge to bow as you present your card with both hands, leave the business card back in the 1990s where it belongs.

Delays! There's nothing worse than being late. I have an actual physical allergic reaction when someone is late to a meeting with me or I think I'm going to be late for something. That's very Swedish. And that's why if I'm stuck in traffic and have an appointment on the other side of town, I'll get out and hoof it. I'm known for coming into a meeting sweaty because I've run for thirty blocks. Don't be late. It's disrespectful, but in the event you are, the moment you realize you will be late e-mail everyone and say exactly that. Then, when you arrive, simply say, "I'm so sorry I'm late. It was unavoidable." Don't go into your long, dramatic saga. No one wants to hear it, and it only makes it worse.

Since you're shadowing me, I won't make you run the blocks with me today.

My Meditative Moment. In the car, between meetings, at

least once a day and if I feel particularly crazed, I try to really be in the now. It may sound silly to you. But it's the truth, so I'll tell you. I touch the rainy window. I run my finger along the steel on the side of the door. I feel the buttery leather seat. And I'm just being with it. The trick is to do it without judgment and with no labeling. Don't think: This leather seat is white, or black, or cold, or hot. Just do it and take it in; try to do it without your brain and with your heart, if that makes sense. It instantly de-stresses me, gives me perspective, and shuts off the background noise. Don't take it from me. You can learn from kids, too. Watch them! Study them! They are in the moment. In the zone. They just are.

Try it when you take a bath or shower, too. Don't judge it— just observe. The water. The steam. The sound. Let's call this your Meditative Moment. I do it in meetings with people or when the car drives through Times Square. I do it in the security line at the airport. The noisier and busier, the better. It's über-important to take a moment in your day and *shhhhh*. Shut it all out by really being present for a minute or two.

Ever hear of the book *The Power of Now* by Eckhart Tolle? Read it if you want to learn more. And try this fun one: Look at the nothingness between the letters on this line. Blur your eyes at that v o i d. Listen to the sounds in the room and then the sounds behind the sounds. There is suddenly a gap everywhere. It's freeing. I promise your Meditative Moment will flush away a lot of worries. With it, you are always one second away from complete bliss. As crazy as life can become, you have salvation.

Okay, now we're back in the room!

6:00–7:00 P.M. Here's where I play catch-up. I run by my office to go over the pile of paperwork that Jordan has waiting for me, and I check in personally with my team. I look over materials for the following day's development meetings and request any necessary changes. I often reserve this time for interviews. Today I did an interview with *The Wall Street Journal* on the state of the real estate market and took a photo sitting on a chair in the middle of Fifth Avenue to promote my book on Facebook.

7:00–7:30 P.M. My day begins to wind down. I often have work events, openings, or evening showings. I need to show up and still be my most enthusiastic self, which is sometimes difficult depending on how demanding the day has been. If that means you need a green tea latte with eight scoops of matcha powder, grab it. I don't like to look or feel disheveled, so I always have a comb, toothpaste and toothbrush, and a new shirt and suit in the backseat of the car.

7:30 P.M. What's for dinner? If I don't have an event, Derek and I try to plan dinner together. Sometimes we go out. Sometimes we eat in. (I'll talk about diet later.) Regardless, I'm still on. That means I return e-mails and texts and take important phone calls until Derek tells me to stop.

8:00 P.M. I'm home in my beautiful apartment. It's that time of the day. Sometimes it's hard to unwind. I mean, what the hell just happened?! Certain days we make $1 million in commissions, I answer hundreds of e-mails, work on new buildings containing more than a thousand apartments, film multiple scenes, kick higher than I have ever kicked before, all while being sore from the gym. After a day battling an informational storm, it can be hard to turn off. Derek is painting. He tells me about his day. I envy the peace he seems to have, the stillness within his paintings. I want to enter that painting and live in it. I notice that only one of my ears is listening. The other ear is still listening to my day. Not good. Sometimes I take a bath to wash off the stress. I sit on the sofa with the dogs. Sometimes I have a glass of red wine.

I don't watch TV, hardly ever go to movies, and I don't read many books. I sit down on the sofa, completely beaten in the best of ways, and know that I have given it my all. I gave more than I thought I could give. I went to war and back again. Derek keeps on painting, the dogs fall asleep, and perhaps I spend some time on social media, reading and making comments. I look at the photo of New York I took in the office tower in the morning, and it feels like it was last year. It's beautiful; it makes me happy, because I was there—I mean, really there.

But at some point, it's time to bury the bodies, dump the phones. I've heard you're supposed to stick it in a box in a cabinet like it's an evil spirit you want to contain, but I haven't mastered that yet. Note to self: Work on this. However, I no longer wake up in the middle of the night like I used to and check my e-mail. It always caused my pulse to race and screwed up my sleep hormones. All because of one middle-of-the-night e-mail.

9:45 P.M. Sleep! Stop. Stop right now. I know this is difficult to hear and contrary to what most will tell you. I have never believed in late nights or staying up to get ahead. Sleep is perhaps the most important thing on your daily calendar. There is no appointment more valuable to your success. I have actually put an appointment for sleep into my calendar every day. Jordan knows that eight hours of "SLEEP" in there cannot be touched. I'm the only one that can negotiate that engagement.

Wee hours. Late-night head spinning is a universal human condition, especially when you are successful. This is something that can happen to all of us at night, but don't feed on it. In the darkness, you might have weird anxiety, and thoughts and problems become magnified and percolate until you feel as though you're in an existential crisis. Perhaps it's the darkness; perhaps it's the brain's way of cleansing itself. I'm not talking about dreaming; I am talking about that sleepless negativity in your head, like a nagging, old, worried schoolteacher that just won't stop. At times I have woken up and asked myself why I do the things I do, have told myself that I've strived for too much, that I've built a card house that might crash around me . . . that I don't give back enough, don't care enough. This happens only occasionally but always at night when I'm alone with my thoughts. During the day I'm too busy living life to worry about anything else.

When I was a kid, I was afraid of darkness and reeeeeally scared of the monsters that lived in our downstairs bathroom behind the washer and dryer. At five years old, I turned off all the lights in the house and forced myself to walk around in the darkness. I sat down on the floor in that bathroom and made myself realize there were no monsters. That's what I do today, still: I acknowledge that negative, nagging voice and detach from it. I realize it's just a thought and everyone has it from time to time, and then I go back to sleep. My advice is you do the same.

Now get out of my room, fly on the wall! I've got to get some sleep.

SET YOUR SIGHTS ON A SUPERSTAR

Did you learn something by shadowing me for a day? I hope so. Some might say the easiest way to be successful is to set out on your own and go it alone. I've read a lot of business books that encourage people to not listen to experts or the pros but to do their own thing instead. While that might occasionally work, and while you certainly don't want to follow anyone blindly, the best way to be successful is to learn from other successful people.

When I began my career, I did what many neophytes do: I sat alone and tried to figure it out by myself, greedily thinking that if I did it alone I wouldn't have to share the money or the glory with anyone else. That was shortsighted and silly. If I had to do it all over again, I'd do it differently. If you really want to succeed quickly in your career, snoop out the people who do what you want to do and consider working for them for free for a little while. Find yourself a professor-mentor.

How do you find this professor-mentor person who is at the top of his game, working in your dream job? Easy. Research! Google it. Every single industry has its top-producing lists, and those top producers can help you a lot. A single day shadowing a winner is like absorbing the information from an entire semester in college.

What will you learn by riding the coattails of the stars and watching them in action? For starters, you'll see how they dress, listen to how they speak, and learn how they arrange their day. You will see the dynamics within the team and the way they deal with others. You'll tag along, for free, get them coffee, and be like a sponge. Soak it all in: the knowledge, the deal making, and the atmosphere. Watch how those at the top of their game talk on the phone, handle meetings, do research, and schedule a calendar. It is all priceless schooling—decades of knowledge and experience injected straight into your brain. When you're watching a winner, make room on that hard drive because there will be a lot of information coming your way.

As an added bonus, if you prove yourself worthy to hang

around long enough, for the rest of your life you'll get to name-drop and say you worked with so-and-so on that big so-and-so project. Talk about a kick start for your career. My assistants will, for example, always get to say they were part of the team hired to sell Trump SoHo, a 391-unit condo-hotel tower. That will certainly spice up their resumes and contact lists and open a lot of doors. When they go to interviews later, they can say, "Fredrik Eklund taught me so much, and it was amazing to be working closely with him and his team as they rose to number one."

So how do you go about landing such a plumb position?

I get at least three e-mails a day from people who want a job or for me to mentor them. Lengthy, and let me add nice, e-mails about their lives, what makes them different, and why I should hire them, attached resumes and all. Let me just go ahead and break it to you: E-mails don't work, and the more e-mails we all send in the future, the less important they will be. Just stop. I don't have time to read your college thesis on the real estate industry or hear how you're a mom of three planning to get back into the workforce. Neither will other superstars in other industries. We are busy trying to keep up with our demanding careers in order to make millions and stay at the very top.

But it isn't so much the e-mail itself that's the problem. It's the fact that everyone sends that e-mail. Did you get that? *Everyone tries the same approach.* For superstars to pay attention and actually consider *you* to become a member of their highly sought-after teams, they have to see something different, something special.

Here's a secret: Not once has anyone ever come to my office. Can you believe that? In twelve years in New York, no one has ever knocked on my door. Some cute Australians with cameras come now and then, and when that happens my assistant Jordan alerts me to take the back elevator. But never has someone knocked on my door looking for a job!

Now, I am not hiring, so don't let me lead you on by encouraging you to stop by my office for a visit. I'm just trying to inspire you to go after the superstar in your industry, in your country and town. Suppose you stood outside my office door, shook my hand, and said, "No, I didn't e-mail you or try to make an appointment like the others, because I knew you needed to meet me in person." Then let's say you hand me a Starbucks green tea latte with eight scoops of matcha powder, skim milk only, and no sweetener and tell me, "I know this is your favorite, especially around this time of the day, three hours after lunch, when you need a kick." That's not talking about what you can contribute— that's proving it. That's showing you've done your homework.

I once interviewed a young man named Nathan who came in for an interview with me with a long list of every high-end building in Manhattan (about twenty-five pages) and of every developer in town (another forty pages). He had memorized this information and said he was now ready to get into real estate and help me become number one. (I was number nineteen in the city at the time according to *The Real Deal*.) Nathan now works on my team and closed $60 million worth of real estate in his first eighteen months.

One of the greatest superstars of all time, Elvis Presley, sang, "A little less conversation, a little more action please!" Superstars are busy, and you have to show them not just that you've got it, but also that you understand his or her challenges and needs. You know his or her time is valuable. If you've done your homework, you already started working for Superstar without even asking for his or her permission. Yes, that's just how valuable you *know* you are. *Know* is the key word here, not *think*. Let me give you some secrets.

HOW TO REACH SUPERSTAR AND GET ON A TEAM
Know the Gatekeeper

Who is Superstar's assistant? He or she holds the key to the castle. He or she decides who's in and who's out, literally, because Superstar doesn't handle his or her own calendar. The gatekeeper does. Let me be frank: This person's job is to keep you away from the superstar. Let me be franker: If you are mean, rude, or arrogant with this person, you're never getting anywhere. Let me be frankest: Kindness gets noticed.

My assistant is Jordan Shea. Before hiring Jordan, John and I had been looking for a new assistant for a while. We'd interviewed more than ten candidates and just couldn't find the right one. Then we heard about this amazing young guy and met with him. I will never forget that night. I remember thinking that this guy was an angel, sent down to become part of the team. He was so accurate, in every word, every almost robotic movement, like he was supernatural, too good to be true. He had so much knowledge about what we were looking for, I almost felt embarrassed. It was as though he'd read our e-mails and had been eavesdropping on our conversations.

He looked me in the eye and said, "What you guys are lacking is a COO, somebody that will run the team for you and with all the simultaneous processes, making it a well-oiled machine. You are all running around like chickens without heads. Let me organize you. I'll get it done just like that." He snapped his fingers with what seemed like endless confidence and kindness. I was speechless and just gave a "He's the one" nod to John.

I call Jordan our "flight control tower." He has organized us. He has made the difference. He *is* the oil in our machine. On top of that, he mans all the calendars, phones, e-mails, and, yes, he will be the one you meet if you knock on the door to my office, and, yes, by that time he will have sent me out the secret back elevator and will tell you I'm traveling. Your goal is to get on his good side and therefore mine. And you don't do that by sending him an e-mail saying, "Hi, Ms. Shea!" Do that and you're headlining the fact that you haven't even done enough work to find out that he's a *he*!

How might you know that he is a he? Or that he just got married, or what his favorite restaurant is? Most assistants or secretaries are active on social media and are probably easier to reach directly because they have fewer followers and might therefore be more communicative. At the very least, by poking around the Internet you'll gather some useful information, and it will certainly get you further than blindly calling the switchboard at our offices.

How do you really score with the gatekeepers? Understand that they want to be cocreators in their superstars' success and that they want their jobs made easier, not more difficult. Wow gatekeepers by giving them an idea or a piece of information that knocks their socks off. Give them a suggestion or a lead that is so good they want to run and share it with Superstar. Trust me, if Jordan gets excited about something and thinks I'm going to like an idea, you're getting attention. I trust Jordan. I listen to Jordan. Let him be a part of the excitement. Ask his opinion. Allow him to paint on the canvas a bit, too. In short, if you win over Jordan or any gatekeeper, you're in the door and can ask for the opportunity to meet Superstar face-to-face.

Make Yourself Credible

Facts instill confidence and give those who know them authority. You want to have done your research not just on Superstar, but also on his or her industry and its facts and numbers so that if you're given the chance to meet you can say, "I'm very familiar with what you do [or your company does]." The Bible has the Ten Commandments. The United States has its Constitution. Every industry has its standards. What are they? You better know them if you're trying to sell yourself to a superstar. Anything short of that is embarrassing.

If, for example, you're looking for a job with me and don't know certain things, I know you haven't done your homework. For reference, in New York real estate a job seeker better be aware of the following:

- There are generally four types of residential properties to sell: condo, co-op, cond-op, and townhouse.
- At the time of this writing, the average price of an apartment in Manhattan is $1.7 million.
- The most expensive neighborhood is SoHo.
- There's no such thing as a "standard" commission, but mine is 6 percent.
- The four websites you have already studied and visit daily are: Curbed.com, TheRealDeal.com, StreetEasy.com (owned by Zillow), and NYTimes.com.

- If you really want to impress me, you could name the ten most expensive buildings in the city and the ten largest developers.

Figure Out What You Have to Offer

Do you know your talents, what makes you special? In chapter 1, "Be *You*," we decided you were going to be 100-proof you. Here's your chance to do it. Razzle-dazzle 'em. What are you going to say in the first thirty seconds when you finally reach the superstar to make your case as to why you're someone he or she wants to know? This is a blend of your own capabilities and what a superstar needs to hear. For example: "I have the perfect combination between brain and heart, an endless Excel spreadsheet up here [point to your head], and a lot of fuzzy warmness down here [point to your heart] that quickly connects to other Excel spreadsheets, even if they don't have fuzzy warmness. I'll make you rich and laugh a lot. We'll laugh together on our way to the bank. I'm constantly seeking to learn more, and anyone who has ever worked with me will tell you I'm an asset to the organization, whether I am sweeping floors or helping bring in a million-dollar client. I'm flexible, a team player, and ready to start today."

Weeeeeeeee! You piqued Superstar's interest and have made a solid first impression.

Don't Be Afraid to Flatter

Flattery will get you far, if it's sincere. Tell the superstar that you are here because of him or her. Not just here in the room, but here on your journey because the superstar has inspired you not only to become who you are, but to be ready for the next step, too, which is, cleverly, working with Superstar. Tell Superstar it all started with Superstar, and will end with Superstar, because you are a loyal soul. By the way, call Superstar a superstar. Not only because it's funny, but also because a superstar loves to hear that he or she is super. Everybody does. My first broker told me my first year, "I'm going to make you a star," and I've never forgotten that. Saying something nice like that doesn't cost anything but will make someone remember you.

Here's an important thing about flattery: It needs to be authentic. Say it because it's true, not because you want something in return. Don't say you like someone's hair if you really don't. I once visited an apartment for the first time and told the owner I loved the zigzag striped wallpaper in the bathroom when really my first thought was *OMG, WTF*. The owner grimaced and asked, "You really like it? We've always joked it looks like the EKG of a heart attack victim. We think it should come down before we put the place on the market." I could have easily found something I really liked rather than nervously blurting out phony flattery to disguise my opinion of their questionable taste. Later, in that same meeting, I said (truthfully), "I love that old mantel above the fireplace!" The homeowner was able to say, "It's from my grandmother's house in Turkey. I'm so happy you noticed it." And like that I made The Sell. The listing was mine despite the wallpaper misstep.

Be real in your flattery. You can find something genuine to like about anyone and anything.

Craft Your Elevator Pitch

What are your skills and what do you want? Be able to say it to Superstar in three sentences or fewer. Powerful people have short attention spans and a lot of people trying to grab some time with them. By the time you do succeed in getting a superstar's time and attention—whether in person or on the phone (don't settle for an e-mail exchange)—you should have etched on the back of your eyeballs a targeted summary statement of what you want. If we're in a fast-moving elevator together, you have thirty stories to speak; perhaps you'd say: "You are the best at what you do. You do it with flair and seem to have fun doing it. I have a lot of energy, just like you. I'm obsessive about setting records. Remember when you were just getting started? That's me. Look at me! I'm a machine and not interested in wasting time with anyone else. I'm ready to work for you because you're the best." Ding! Everyone exits the elevator at the lobby level and you, high-kicker, have made an impression.

Say Thank You

Whether Superstar responded with enthusiasm or not, send a *handwritten* thank-you note telling Superstar something amazing he or she helped you realize, thanking him or her for something specific he or she did, and giving an idea you've had as a result of the meeting. Send a note to the gatekeeper, too, and then call the gatekeeper after to follow up.

What does all this demonstrate? It indicates preparation, guts, ingenuity, and follow-through. Success in any business starts by getting in the door. It also indicates something every superstar will appreciate: a bit of bold insanity. Successful people have a spark, a drive, and a need to succeed. You can see it in their eyes and the actions they take. You want superstars to see themselves in you, and although your friends will advise you not to be this aggressive, the superstar will appreciate it because he or she didn't get there by being tame.

Remember, you're not asking for a job, because a job requires something from the superstar. You're saying, "Let's not talk about money. I'm telling you: You're going to be so impressed with my performance, you'll never want to let me go, and then we can talk about the logistics." I don't care what you have to do—call your rich aunt for a loan, bartend, sell your bike, clean bathrooms at night—just have enough money on the side to float yourself for a little while on a boat with a superstar or a dynamic team already succeeding in your dream career.

YOU'RE IN THE DOOR! NOW WHAT?

Do *not* stop or slow down! Hit the gas. Once you're in, if you prove your mettle, you are golden like the shiny, embossed letters on the cover of this book. The first days of working with anyone are a test-drive, and you want to be a sports car, not a golf cart. How might you get noticed, appreciated, and brought on as a permanent member of the team? What do you do to prove you're someone I want to hire?

Be in the office when everyone walks in. It's such an easy thing to do, and no one does it. Be there when the superstar boss arrives and when the superstar leaves. Say, "Good morning, Fredrik" with a smile on your face. Say, "Have a good night, Fredrik" with that same smile.

Introduce yourself to everyone. People will be impressed and flattered if you make an effort to meet them. When you see them again, greet them by name, and you'll be remembered. If necessary, keep a cheat sheet of names—from the guy in the mailroom to the names of the boss's children (or dogs!) When people ask me about Fritzy and Mousey, it always gets them a check in the "Like" column.

Be the one to brew a pot of coffee. Think of your work environment as an extension of your home and be thoughtful. Clean up the kitchen or break area. Bring in a batch of cookies. Put flowers in the reception area. Little efforts go a long way. People notice.

Make a friend. Don't ask the boss how to set up a conference call or use the copy machine. Find a friendly office ally who knows the lay of the land and is willing to give you the royal tour of office mechanics, politics, and personalities. You don't want to be the one who starts a brouhaha because you used too much space in the refrigerator.

Be eager, but not too eager. Show you are genuinely interested in helping and be readily available. Answer your phone and e-mail in real time during your apprentice period. If the superstar needs to reach you, be on call. If you're fighting for a position on someone's team, you want to be enthusiastic, but not so excited that you say yes to everything, even tasks out of your skill set. If you agree to do something, make sure you knock it out of the park.

Compliment your boss and his or her business on social media. Taking ten minutes to crow about your superstar on social media will get his or her attention. Saying "I couldn't be prouder to be working with @FredrikEklundNY" or posting a photo of one of my properties and saying "I'm saving up" makes me happy. And if you make me happy, I want to keep you around. The same applies with any boss or company you work for, unless you're in covert operations at the CIA.

Offer solutions. It's not enough to say the bathroom smells or that booking the conference room is impossible. Be proactive. Buy air freshener or buy a dry-erase board and marker and suggest a system for booking the conference room. Every manager or superstar wants someone on the team that can solve problems, not just point them out (or be one). Become a solution generator and you're increasing your value.

Know what you want. At every meeting I go to, I know exactly what I want to accomplish. I know its purpose. If there is no purpose, there's no reason to have a meeting. The same applies to every day of work. Know what you want to accomplish in the day and set out to make that happen. Otherwise, your day (and you) prove dispensable.

After a couple of weeks of being sincere, enthusiastic, and helpful, you'll find that sudden moment when you're alone with the superstar. When you do, you must leap on that opportunity. Plan and practice exactly what you will say. "After what I've learned about you and this company, I think I'm a great fit for your team. Is there anything else you need to know for me to prove I want this job? What's the next step?"

Do these things and you're no longer shadowing a winner; you *are* a winner.

CHAPTER 4

DRESS THE PART

Make Yourself as Beautiful and
Appealing a Package as Possible

Every Christmas season during my childhood in Sweden, my family went to the NK department store to shop for one another's gifts. We'd get to the store and then separate to pick out gifts, pay for them, and go to the special counter at NK to have everything gift wrapped. The only one who didn't get her gifts wrapped was my mom, Jannike, who wrapped her gifts at home in the kitchen that night. You see, at NK, gift wrapping is an art form. The store even has a special training program for its gift wrappers, and in the late 1960s, my mother took the training program and worked at the store's holiday wrapping counter.

My mom wraps a beautiful package. I used to get to watch her wrap everyone's gift but mine. I was fascinated with her unique technique, where no paper borders or ends were showing, how she hid the tape and folded everything away. It was truly a masterpiece, and when she was done, we would compare her wrapped gifts with the rest of the family's. The only difference between my mom's wrapping and NK's was that her paper was different.

My mom passed along some words of wisdom to me that she learned at the NK training program: "No matter what you spend, a gift bought with love and wrapped beautifully is the perfect present." Even if I had only five kroners to spend on her gift, she'd ooh and aah at the beautiful wrapping and the perfect ribbon as if it were a diamond necklace from Tiffany's. To her, the care in the wrapping was a gift in itself.

Now, let's talk about how *you* wrap yourself up and present yourself to the world. If you get up in the morning and don't fix yourself up and walk out that door not looking your very best, it's like presenting your Christmas gifts in a brown paper bag. No matter what's on the inside, the presentation ruins it.

At the risk of sounding like Christian Bale's character in *American Psycho*, every successful person starts the day by acknowledging that his or her look and feel is 100 percent correlated to his or her performance that day. Simply put, if you've got on an ugly outfit, dangling nose hair, and dragon breath, you're striking out. Your first mission every day is to be a well-wrapped package that fits both your personality and what you're selling.

The first expensive suit I ever bought was black. I was in Jeffrey, arguably the Meatpacking District's most expensive men's clothing store, on Fourteenth Street. In walked Carson Kressley, my new client and star of *Queer Eye for the Straight Guy*, which was a big hit at the time. At his encouragement, I tried on an expensive Christian Dior black suit. "It's so chic!" he told me.

"You have to get it!" I bought it because he was standing there and he said it looked good on me but mostly because I wanted to impress him. It did look good, but it was so expensive that I couldn't afford to high-kick in it. I was simply too embarrassed to admit that it was out of my budget.

Spending $2,100 on a suit was insane for me at the time. But over the next few years, I realized something. My expensive suit gave me superpowers. I've probably done more sales in that black armor than any other, and it still hangs in my closet. Let's say the peer pressure from Carson was a divine intervention and forced me to upgrade my wardrobe, and with it, my confidence to convince people they absolutely have to buy what I'm selling. I've made millions of dollars wearing that suit because I felt like a million bucks wearing it.

Now, it's time for me to give you a little peer pressure.

HOW TO LOOK YOUR PERSONAL BEST

Move over, Heidi Klum; it's time to kill the darlings, darling. This is my etiquette, fashion, and style advice, and it's a show-stopper. Are you *in*, or are you *out*? (Say that again with a Swedish accent, not German!)

I always tell new salespeople to put aside 10 percent of every commission check for their wardrobe and grooming, because that money will duplicate itself many times over in new sales. Yes, I know other life-advice books might have told you to put 10 percent away for retirement. Forget about that right now. If you want to up your ante, I say putting that money in your wardrobe will lead to bigger sales and soon a bigger stash to put away for retirement. Let's get into some specific ideas on how to spend that money.

Hire a tailor. The biggest mistake both men and women make with clothes is buying them off the rack and not getting them tailored. Your clothes must be altered to your body in order to accentuate the positive and minimize the negative. Have you ever looked behind the mannequins in a store? Every single one of them is pinned or clipped to an inch of its plastic, perfect life. Pins and clips are rather uncomfortable to wear, so you need a tailor. Trust me on this: If your job entails meeting anyone face-to-face, find yourself an expert tailor who will shape your clothes to you. I tailor all my shirts and suits in on the sides. I buy pants at their raw length and have them hemmed up to my perfect length. Every professional man should do that with his shirts and pants. Every professional woman should do that with her blouses and skirts. It usually costs me forty dollars a shirt, a hundred dollars per suit.

My tip to you: Buy a less expensive brand and take it to a tailor. You can make a $400 suit look like a $4,000 one with the expertise of the right tailor.

Avoid the black cloud. There are "fifty shades of gray," but when it comes to suits and dresses, they're not sexy. Black and gray suits and dresses tend to be generic and drab. Want to look *GQ/Vogue* fantastic? Buy a suit in unexpected materials, patterns, or colors. It grabs attention in a really good way. I haven't bought a gray or black suit in the last five years because I like a little excitement in my wardrobe and think it works well for getting noticed in business. My favorite? My blue-jean suit. It's on the cover of the book you're holding.

Another one of my favorite purchases is my red-wool suit. When I was named to *Us Weekly*'s best-dressed list, I wore it to the party on a hot August night in New York because I knew I looked *hot* in it. The problem was I didn't think about the *wool*! It was in the nineties in the city that night, and humid, and I was definitely hot—steaming *hot!* By the time I got into the party, I was sweating like a pig. I met Andy Cohen inside, and he immediately asked, "Why the hell are you wet?" At that moment, Eve, the famous rapper, yelled across the room, "*I love your suit!*" I ran over and we took a picture. We tagged each other on social media, and I got cheers (and more followers) from tens of thousands of people around the world. High-kick!

Whatever your business attire, remember this: Business attire is by nature a conservative statement in and of itself. So, why make it doubly conservative? Are you conservative squared? *No!* You're conservative × *fabulous.* You're a high-kicker!

Sometimes I think of the Olympic Games and how everyone wears the same sportswear but in different colors because they belong to different teams. So should you: Wear your own team colors because everyone else plays for the black or gray team.

Find your signature. Please don't just wear a suit or dress to wear a suit or dress, especially if it's ill fitting! I'm not really sure why people are so obsessed with boring suits and dresses. You want to feel comfortable and fully *you* in what you wear. You want to feel like a million bucks so you can make The Sell. Your clothes are, after all, your selling costume. If your signature look is dark jeans and a polo shirt or a blouse and short skirt, work that out!

I have several ties with miniature dachshunds on them. Wearing one of those ties gives me an opportunity to talk about Fritzy and Mousey. I have a pair of ski pants I wear in the winter with a suit jacket. It looks fantastic and allows me to joke, "I'm from Sweden," and get a laugh. I have eight pairs of glasses. The truth is I had LASIK surgery and don't need them, but I still wear them because I have a baby face and think they make me look distinguished. Whether I do or not is a matter of opinion, but at least they make me *feel* that way, and that confidence makes me more successful.

Add a splash of color. Okay, so you're not ready to wear a red-wool or blue-jean suit. Fine. But please do me this favor with your boring gray and black outfit: Break the monotony with a sharp splash of color, something that shows you've got personality and aren't taking yourself too seriously. A colorful tie or scarf says *I'm confident*, as do colorful socks. I have made colorful socks one of my personal trademarks. I love to go out hunting for them. I have half a closet filled with colorful socks. I have socks with flags, with polka dots, with pink dollar signs, but I take it one step further. I mix and un-match them. I'll wear a turquoise on my left with a pink on my right. Why? Because I like it, people ask about it, I get to answer "Fun, right?" with a smile, and they never forget me. Those socks help me make The Sell.

P.S. I've gotten laughs (and made friends) so many times by making references to my colorful underwear. I've got on my purple polka-dotted pair right now. Do you want to see them? ☺

Polish your shoes. Everyone notices your shoes, and, believe me, what's on your feet can either give you a strong leg to stand on or hobble an outfit. What you want is for your shoes to make a positive impression with every step. I did my first real estate deal in a pair of yellow sneakers with holes in them. It wasn't cute, but in my defense I couldn't afford better ones at the time. Look down at your shoes. What are they saying about you? Are they styling? Or are they dirty or old? Someone doesn't have to be Sherlock Holmes to deduce a couple of things if they are. You obviously don't make money, but perhaps worse, you're not attentive to detail.

There are two extremes in shoe buying. Women buy too many shoes; men don't buy enough. You don't have to be Sarah Jessica Parker in *Sex and the City*, but please have some nice shoes in your closet. By the way, did you know the average American buys a new toothbrush every eight months? You're supposed to change that out every thirty days, people. Yuck! I'm mentioning it because I think the same theory applies to shoes. Don't wait until your shoes fall apart in order to replace them. You want to replace them or get them polished or resoled *before* they look like they need it. I regularly take shoes to the cobbler for him to do his magic. (That's cost effective!) And don't forget to give the shoes you no longer need or want to charity. (That's tax deductible! And nice!)

We high-kickers walk a lot during our days. So let me give you some advice on how to find the perfect pair of shoes. Buy shoes with organic materials with stitched soles (not glued). A friend in the shoe business told me that your feet swell during the day, so trying on shoes at the end of the day will give you a more accurate measurement of your foot size. Oh, he also said that generally one foot is a little bigger than the other, so try on both shoes and make room for your biggest foot! There's no such thing as "breaking in" a shoe, which means if they don't feel good when you're walking around the store, they are going to feel horrible when you're running to that appointment.

My mom always said you could pick a life partner based on shoes. I'm not sure that's the case, but make sure your shoes say you're polished and well put together. Spend money on a few pairs of good, high-quality shoes that will last and be stylish for a long time, and spend money on keeping them shined and soled. It's a quality investment. I respect women so much for their endless shoe show, where shoes go out of fashion quicker than men's, and I acknowledge it's a whole different ball game than the one for men. So spend according to budget, invest in a few staples, but always walk in something that makes you feel awesome.

Flash a nice watch. A watch is a billboard. It's something that everyone always looks at and appraises, even more than a wedding band. Buy yourself a nice watch, and if you can't afford one today, save up for one. Rip out an ad of your dream watch from a magazine and tape it to your bedroom wall. (And, by the way, I love a big, bold man's watch on a woman. It says, *Don't f*ck with me. . . . I'm a woman in a man's world, and I rule it. My watch is bigger than yours, so back off. I can afford it and pull it off.*)

I wish I had a grandfather or father who gave me that watch, not just for the sake of an heirloom, but also for the sentimentality and symbolism of wearing his ethics, his honor, his success on my wrist. Maybe you have something in the attic, a keepsake from someone you love. Wear it with pride! I didn't have that, so I had to buy my own and will one day, hopefully, pass it on to my son or daughter. See my watch on the cover of *The Sell*? I like the weight of it. It's very heavy and pure gold. It's a $29,000 watch. But you don't have to be as stupid as I was and pay full retail price, I know you can buy one for half that used (and you can imagine that it was worn by someone successful, very quirky, and wonderful!)

People have opinions on watches like they do on cars and ice cream flavors. There's nothing wrong or right about style or brand (or even how much you spend). Buy a watch that works for you and flaunt it, or don't, but at least own it! It becomes a part of you like an old friend who is there with you in the darkest hours and the brightest moments. Oh, if my watch could talk. High-kicker, with the proceeds from your next big deal, buy thee a nice watch.

Invest in your hair. In your monthly budget, you should also set aside money for a really good hairstylist. If you see someone on the street (or better, a client!) with really good hair, ask where he or she gets it done. Then put a blindfold on and an apple in your mouth, and trust that really good stylist to do his or her craft. We all have been there: directing the professional and ending up with the exact same (expensive and dull) haircut for a decade.

Trust me, there's a difference between a haircut and a hairstyle. I've heard it said that hair is a ball gown you never take off. Think of it this way: You spend a small fortune on a dress or tailored shirt that you wear perhaps twice a month. But you wear your hair *every day*. Don't you want it to look good? Find yourself a good hairstylist. It will pay off. Good hair is a proven business winner. Don't believe me? According to a Harvard research study, a good hairstyle is a professional's most important physical attribute. The study discovered that 83 percent of senior executives said "unkempt hair" undermines a woman's executive presence and 76 percent said it detracts from a man's. There's a reason people feel great on a good hair day.

I'm often asked what hair products I use, so I'll tell you. The only thing I use in my hair is a dab of Kiehl's Ultra Facial Moisturizer. Yes, that's right: facial moisturizer. It makes my hair soft, stay where I want it to stay, and makes it perfectly shiny, but not too shiny. I don't have any scientific evidence for why it works, but it does. Sound silly? Fine. Use what you want. I have tried it all, and those waxes, pomades, muds, and hairsprays . . . Ewwww. Who wants to run their fingers through a helmet of goop?

P.S. I'll confess that every three weeks I spend $275 on my haircut. Does that sound terrible? Sorry I'm not sorry. You don't have to spend $275, but you *do* have to find someone that gives you an awesome style. If you want perspective on how my life and ability to spend has changed, I'll give it to you. When I first moved to New York, I went to the barber every two months and paid $12. I look at photos of myself from that time, and I burn them. There is one photo in particular where my cheap haircut is too ugly to print in this book. I am in a pool with a walrus, and we both are sticking out our tongues at the same time. And we have the exact same haircut. Oh, what the hell, let's print it!

The exact moment I realized this guy had a better haircut than me and that it was time to switch stylists

Get groomed. When I was younger, I had one weakness I couldn't kick. I bit my nails. It was a horrible habit, I know. My mother used to paint this nasty-tasting stuff on my fingers that I would promptly wash off as soon as she left the room. I've finally stopped, but I have to tell you, every now and then I'm still tempted. My business partner, John, is the one who made me finally realize how bad my habit was. John, who has perfectly manicured nails, pointed out to me that in real estate we shake hands, point at floor plans, showcase appliances, and hand clients pens to sign contracts. "Your nail biting is making you look like you're not in control," he told me. "If you're negotiating with someone's money, they don't want to see you nervously gnawing your nails." It was an aha! moment for me. I went out and bought a nail file that I now keep in my bedside drawer.

I realized that I would never want a client to look at my hands and decide I don't have self-control. You wouldn't want that either. You have no idea how many closings I've been in where the other broker, attorney, or client is biting their nails. It's a billboard for stress and anxiety. And really weakens their position. I used to be one of them, and now, like a reformed smoker, I notice every nervous nibble. On the other hand (pun intended), if you are a guy and take it too far with shiny polish or a girl with claws, you're announcing that you're a poser and an animal, respectively. You want to look natural, relaxed, and in control—not fake, forced, and extreme.

Ear hair and nose hair? Keep it trimmed! No one wants to see a shrub growing out of your left nostril. You think this stuff is basic and obvious? Good, I'm glad to hear it. But a lot of people don't. Eyebrows (that's plural, as in "two" not "one") should be shaped. Hickey? You can't see me right now, but I'm shaking my head *noooo*!

What's that smell? Please don't make me go there. Let's just say always use deodorant or, if you tend to sweat, a strong antiperspirant. And don't be one of those people who waft into the room smelling like the entire perfume counter at Bloomingdale's. Over-scenting yourself can be just as bad as body odor. I've always used Chanel Egoiste Platinum, and I spray a bit on each wrist and then rub those wrists under my ears, because my mother used to do it that way when I, as a kid, watched her getting dressed in the morning.

Hopefully, these things seem obvious to you. If they don't, please read this section again, or ask your bestest friend and most honest ally to tell you the truth about you. People pay attention to your personal grooming. You don't want anyone paying attention for the wrong reasons.

Smile! There is nothing more attractive than a smile. Why aren't you smiling? Are your teeth yellow? Get those things whitened! There's a kit at your corner drugstore. We are drawn to people who smile just as sure as we try to avoid anyone with a scowl. Smiling people look more confident and are more likely to be presented with more opportunities. It's just that simple, and you know it inherently. People want to be around (and give their business to) people who smile.

I learned to smile the hard way. Early in my career I was terrible in live interviews. I'd watch playback of a TV appearance and note that I looked frightened and awkward. No one would want to work with that guy. It occurred to me that if I wanted to win business, I needed to smile throughout the interview, even when we were talking dull market numbers on CNBC. I began starting the interview with a big smile on my face, picturing myself opening my whole soul to the world. Everything changed, and interviews became much easier. Now with each interview, I pack in the smiles, and my phone starts ringing.

But there are more reasons to smile than just because it's a proven moneymaker. There are amazing health benefits to smiling. A smile relieves stress, boosts your immune system, and lowers your blood pressure. Those are facts! It's also a natural drug. Studies have proven that smiling releases serotonin, endorphins, and natural painkillers. That's a happy cocktail. Further, smiling gives you a natural face-lift because the muscles we use to smile pull the face upward. And who doesn't want to look better without surgery?

Try it right now. *Smile!* I'll wait. *Smile bigger! And hold it!* So what if people are looking at you right now holding a book and smiling ridiculously big? That's exactly what you want, to get attention with that infectious smile of yours. I'm 100 percent positive your mood just brightened. That smile just told your whole body, *Weeeeeeeee!* For a week put on a smile every morning as soon as you wake up and let me know the results. I'm betting you'll find it makes everything better.

When I have a good tan, freshly cut hair, and am wearing a smile and my new, tailored suit and gold watch, I know I can conquer the world. No matter what you do in life, even if you're a telephone operator sitting in a cubicle, looks matter. Why? How you feel directly correlates with your attitude. If you feel polished and put together, your performance is polished and put together. That telephone operator sees a lot of people on the way into that cubicle, from the guy at the gas station to the boss in the corner office. If she feels positive about how others perceive her, she feels more positive about how she perceives herself, and the result is, at minimum, a nicer day and, more likely, a better chance at moving ahead in life.

A first impression happens in a blink. Literally. Do not underestimate the power of that moment. According to research by Harvard Medical School and Massachusetts General Hospital, people evaluate your competence and trustworthiness in the first quarter of a second (that's 250 milliseconds!) of laying an eye on you based *solely on how you look*. Therefore, I imagine every day as a first date and get myself ready accordingly. We encounter a lot of people in a day. Each of them presents us with an opportunity to influence, impress, and make The Sell.

There are so many things about the world we can't control. Appearance and presentation are ones we can. If we're wrapped nicely, like a present from NK department store, we're offering our best gift to the world. Many people fail big in the presentation of their bestselling point: *themselves!* Make wrapping yourself up beautifully your everyday habit, your ritual of self-love. Kick it up a notch and see how you suddenly knock it out of the park! You'll never look back (except at old photos, which you'll promptly want to burn).

Oh, and one last tip: If someone ever offers you a breath mint, take it.

CHAPTER 5

TRAIN LIKE A PRIZEFIGHTER
Work Out, Eat Right, and Get Your Beauty Sleep

Remember when I told you I did $50 million in business during my first year in real estate and was nominated for "Rookie of the Year"? Well, bad news. I lost! I went into the men's bathroom after the awards and stared at myself in the mirror, wearing that expensive tux I shouldn't have bought. The same tux I had imagined I would win in, pose for photos in, and celebrate late into the night in. Now I was standing in bad light, looking at my mirror image.

I saw bags under my eyes, and my skin looked sallow. I looked down and realized my belly looked swollen. I was twenty-five but in that moment looked thirty-five. Yes, I'd sold $50 million and finally had some money in the bank, but what did it matter if I let myself go to pot? I'd dropped the gym, was eating poorly, and wasn't getting enough sleep. And on top of all that, *I lost*! I looked myself in the eye and decided to make a commitment to myself, a promise that my health was more important than my wealth. Perhaps then I'd be a winner on more than one level.

It's time for you to make a lifelong commitment to a healthy you, too. Yes, like me entering my second year of real estate, you are marrying the new you. Repeat after me:

I, [Your Name], take you, [Your Name], to be my partner in life. I will cherish our friendship and love you today, tomorrow, and forever. I will honor you, treat you with respect, and make sure you receive the things you need to stay healthy, happy, and sane. I will love you faithfully through the good times and the bad, through the easy and the difficult, and will always be there for you. I give you my life to keep. So help me God.

Now the success you *are* can kiss the success you're *going to become*. Everyone is applauding and throwing flowers, and I'm in the front row high-kicking!

What am I talking about here? I'm talking about you and your health, both physical and mental. It's all related; it's all you. There are a million books written on the topic of diet and health. So, why are there so many unhealthy, out-of-shape, hardworking people? US government data shows that 61 percent of Americans weigh too much and 26 percent of its citizens are classified as obese. That's one out of four people! Most people don't realize that how you feel doesn't just affect your bottom; it affects your bottom line. I certainly didn't in the beginning. I now know there is a direct correlation between how I feel physically and how much money I make. Need proof? In a study published in the *Journal of Labor Research*, researchers found that employees who exercise make 9 percent more than those who don't.

But how do you fit it all in?

Who has the time to sleep well, eat well, exercise, *and* still be able to work a fifteen-hour day? You do! With some planning, it's really quite simple. I schedule in those three activities as important appointments in my life by making them part of my daily calendar. And I prioritize in exactly that order—sleep, eat well, exercise, work—so that I will do well. I think of myself as a marionette doll dangling beneath the control of my puppet master calendar. Yes, I create the calendar, but the calendar is in control of me.

It all starts and ends with taking care of ourselves. Most of us know that eating well and regular exercise reduces risks of things such as heart disease, cancer, and osteoporosis, but new studies suggest that exercise actually improves concentration, lowers stress, enhances creativity, and makes us smarter. Now that you know these things (including the research indicating that exercise leads to more income), let's talk about how to make this happen.

Olympians aren't just born with the ability to do those feats of physical prowess. No one is. They make a lifelong commitment to the sport and the training program that will get them to the top. They make huge sacrifices, investing four to eight years of their lives to practice, often away from their families. They study nutrition, physiology, and visualization. They get eight to ten hours of sleep a night. In other words, they make the regimen their job, and the payoff is often golden.

I want a golden payoff, and you probably do, too, right? *You* want to be at the top of your game? Well, your sleep, diet, and exercise are part of your job. Your physical and mental health aren't just what make you able to run the race; they help you *win it*.

When I moved to New York, the gym became an important daily ritual not because I realized it would help my career but because I was vain. I signed up with the David Barton Gym in Chelsea, where the boys wore very little and every surface was covered in mirror, including the ceilings. There was a live DJ who spun tunes from inside a gigantic disco ball. Yes, I felt better, but for the wrong reason. I had no consistency and no real goal except looking good and showing off in that gym. That grew stale very quickly.

By the end of my first year in real estate, I was making the mistake that so many hardworking people do. I became so consumed with busyness, my physical well-being wasn't a priority anymore. And what happened? I slowly began to look and act like some of the other sellers in this town: like the life had been sucked out of me. I learned the hard way that my performance, my emotional life, and my productivity had been left back at the gym.

Today it is all about *feeling* good and trying to do something that physically helps me feel good every day. That's the goal. But instead of looking at exercise as an indulgence that takes me away from work, I'm saying my health is part of my work itself. And it doesn't have to be restricted to a gym. I've actually found that I enjoy being outside more than I like being inside a basement gym. Hiking is my favorite energizing activity; running by the river is my most calming activity. Parks are nice, as long as they are big enough for me to move around in. But the point is I'm making it part of my scheduled day.

My career is a long and winding road, and I know I need a

solid pair of legs, a strong heart, and a clear mind to stay on top. If you're striving for success, your days are going to be packed and hectic, and you're going to find you have less time to eat right and get to the gym—and that is exactly why you *must* eat right and get to the gym. Don't you get it? The *less* time you have to eat well, exercise, and sleep, the *more* important it is to block out the time in your calendar for it. How do you keep it all together when the world spins fast and you need to speak, scream, run, juggle, and keep track of five hundred different things in your mind?

Trust me, high-kicker, your biggest challenge doesn't come from outside; it's your own mind and body. These three things— the nutrition from what you eat, the intensity of the exercise you get, and the quality of your sleep—are directly correlated with your output. I will *not* negotiate on my health and well-being, and you shouldn't either. Yes, I bargain with myself, too, while trying to make the best of my body and mind. There certainly are days when I'm hungover with cold, clammy skin and a pounding head and feel like I'm one step behind. On the flip side, when I'm leaving the gym after early-morning exercise with a green juice in my hand, after eight hours of sleep, I look up at the sky and know I can conquer the world.

It's a lifelong discussion with ourselves. For example, I love love love wine, but I know that when I have too much of it, I underperform the day after. Do you also like expensive wines? I really do. But if I have a big meeting or am involved in serious deal makings the next day, I know that a bottle of wine will adversely affect my abilities. (Let's not even comment on how my face looks blown up for the uncompromising cameras of Bravo.) If I lose a $5 million deal because I'm not fast on my feet, that's an awfully expensive bottle of wine ($5 million at a 6 percent commission = $300,000). Yikes! So, put a dollar value on each glass of wine, burger, or hour of late-night TV watching.

You think your TV bill is only $79 per month? For every hour you watch TV, you could be building your dream company, going to the gym, sleeping, writing that book you've been talking about for years, reading that book you've been thinking about for years, planning that big event, *creating something*. Don't just consume nothing on the couch. If you consume anything, I'd rather you consume your own sweet dreams while resting your tired brain for another big day tomorrow. Now do you see how much money you are *losing* by flipping channels for a lifetime?

You're catching on, right?

Since showing you my day seemed to work out well, let me dive further into it to show you how, even if I'm busier than a bee in spring, I can stay fit, eat well, and keep my head together. And you can, too. Here are my daily tricks that help me perform my job like a prizefighter. By the way, this foolproof program has cost tens of thousands of dollars and taken years in research and development. So pay attention!

IT'S MENTAL

What's the key to a prizefighter's ability to win? Focus. Focus is like a muscle that is strengthened every time you use it. No other humans in history have had as many daily distractions as us twenty-first-century prizefighters. The caveman with his club didn't often fall prey to distraction. While hunting for food, he was on high alert, absorbed fully in the task at hand. He concentrated like his life depended on it . . . because, well, it did. One momentary lapse in focus and rather than finding lunch, he was lunch!

The same is true today. Those who are focused on their hunt become the most adept at capturing the biggest trophies. Those who lack focus don't even get unframed participation certificates.

I've developed quite a knack for concentration, so let me tell you, high-kicker, my proven ways to sharpen your focus.

1. **Stay hydrated.** John tells me at least five times a day to drink more water. My driver Albert keeps bottles of water stocked in the backseat of the car, and John often texts Albert to tell him to make me drink it. I still get dehydration headaches, so note to self: Drink more water, Fredrik. It not only gets rid of those nasty headaches; it's a proven thought booster. Think that sounds silly? A study by *The Journal of Nutrition* found that mild dehydration (the kind where you don't even know you're thirsty) leads to inattentiveness and impaired abilities on cognitive tests. In fact, a decrease in your ability to focus is a red flag that you need more water. I won't go into all the health benefits of water because you've heard them before. I'll just say your body is more than half water, so it needs to be hydrated. If I don't have to pee every other hour, I know I'm not drinking enough. Try it; it's a lot of water and it will change your life (and your skin)! Plus, if you're trapped in a long meeting, you can, like me, use your bathroom break to check your e-mail.

2. **Avoid time wasters.** What are they and how do you spot them? According to Nielsen, the average American spends an hour of spare time a day on the Internet, an hour and

seven minutes on a smartphone, forty-six minutes listening to the radio, and—get ready for it—five hours a day, every day watching television! Even a Stockholm School of Economics dropout can figure out the math: That's thirty-five hours a week—or seventy-five days a year—*watching television*! I know it's scandalous for a TV star to say don't watch TV, but, unless you're learning your ABCs on *Sesame Street* or watching my dynamic sales techniques on *Million Dollar Listing*, you are wasting your time. Do you know all the good things you could do with seventy-five days? Fun? Family? Sleep? Exercise? Meditate? Sail to China and back? Make more money? Play with your Mousey and Fritzy?! You've probably said to yourself, *I wish I had the time to do that.* In her book *168 Hours*, Laura Vanderkam shows that most people who complain about not having enough time don't actually realize how much time they're wasting on idle activities. In a chapter entitled "Don't Do Your Own Laundry" she suggests time is money. Figure out how much the time you spend on the chores of life costs you, and you might decide it's better to outsource some of them so that you have time for some life-enriching activities instead.

3. **Exercise.** My New Year's resolution at the end of my second year in New York City was about exercise. I had finally fallen in love, I had been able to travel abroad, and I had gotten a great tan on an exotic vacation to the Caribbean. . . . But my pulse never quickened except when I negotiated. I never ran, never biked, and wasn't really ever sweating. Then, that New Year's Eve, I read something about the body being our temple, and I decided I don't need to worship it, but I certainly

need to start polishing it, repairing it, adding some ft.
and incense to it.

I cut down on caffeine and sugar, at least tried to (both useful stimulants), but switched to something better. I started getting my heart rate up for the sake of sweating. Physical activity has been proven to sharpen focus and release chemicals in the brain that aid learning and memory. The adrenaline I get working out powers my day. You have to figure out your daily workout. (More on that in a moment.) We all know how focused we feel after a good workout. Life's noises fade away, and we only hear what's important. We feel strong, mentally and physically, and our mood brightens. I've never met a sweaty depressed person coming out of the gym after a two-hour workout.

4. **Get more sleep.** I have a confession. I should have known I needed more sleep when, during my first year in business, I fell asleep while I was pooping in the office bathroom. Literally, I nodded off with my head against the toilet paper roll. (Go ahead and laugh. I laugh at myself, too, but if I can't be honest with you, who paid money for my book to read my story, then I'm just a liar.) I woke up to a flush in the next stall.

If you're not getting enough sleep, you need to wake up! A recent study from Duke-NUS Graduate Medical School–Singapore found that the brains of people who don't get enough sleep age faster. If you're getting less than six hours of sleep per night, you reeeeeally need to spot your time wasters. Turn off that TV! I got help by hiring a dog walker for Mousey and Fritzy and a housekeeper for me. That extra expense paid off with what I'm able to achieve with those extra hours. Exchange wasted time for some good old snoozy time. There's all this mumbo jumbo about REM sleep and delta sleep that I could waste your time with, but let me just say, if you're not getting six to eight hours of sleep a night, there's a problem with both your schedule and your mind.

5. **Find a trigger.** If you watch *Million Dollar Listing New York*, you've probably noticed that I occasionally purse my lips. That's me summoning my überconcentration. It's like my personal Ritalin that stimulates a sudden, focused intensity. Figure out what you can do to bring yourself instantly back in the room. You can wiggle your toes, touch your nose, bite your finger—whatever it takes. Find a trigger to snap yourself back into focus, and use it as your secret superpower. Do it. Really. Right now!

6. **Dump the negative.** By my fourth year in business I was known as "the listing machine." I was making serious bucks for my young age and was proving myself to be a real go-getter. I remember the year I hit $1 million in income for the first time. My problem was I couldn't enjoy the success because I had some friends who weren't celebrating this new path with me. Instead, they seemed eager to share their negativity and pull me down. It came to a crescendo one night when I was out with a group of friends and they told me I didn't need more success but that I needed more distractions. They didn't realize they were basically saying, "Be stuck like us." Luckily, my grandmother called the next day, and I told her what they'd said. She told me: "Att flyga som en fågel, du måste först klippa av det som tynger dig ned," which trans-

lates to something un-grandmother-like: "To fly like a bird, you have to first get rid of the poop that weighs you down." If you have friends holding you back, an ex who stalks you, a mother-in-law who demeans you, or a hurtful memory from childhood that sticks with you, you have to deal with it. My suggestion is to cut it out like Mary J. Blige in her song "No More Drama."

If you've got a nagging problem, get some therapy or find someone to talk to. If your friends are dragging you down, find new ones. The extra burden of carrying that around is holding you back. As a friend on Facebook recently posted, "An entire sea of water cannot sink a ship unless the water gets inside the ship. Just as the negativity of the world cannot pull you down unless you allow that negativity to enter your being."

I love Eckhart Tolle's reminder in *The Power of Now* that we don't have to replay the pain and sorrows of our pasts over and over on repeat in our minds. "How do you drop a piece of hot coal that you are holding in your hand?" he asks. "By recognizing that you don't want to suffer the pain or carry the burden anymore and then letting go of it." If you're holding a hot coal, *drop it*! Once you do, it can't bother you anymore and you'll be able to focus on what's really important. Accept whatever pain you are going through, fully take it in, and be it; then it will vaporize. It really works; I promise. Try it!

Another example is when my partner at the Internet start-up, Maria, and I became enemies because we started fighting over money. She met a new boyfriend, and he decided he didn't like us together at all, and he wanted a stake in her money. In addition to being partners in the business, we also owned an apartment together. In the end, Maria and I were partners in being equally stupid, and I will never, ever fight over money with anyone again. The situation became very dark, full of friction and drama, until one day I decided I'd had enough and that it was time to leave the company and the friendship behind. Come to think of it, I actually did the same thing when my parents divorced. I let them deal with the drama without me. I don't know if it was the right way to deal with it, but I decided not to dwell in their anger.

If there are things you're carrying around or people in your life who are just pushing your buttons, holding you back, secretly hating on you, don't sit around with them waiting for you to lose. Don't let them take your shine. Keep on movin'.

I'm tired of talking about this! Let's move on!

EXERCISE

As I told you, I like to get to the gym by 6:00 A.M. every morning at the latest. It gives me a rush and starts my day off right. I realize, however, that getting to the gym every morning (or even at all) may not be possible for everyone. Gyms are over-rated anyway. They are usually in basements with no windows, too cold or too hot, and can smell like someone's socks. But getting some sort of exercise every day is possible for everyone, and that is a fact. There are other options: yoga, swimming, walking, running, dancing, hiking, martial arts, aerobics, Hula-Hooping, Zumba, CrossFit, Bar Method . . . The list is endless. But you don't even have to do any of those; there are ways to get a workout in anywhere, because you have a body, and, unless you're Sandra Bullock, there is gravity everywhere.

The hardest part of exercise is getting started. There's that moment when one side of your brain says, *I should work out, and probably right now*, and the other side says, *Nah, I'm just going to watch some TV, and then maybe I'll consider it again.*

Have you ever seen the classic Donald Duck cartoons from the thirties and forties? When Donald was conflicted, a cute, little angel duck with white wings would suddenly appear over his left shoulder, and then, over his other shoulder, in a darker cloud, a little evil devil duck with a long tail showed up. Both whispered opposite ideas in opposite ears. We all have the angel and the devil. I'm your angel, by the way. And I'm cute, so listen to me now.

The brain and the body are always looking for ways to get out of working out. Being lazy is just so easy. Listening to the devil and his temptations is always easier in the short run. But your commitment to yourself is for life, not just the next five minutes. If you want to be at the top of your game—any game—you have to exercise. And don't give me any excuses.

What I'm about to share with you can be done anywhere, whether you're delayed in the airport, stuck in the office, traveling for business, or stuck at home with a blizzard outside. This is called the "Dirty Dozen," and I got it from fitness guru Greg Gomez, who has trained everyone from Bruce Littlefield (my high-kicking, in shape coauthor on this book) to Beyoncé. You can make this part of your daily routine no matter where you are. These exercises require zero equipment, build strength in all the right places, and are easy to do correctly. Ready, high-kicker? Let's do it together. I stretched while I was writing that paragraph about Donald Duck. So, I'll wait while you spend a few minutes stretching the muscles of your arms and legs. (I'm returning an e-mail.) Okay, ready?

- **Twelve old-fashioned jumping jacks.** Stand with feet together, knees slightly bent, and arms to sides. Jump while raising arms and separating legs to sides. Land with legs apart and arms overhead. Jump again while lowering arms and returning legs to center. Land on feet with arms and legs in original position. That's one. Keep going!

- **Twelve body-weight squats.** With your feet flat on the floor, a little wider than your shoulders, extend your arms out in front of you with your palms down. Slowly bend your legs, while keeping your back as straight as possible and your head facing forward. Squat down until your thighs are parallel to the floor. Stand back up. And again!

- **Twelve push-ups.** Get facedown on the ground and set your hands slightly wider than shoulder width apart. Think of your body from head to heels as one straight line. To keep your form, clench your butt and tighten your abs. Look slightly in front of you, not straight down. At the top of your push-up, your arms are straight and supporting your weight. Lower yourself down until your elbows are at a ninety-degree angle. Keep your elbows in! Pause slightly, and then explode back up until you're back in the starting position. We've only got eleven more.

- **Twelve walking lunges.** Stand with your feet to-gether. Step forward with your left leg, lowering your hips toward the floor. Bend both knees (almost at ninety degrees). The back knee should come close but not touch the ground. Your front knee should be over the ankle, and the back knee should be pointing to-ward the floor. Push off with your right foot and bring it to the starting position. That's one. Next step forward with the right leg and repeat. That's two.

- **Twelve sit-ups.** Lie on your back with bent knees. Put your feet flat on the floor one to two feet in front of your tailbone. Cross your arms on your chest and squeeze your shoulder blades together. Exhale, then tighten your abs while curling up toward your bent knees. Tilt your chin forward slightly as you come up. Keep your feet on the ground and your lower back against the floor throughout the exercise. Pause for a one count at the top. Lower yourself back down until your back is fully in contact with the floor. Keep pulling your abs in as we do eleven more!

- **Twelve chair dips.** Sit with the heels of your hands on the edge of a sturdy chair. Slide your butt off the seat, and support your weight with your hands. Keep your legs out in front of you at a ninety-degree angle. Pull your abs in. Bend your elbows and slowly lower your butt toward the floor. Keep your elbows tucked in as your body just clears the seat. Push yourself back up until your arms are straight. And repeat!

Now repeat the series again, anywhere from three to five times. Don't argue with me! This routine will get you going, and, if you don't do anything else, make this your daily baseline workout. Take a "before" photo. I want to see you "after" a month. Tag it proudly everywhere #TheSell #DirtyDozen.

P.S. Want to know something else I do during boring meetings, on flights, or while driving the car? I sit up straight, flex my core by pulling my belly button in toward my back, and breathe. I do that intermittently for an hour or so and achieve real results. I have an eight-pack now because I've been practicing it while writing this chapter, and I'm feeling great!

DIET

Everything physical comes back to what you eat. You don't have to live on a farm and pick your own apples and milk the cows to get good food. You can live in a city and still stick to those vows you made to yourself. This is pretty simple. It's about being smart and logical. If it's made in a factory, you shouldn't eat it. Anything that comes sealed in a plastic wrapper or crammed inside a can is probably not the most nutritious, okay?

I've always heard that if you're really hungry, you should eat an apple. If I'm really hungry, a protein shake does it for me. I try to eat a lot of protein and very few carbs. That's what I've found works for me and keeps my machine running well. Fish, steak, chicken, and salad or soup. I like colorful food. I feel like that has more nutrition. I never eat pasta. No rice. No potatoes. Just good, clean, unprocessed food. A lot of white fish, sometimes salmon, a lot of salads, nuts, and raisins. Speaking of salads, dinner doesn't have to be expensive to be healthy. Sometimes Derek and I go to Olive Garden and eat all the salad we want for $9.99.

My vice was Diet Coke. . . . I was obsessed. Especially in the summer . . . a tall glass full of big, perfect ice cubes, a slice of lemon, the crackling of the ice and explosion of foam at the top, the condensation on the outside of the glass, my own reflection in the bubbly surface before my lips touch the liquid . . . Can you tell how much I loved it? It was my little treat, my little vice. I gave myself permission to do that one naughty thing. You probably have some sort of vice, too. And since you've got your big-girl panties on, you can decide for yourself if you want to give yourself permission for that.

For years I'd read about how bad Diet Coke and aspartame are, but the information went in one ear and out the other. I recently kicked the habit. It was tough, but I thought, *I'm drinking this black liquid. What is all that chemical stuff?* Then I stopped. The second day I had a headache, which by the third day grew to be incredibly painful. I got more motivated by the headache, almost enjoyed it, because I knew that was a sign the chemicals were leaving my body. After the third day, my headache disappeared, I became more energetic, and I've been sleeping really well at night. The surprise benefit is that I have a lot fewer urges for sugar.

It was a doable task. I made a commitment to myself, and I have been true to that commitment. I'm no hero for gosh sakes, but I do feel proud of myself. Too often we try to take on too many things at once. We think, *I'm going to lose twenty pounds, stop smoking, start going to the gym, get a new job, spice up my relationship, and look for a new house.* And then we wonder why we fail. If you try too much at once, it's a fiasco. Don't make the "New Year's resolution" mistake and try to change your life all at once. Take one at a time. Two or three weeks in, when you feel accomplished in one goal, move on to the next.

I'm not a doctor or a nutritionist, and I'm not giving you medical advice. But I will tell you I take a multivitamin every morning. I also take an odorless garlic tablet, flaxseed oil, and fish-liver oil at bedtime. During my teenage years, I used to get sick often, but I never get sick anymore. I also always stock up on Emergen-C. Any time I'm traveling on a plane, I take one at takeoff and one at landing. It's loaded with vitamin C and energizing B, D, and E vitamins.

What I don't do is eat things that I know are going to make me feel bad or make me fat. And you shouldn't either. I listen to my body. I like the taste of orange juice, but it's all sugar and sends me into a frenetic tailspin. So, I steer clear. I also don't do french fries, white bread, and white rice because they're fattening and full of empty calories. Pizza must be the worst food invention in the world: melted cheese, oil, and white bread, all of which don't really contain anything good for you. I also don't ruin a fabulously nutritious salad by dousing it in cholesterol-laden, fattening dressing. I use a little olive oil, balsamic vinegar, and a squeeze of lemon instead. I used to eat protein bars thinking that they were healthy. I guess some of them are okay, but replacing every other meal with a glorified chocolate cake with added protein turns into a bad habit quickly. I simply try to stay away from any factory food. I also used to go to the movies and get those nachos with the fake cheese. Mmmmm . . . I loved that. But I always felt sick and disgusted afterward. So, I said, "Adios, nachos."

I also want to share my theory on ordering at a restaurant. Just how the first thirty seconds of your morning sets the tone for your day, your thirty-second answer to "Can I take your order?" is going to have a ripple effect on not just the next twenty-four hours, but your entire life, too. The only time to change your life is today. Try this trick: While holding that big, folded menu in your hands, think about how you would answer *after* the meal. At the end of dinner, if you had to order again, you'd order differently. Because you are full, too full, you feel guilty. You would select something healthier—something you *know* is good for you. So, when that waiter asks, "What will you have?," choose your words as though it's two hours later.

We've all asked ourselves, *Why did I eat that?* Is your blood sugar normal? Do you have heartburn? Feel like a six-day-old cream puff? Do you have gas? Do you need to run to the bathroom? Do you secretly pinch to see if you can feel belly fat under the table? Do you suck in your stomach while leaving the restaurant? Do you wake up in the middle of night hurting?

Are there times I've overeaten? Gone off the rails? Absolutely. I sat in bed the other night and ate a bag of potato chips while watching *Godzilla*, and I'm not referring to Fritzy. But I make those moments the exception, not the rule. I'm six foot four, and I'm almost two hundred pounds, but I don't have a lot of body fat. I can't wait until I'm eighty-three years old, wearing a grass hat and sitting under an olive tree with a big bowl of pasta and a bottle of white wine behind my giant mansion outside Venice. I live an active, crazy life, and I do eat a lot. My calorie intake is high. When I go to restaurants, I apologize to everyone at the table and usually order two starters and a main course. I always pick one starter containing 100 percent protein, like tuna tartare or beef carpaccio, and then one salad. The main is almost always fish, the biggest, whitest fish they have, and preferably grilled. Sometimes I add chicken or a second fish if the plates are small.

Desserts are a complete fiasco. No, I mean like a total

disaster every time. You have to live, I know. Most of us have a sweet tooth. My business partner, John, is obsessed with sweets as much as he is obsessed with money. For a long time, he actually developed a problem habit. He used to go from his apartment every night in a cab and travel forty blocks to get his favorite chocolate cake, in a paper box, and bring it home and eat it in his kitchen. He just couldn't stop, until he realized it had become a sickness.

I'm not going to tell you to take the joy out of life by never eating dessert again. But just know the aftereffects. The first spoonful is incredible, we all agree, but by the fourteenth spoonful it's not really doing much for you. I never, ever, order desserts. I let the others do so, and then I have one little taste of theirs. That's it. I get 90 percent of the enjoyment but 0 percent of the guilt or stomach fat.

In the end, you are what you eat. And if that doesn't make you want to eat well, try this on for size: A study based on data from the US Bureau of Labor Statistics found that the paychecks of obese workers are about 2.5 percent less than the paychecks of their thinner counterparts in the same professions. So, eat as if your life (and your bank account) depends on it. Look down at that plate, and think, *That's me lying there*. Open your mouth, and give it one last look. Do you want to become a lean, fast-swimming fish, or a clump of melted cheese?

Now dig in.

SLEEP

It is estimated that nearly 75 percent of American adults experience some sort of sleeping disorder. Most people I know in New York complain of having insomnia at least a couple of nights a week. Does that make you yawn? Researchers have found that sleeping too little—less than six hours a night—is one of the biggest predictors of on-the-job burnout. A study by Harvard estimated that American companies are losing more than $63 billion a year in productivity due to sleep deprivation.

According to a poll conducted by the National Sleep Foundation, more than one-third of Americans say their sleepiness interferes with their daily life. I think the other two-thirds are lying (or fell asleep from exhaustion while filling in the form).

I take sleep very seriously. I'm obsessive about it, and you should be, too. A successful person can't afford to be sleepy. Sleepy is unsexy, unexciting, and unproductive. All of which costs money! It makes me anxious to know I'm not going to get more than six hours of sleep in a night, because I know it's bad for me, for my health, for my looks, and for my presentation. Everything is a fiasco with no sleep.

Some people are proud to say they don't need much sleep. "I only have to sleep three hours a night!" they brag. I always look at them like they are insane, since they probably are. Who in their right mind wouldn't let their mind and body rest?

I love early mornings but know I need eight hours of quality sleep, which means if I'm getting up at 5:30 A.M. I like to be in bed at 9:45 P.M. That's fine with me. Call me old and boring, but call me a multimillionaire. I am not interested in staying up to watch the late-night shows. If it's a really interesting show, DVR it and watch it the next day. The only late show I'm interested in is *Sleeping with Fredrik Eklund*. Trust me, it's a really interesting show.

You should also know what makes you the most comfortable when you sleep. It's a very individual thing. I like to sleep on the right side of the bed, on my stomach, with my head on a medium-soft pillow in a very cold bedroom and have my naked body covered in soft sheets and a down comforter. For years I couldn't afford a decent mattress, so when I finally could, I got one with a memory-foam top. After a week, Mousey developed a skin rash with big, nasty bumps all over her soft little body, which I soon discovered was an allergic reaction to the chemicals in the mattress. I was furious, and Mousey was itchy. The company said to give it a few weeks and the chemicals would dissipate. *Yes, right into my lungs*, I thought. I threw the mattress out. And then I let Mousey pee on it. I'm very happy with my all-natural (and Swedish) Hästens horsehair mattress and so is Mousey. It wicks away the moisture, and you're never hot and never cold. And no horses or dogs were harmed making it. Invest in a mattress that is right for you. You're going to spend one-third of your life on top of it, and the other two-thirds of your life depends on it.

It took me thirty-six years to realize the life-changing wonder of earplugs. Now that I know their silent magic and how to properly insert them—roll each plug into a skinny little tube and pull up on your ear to slide it into your ear canal—I'll put them in every night for the rest of my life, even when I sleep by myself. I figured out that if someone can see the plug in your outer ear, it's not really in tight enough. Now that I know how to properly insert them, no sound disturbs me—not panting dogs, snoring husband, screeching sirens, whining air conditioner, or rowdy street noise.

I've forgotten them a few times while traveling, and it was a disaster. One time I tried to make my own with napkins on a United flight, and I could clearly hear the flight attendants giggling at the six-foot-four TV star with napkins sprouting from his ears like paper flowers. Please don't make the same mistake. Buy a pair and see if you sleep more soundly.

Find your tricks to help you fall asleep. Drink a glass of warm milk. Have sex. Go on a long walk. Take a steamy, hot bath. Read Nietzsche. When I have trouble getting there, I lie on my back and visualize relaxing my body parts from my toes to my head, trying to feel that there's space between the mattress and my body. I imagine there's a thin layer of air below me and I'm ever so slightly floating above the mattress. By that time, I'm falling asleep. I breathe in, filling my lungs with crisp, blue air. I breathe out red-hot air, breathe in blue, breathe out red, breathe in blue . . .

Let's get to the next chapter. This just put me to zzzzzzzzzzzz.

CHAPTER 6

MAKE 'EM SMILE

Cultivate Your Charm and Sense of Humor

The second time I met Justin Timberlake was with Jessica Biel, and we were all squeezing into a tiny little elevator in a building on Nineteenth Street. I immediately looked down at Jessica's shoes, pointed, and said, "I'm obsessed with your shoes! No, I mean really, really obsessed." Here's what that accomplished in about five seconds. It said to her, *You've got great taste.* It said to him, *And you've got nothing to worry about.* It said to both of them, *I'm a funny character.* We instantly connected, and they were thinking, *We like this guy, Fredrik Eklund, who is walking us into this multimillion-dollar home.* By the way, I met Justin a few years earlier when he was with Cameron Diaz. That time I high-kicked in front of Cameron up on the rooftop terrace in the sunset and told her to watch my profile. The kick always looks amazing in profile.

YOU'VE GOT THIRTY SECONDS

I believe that the first thirty seconds of meeting someone sets the tone for the rest of your time together, whether that ends up being five minutes or fifty years. Read that sentence again because it is a strong one. Yes, *you have thirty seconds to capture someone's attention.* Perhaps that means I might come off as a character—so be it. But I believe successful people are (and should be) a little larger than life.

Perhaps the biggest deal of my life—meeting Derek— happened within my thirty-second rule, so of course I'm going to tell you the story.

I had basically given up on love. I'd spent my years in New York working and secretly feared that I might be forever single. So I traveled to Greece alone. And on one of my last vacation days in Mykonos, a place I'd always felt destined to go, I saw this six-foot-five guy from behind. He was the only guy taller than me, but I didn't know what he looked like. I went up to him and tapped on his shoulder. When he turned around, I said, "Why are you so tall? I don't understand." He looked very confused. He smiled. I then continued, "I grew up on Swedish meatballs, which made me tall. What did you eat?" In those first thirty seconds, I had made a good impression and more than a friend.

Tick tock. Tick tock. Tick tock. Be smart about how you use that time. Not many people break the ice and take charge in the first thirty seconds of meeting. The person who does controls the moment and sets the tone for not just that encounter, but also for the relationship for a long time to come. A positive tone.

My theory is that everyone in the room—even the most boring person—secretly wants to laugh and have fun. I'm here to tell you there is no rule against having fun and being professional at the same time. Many years ago I told John that our number one goal in business was to have a good time and that we had to crack ourselves up at least once every day. Laughing until we cry. And we have. Yesterday in a very serious meeting on the forty-first-floor conference room with a view over the entire city, we started laughing so hard we actually cried. I don't even remember why we started laughing, and that really is the beauty of laughter. It's highly contagious. Suddenly, everyone in the room was crying with laughter, without anyone really knowing why, and then *that* becomes even funnier, because no one knows why everyone else is laughing.

You only have one life, and laughing will not only make you live longer, but will also help you attract money like a magnet.

Let me get serious and tell you the health benefits of laughter. A recent study by cardiologists at the University of Maryland Medical Center found that people with heart disease were 40 percent less likely to laugh than people the same age without heart disease. Need more reasons? Laughter has been proven to boost the immune system, trigger the release of "feel good" endorphins, and relieve physical tension and stress. Laughing is sexy. Everybody wants to laugh more than anything. Everybody wants to be with somebody who makes them laugh. When looking for love, most people will say they want to find someone who makes them laugh.

Further, humor is infectious. Infectious in a good way. When laughter is shared, it brings people together and helps them connect. In business and in life, rapport is everything. If you're the one at work who makes others feel good with your sense of humor and charisma, that's cash in your pocket. My funniness is part of . . . no, it's *the core* of my winning formula.

When I'm about to enter a conference room filled with people, I stop for a second outside the door. I grab the door handle and close my eyes, and I let my body be filled with joy. I tickle myself. Maybe a little kick. I visualize laughter, and then I open the door with a big smile. Regardless of what is going on in there, I physically jump into the room like a happy child and scream out, "Hi there!" All heads turn, and I open my arms. "I'm here! Good to see you all." And, once again, a big smile.

You, my high-kicker, want to be remembered for being the person who brightens the mood in the room. Truly successful people are happy (I'm not talking about money!), and only people who love what they do are truly happy. Happy people are winners. Happy makes happy. A sense of humor and charisma is great for business. Everyone wants to be around and work with happy people—and buy what they're selling. Are you following me? Humor and charm immediately put you on a pedestal; the person or people you're with might be more experienced, more successful, or more famous than you, but you have something they all want: energy and happiness. And that's contagious.

CHARM 101

Everyone is born with varying amounts of natural charisma, but charm can be acquired through practice. Since a lot of people on social media have asked me how to attract people and get people to like you, let's go to Freddy's Charm School.

Charm, my friends, is the art of having an appealing personality. Though I do know successful rude people, I always think their success will be temporary or at least empty because they are unhappy. We're more likely to build great personal and professional relationships with people we like, people who are agreeable, nice, funny. . . . In short, charming people get their way. You already know this, but then why are there so few funny and happy people out there? Our entire lives we have been told to tone it down. I'm here to tell you to tone it up.

Let me show you how I charm people on the phone. When I call United Airlines or the Ritz-Carlton or my cable company, I'll say to the person on the other end (who is probably stuck behind a desk in a windowless call center somewhere far away), "Hi! Where are you today?" They'll say, "Seattle." I'll say, "Oh, a call center or working from home?" They'll say, "Call center." I'll say, "Well, you're almost home." If we're talking about my travel plans or I'm booking a hotel, I'll ask, "You want to come with me? You can fit in my bag!" They'll laugh and say, "I wish!" Customers are often rude to customer service phone representatives. If you're nice, you're getting more than the guy who isn't. You're probably getting your way. Besides which, it just feels better. It's better karma. Why have an unpleasant encounter when you can have a pleasant one?

That's why I'm also always nice to the people in Starbucks. Instead of just barking out my order, I'll ask, "What's your name?" Or "How's your day going?" People don't ask. People don't care. And being fellow humans, we should. It only takes a moment to make an investment in others, and then they're definitely more willing to make an investment in us. If that means they put a little extra love in making my coffee or just a smile, it perpetuates a charmed day. It gives each of us a pause between all the noise. I want to be the nice guy who is remembered amid all that rush, and you, high-kicker, want to be the nicely remembered one, too.

You also never know who will make you rich. By being rude

to people, it will catch up with you one day. You might forget, but other people don't.

When I first moved to New York and was taking my real estate course, the classroom was near Bryant Park. During my lunch break, I'd buy a salad at a local deli and sit in the park and dream. It was fun and inspiring to watch all the people buzzing about. I nodded and smiled at them. I'd occasionally say, "I love your shoes" or, "Great bag." People liked that. A sincere compliment rewards both the receiver and the giver. And it's *free*! Try it and see. Smile while doing it, to double the effect. A brief but uplifting encounter picks you up because you've picked someone else up. I loved watching those busy New Yorkers get a sudden extra bounce in their step.

Being genuinely glad to meet or talk to someone is charming. Charming people smile. Charming people nod. Charming people look you in the eye and smile and nod. We don't always agree with others, but respecting another person's opinion is charming. Charming people know that opening the door for someone is nice. Charming people know that everyone likes the sound of his or her name, and they greet others by name as often as possible. Charming people know that everyone likes to be listened to, and they are genuinely interested in other people's stories and life experiences. Charming people want to know others' thoughts and opinions.

Charming people want to agree. We look for common ground and try to find something to agree on, even if we have a completely opposite opinion. Rather than attempting to one-up someone with our own successes, charming people are impressed by others' accomplishments and triumphs. We say, "Wow! That's fantastic. I hope to do that one day."

Charming people also show a little vulnerability. Charming people are willing to talk about our mistakes, weaknesses, and failures. Charming people don't mind looking a little silly. Charming people don't mind making fun of ourselves. People respect you more when you're the one willing to let your guard down.

Think of something stupid you've done that will make you laugh out loud. (I'll tell you mine, if you tell me yours! And then tell the world, because it shows you are not taking yourself too seriously.) I once was sitting at a huge conference table with twenty or so people in this important development meeting uptown. I had to pee urgently, and, as you already know, my pee breaks are also my time to hammer out e-mails and put out fires. There was someone in the stall. Knowing I didn't have a lot of time, I walked up to the urinal, pulled out my phone, and then pulled out my peepee. I now know it's not so smart to answer e-mails while standing up peeing. After sending off a deal sheet for a Hong Kong buyer and telling my assistant to deposit a commission check ASAP, I felt the telltale warmth in my pants. I looked down at my suit, which was soaked with urine. I wasn't laughing; I panicked.

I could not exit the bathroom. I whispered "Oh my God" over and over again like a mantra. This was an important meeting! I could not go back into the conference room covered in urine. I would get fired! And I was worried someone else was going to come into the bathroom or the guy in the stall was going to finish his business and come out. I stayed completely still listening to the silent bathroom, fearing that someone was going to walk in and discover my predicament. I momentarily considered taking my pants off and walking out half naked but decided instead to take off my jacket, wrap it around my waist like a Scottish kilt, and dash to the elevator, all while pretending I was reading e-mails on my phone so I didn't have to look at anyone. I'm sure I left a trail behind me. My driver laughed at me when I told him what had happened. We drove away, and I never came back to the meeting. I texted my colleagues to say I had to deal with an "emergency situation." I did not say I wet myself, but now they know.

What's the point of the story? Why am I telling you this? Well, for one thing, I want you to know the importance of sitting down to pee if you're answering e-mails. But I also want you to smile, even at my expense. I want you to know that any time I think of that story, it makes me laugh. I have more of those, and they are a part of who I am, and my ability to laugh at life's foibles rather than let them defeat me contributes to my success.

Let me tell you a secret: The queen of England has peed on herself, too. Did reading that just make you laugh? Does that make you feel better? Well, you know it's true. I've done it. You've done it. I suspect the pope has had explosive diarrhea, even though he prayed not to. And what does that mean? We laugh because we've been there, too. I don't think I'm a comedian, but life is often absurd, and people are funny. If we can't laugh at the absurdity of it all, then why bother getting up in the morning? Put your arms around that. Hold it. Understand it. Help encourage it.

My whole life is about smiling and finding laughter. Why? Because my work is demanding. Laughter is the antienergy, the polar opposite of the old way of working hard. You have to make an effort to have fun and then repeat the fun in your head. If your client is frowning, you have to smile. In fact, if I catch myself frowning, I turn my own frown into a smile. How do I do that? I think of things that make me laugh. I make fun of something I've done. I watch an old episode of my show and crack up at my insanity. The bottom line is that I know to never, ever take myself too seriously. And neither should you.

Jokes aside. Let me be serious for a second and give you some hard facts about laughing matters:

- Numerous studies have shown that laughter lowers blood pressure, increases blood oxygenation, gives a whole-body workout, decreases stress, reduces the frequency of colds, increases the power of disease-killing cells, prevents heart disease, and improves alertness, creativity, and memory. *That's something to laugh at.*

- A study at Johns Hopkins University School of Medicine found that humor increases test scores, which means humor helps you perform better. *I already knew that.*

- Dr. William Fry of Stanford University found that in less than a half second after exposure to something funny, the whole brain, both left and right hemispheres, becomes engaged. *Are you engaged yet?*

- Economists at the University of Warwick found that happiness increases productivity by around 12 percent. *I think they are wrong. I think it is 112 percent.*

- A study published in the journal *Proceedings from the National Academy of Sciences* found that smiling, happy people make more money. *I certainly smile on my way to the bank.*

- Research by Duke University found that a smile makes you more memorable by sending a message to decision makers and influencers that they can trust and cooperate with you. *Show those pearly whites.*

- A study at the University of Cambridge puts a value on the smile during a negotiation at a 10 percent increase in trust. *Are you following me?*
- Research from Wharton, MIT, and London Business School has found that every chuckle brings with it a host of business benefits. Laughter relieves stress and boredom, boosts engagement and well-being, and spurs creativity, collaboration, and productivity. *Do you understand?*

Babies laugh, on average, four hundred times a day, and people over thirty-five laugh fewer than fifteen times a day. What happened? A recent study of Gallup data found that we laugh significantly less on weekdays than we do on weekends. Why? I suppose work is a sobering endeavor. But guess what? There's some good news for me and you, high-kicker. Karen Machleit, professor of marketing at the University of Cincinnati College of Business Administration, has found that humor increases sales. She found that humor in advertisements increases credibility and makes consumers much more likely to accept an advertiser's claims. Professor Freddy's translation: If you're bringing the laughter, you're bringing the business. You may have heard that money can't buy happiness. But actually the opposite is true: Happiness buys money.

Business is often so damn stressful that you just *have* to find a way to laugh. In my world, apartments aren't ready on time, attorneys threaten to sue, and everyone freaks out. If you're the one who brings humor or a smile to the situation, you are the hero.

You defuse the bomb. A joke or the right sense of humor cuts the tension like a warm knife through butter. It always wins. The guy or girl who brings the fun to the party is the one everyone wants to be around (and go home with!).

The business world is absurd. It's hilarious. Here I am dressed up in my fantastic suit to sell you something that you're going to overpay for. And I'm only going to make money if you buy it. We're going to dance this dance together. I'm not solving the problems of the Third World. I'm unfortunately not curing cancer. I'm not flying to the moon. I'm a salesperson . . . a fabulous moneymaking one because I've figured out that charm and laughter bring big money.

The old guard of my competitors will not even understand what I am writing here. They long for a world twenty years ago when clowns like me were still in high school. They are stuck living back in the day when you were successful if you "behaved" and "toned it down." And that is why they are falling behind now, because the world has changed for the better.

I'm not saying you need to become a stand-up comedian, but you have to learn to incorporate humor and charm into your life and into your sales. When I go into Starbucks, I say, "I'm *heeerrrre!*" and flash a smile. Everyone is like "Huh? What?" but they smile with me! You know my quirky facial expressions? I often pull them out to bring levity to a tense situation. I put them on my face to evoke a laugh. I'm no Eddie Murphy, Kathy Griffin, or Chris Rock, but there are several types of comedic devices I use to make The Sell. And they work for me. Perhaps reading these might give you an idea of how you might bring a smile to the people you meet:

Quick-witted/clever. This is humor that comes from nuance or doing a subtle variation of the ordinary or expected and often involves clever wording or phrasing that catches you off guard and leaves you laughing. By its very definition (comedy plus speed), not everyone is going to get it, but those who do love it and you. I use this technique in a negotiation when I'm coming to the other party with bad news. I want to ease it up and make him or her smile. For example, when I call to say an offer is rejected, I might ask, "Are you sitting down? Are you holding on to something? Good! I have amaaaaaaazing news! Your offer has been rejected. [Pause] But I think I have a solution. . . ." If the news is bad, why double the effect by being serious and somber? You're making bad news easier to take by doing the opposite of what's expected.

Cheesy/campy. Cheesy/campy is the snaggletoothed stepsister of quick-witted/clever. These acts are often silly, colorful, and cliché filled. People who are cheesy often use puns, clever wordplay, and pickup lines. In business, I often make light of a situation in a cheesy way. When someone is asking me to accept their low offer, I might say, "*Hmmmmm.* Let me think about that. [I look like I'm really thinking hard. Then I make a silly face and give them the punch.] Um, *no.*"

Off-color/racy. This is a joke or comment you wouldn't tell your mother or a six-year-old girl. It's often tasteless and offensive to many listeners. Said at the wrong time, it can be deadly. Said to the right person, it can be the funniest moment of your life. When Derek is mad because I've been working all day and have missed dinner, I'll text him and say, "I'll cook you some Swedish meatballs tonight . . . ;)"

Sarcastic/dry. Observational humor often states the obvious or finds the real in the moment. It could be an ironic or satirical remark seemingly praising someone or something but really teasing or taunting. Those who pull this off can crack a room up. In a negotiation sometimes, I'll laugh and say, "I can't believe you can read my mind. How did you know that I needed a hundred thousand dollars more?"

Mocking/obnoxious. This is sarcasm on steroids, insulting and in-your-face. Insult comedy is an art, and in sales, potentially a deal killer. Obnoxious people often think they're being funny, but they're not. Use this one sparingly and only with special people. One time while talking to Luis, I bent down, opened his hair to see if there was a bird's nest in there, and then continued talking. With Ryan, I ran out of steel wool while cleaning my pots and pans and called him one night to ask to borrow a piece of his hair. (Note to both: Can't wait until your books come out and you can make fun of me!)

Self-deprecating. This is making fun of oneself, and I love it! If used effectively, self-deprecating humor is one of the quickest ways to get someone on your side because it cleverly makes others feel superior to you. When begging for extra legroom in a sold-out airplane, I look deep into the eyes of the flight attendant and say, "I'm six feet four inches with six-foot legs." Or if I'm ever late for an appointment, I might say, "Sorry! Fritzy's and Mousey's little legs couldn't pull my dog sled fast enough."

Goofy. This comedy is based on practical jokes, collisions, clumsiness, and embarrassing escapades, and often involves absurd situations and big physical action. This is my high-kick in a tailored suit in front of a shocked (but newly rich) seller!

Since we're talking about humor and charm, it's important for you to understand the art of the high-kick. It isn't really about the kick itself. The kick is a leitmotif for some of the most important recommendations in this book: to be yourself, to have a signature, to give people something to remember, to be on top of your game, and to do it with humor and style.

But since you asked, here is how to high-kick:

1. Start by standing still. Both feet on the ground and arms relaxed. The high-kick always comes unexpectedly with great energy and is in contrast to everything else around you, which is planned, forced, and static, and therefore it's important you begin from a relaxed pose.

2. Raise your leg up, bending at the knee and lifting to a forty-five-degree angle.

3. Lift higher and end with a straight leg because the only way is up for you from here.

4. It's important now to straighten your toe and hold this pose for a few seconds. Learn how to balance yourself with a straight leg and straight toe. Control! Don't start laughing if you lose control—just don't fall.

5. Now, when you have control, you can laugh—that's the point really—and anyone watching you will laugh, too, especially

if you are a big, broad-shouldered guy like me in a conservative three-piece suit.

My goal is to make sure everyone knows how to high-kick, even the superheroes.

When you get really good, you can control that slow kick and add your hands. Pretend you are a *Tyrannosaurus rex*, with angled hands downward, then kick and make a sound effect. I like the *"Weeeee"* in a light Michael Jackson voice. You can also finish off with a crazy face after the sound effect, like it's an attack on your enemy. Show your teeth.

When it was announced at an award ceremony that my team became number one in the nation, I let the microphone go and took center position on stage, beneath the spotlights. I high-kicked as my loved ones applauded, screamed, and jumped up and down, and my competition reeled.

When people think of me, they think of the high-kick. It now lives beyond me. Have you read Malcolm Gladwell's book *The Tipping Point*? The tipping point is that magic moment when an idea, trend, or social behavior crosses a threshold, tips, and spreads like wildfire. People run up to me every day and ask me to do a high-kick with them in photos. Taxi cars drive by with people high-kicking out the window. Construction workers yell out from scaffolding, "Fredrik!" and do a high-kick. In customs last week at Newark Airport, the customs officer looked at my passport, stood up from his stool, and did a high-kick!

Imagine having your own trademark move and having it work for you. Have you ever seen a Newton's cradle? Named after Mr. Gravity, Sir Isaac Newton, it's that device also known as an "executive ball clicker" because a lot of CEO types had a version of it on their desks in the 1970s. It demonstrates conservation of momentum and energy by a release of swinging spheres. When one of the balls on the end is lifted and released, it strikes the stationary spheres and a force is transmitted through them and pushes the last one upward. Maybe those CEOs understood the power of continuous momentum. A little effort, a lot of result. That's what humor does. When someone does the high-kick, they are selling me. They are helping me.

I certainly don't mind if you borrow the high-kick, but let me give you a few ideas for your own personal high-kick so you can have your own special trademark and write your own book on the subject. Think of Donald Trump's "You're fired" finger jab, or Tim Tebow's drop-to-one-knee prayer, or Michael Jackson's moonwalk, or John, my business partner, who sticks his butt out, snaps his fingers, and says, "I'm a *growwwwn* woman."

I told my *Million Dollar Listing* costar Luis before season three that he should do a little backward dance when he did a deal. Of course he didn't listen, and instead said, "*Boom*," so *you* can take his backward dance. It's available. Or can you do an amazing cartwheel? Vogue? Show your big bicep and make a tough-guy face? Maybe you do a break-dance turtle? Seriously. If you can, do that in a meeting and you're not just getting noticed— you're getting business.

But most important, do something. Take something that people have seen or already know, but make it yours. Make it your size. Make it fit you. Yes, it may be annoying the first three times you do it, but if you really own it and live it, it becomes part of who you are and makes people laugh *with* you and *love you.*

Let me tell you some news. In the last few years, there's been a shift in this world and certainly a change in business. In the past, particularly in New York, some of the rudest people with the worst reputations rose to the top. Nastiness worked. I won't mention any names, but they are now has-beens. And so are their ways. Today, moving forward, it is all about being charismatic, alluring, fascinating, and magnetic.

Prince and Princess Charming are the future. You are the future.

When you're trying to sell something—whether it's a million-dollar one-bedroom or a vacation idea to your love—be happy and be fun, especially in those first thirty seconds. Joke around. Even with the most boring and irritated person, it works. You'll turn a frown upside down and a no into a *yes*! I make fun of myself. I cut up a little. I'm not making a joke at anyone's expense. I'm making myself ridiculous in a harmless way. It's funny, and I'm not putting anyone else down. In fact, I'm making people more comfortable. If that scares you, go for simple charm. Be positive, spirited, and uplifting.

I've seen it so many times, where the grumpy old fart of a

seller or the bitchy and frugal buyer all of a sudden smiles back at me. Being a little nutty melts the frozen personality of even the crankiest Scrooge, and his cold heart suddenly warms up to you. Why? I'm going to whisper this now because it is the biggest secret of the chapter: *because they realize you are not a threat to them.* Laughter and charm, like a smile, are part of a universal language that everyone understands and always brings people together. Quite simply, people drop their hackles when you make them smile. They suddenly look at you as if you are an overgrown kid, still innocent and young (I'm not talking about actual age). You make them feel younger, too. It's almost like you can see the wrinkles in their faces disappear. You let life and light into the room with your humor. Putting a smile on someone else's face is a gift that keeps on giving.

Leave behind a smile. You do that, and you've made The Sell.

PART

TWO

When I was eight years old, I realized people around me needed some help and that I could make money by offering my services to them. The Sell was simple: I'd help them accomplish their tasks, and in exchange they'd help me by paying me. I folded sheets and towels with my mom, cleaned my grandfather's pool, cut my grandmother's lawn, walked my neighbors' dogs, took out their trash, cleaned their litter boxes, and fed their goldfish. I charged a fee, which I negotiated with each of them individually. Why? I recognized the negotiation as a pivotal part of the process. I could convince my neighbor to give me more money for my services than my grandmother.

I'm now a real estate broker. My job is to identify the needs of my client and then bring two parties together, a seller and a buyer, for the biggest transaction of their lives. My clients run the gamut from some of the world's most famous faces to the

Chinese mogul flying in for a day to buy a parking lot. With each of these clients, my role is often best friend, hand-holder, cheerleader, and marketing guru.

However, what I do today is identifying the *needs* of my clients—actually, inventing needs. Need equals money/services . . . and only then do you have negotiation power.

Whether I was assisting my family with chores when I was a kid or assisting people today with their most important life purchase, identifying needs is a process that requires chutzpah, finesse, and diligence. First, I have to find the clients; then I have to pitch them an idea that solves their specific needs; and then, if I succeed in convincing them to move forward, I have to negotiate the cost. Finally, I complete the transaction and claim my reward.

Chapters 7–10 provide step-by-step instructions on how, in this modern day, to

- find people who want your services;
- craft the perfect message;
- negotiate the parameters of any deal; and
- make The Sell and claim your payoff.

It's time for you to ask for what you want and get it.

CHAPTER 7

EXPAND YOUR REACH

Find an Audience Brilliantly,
Strategically, and Inexpensively

It was a bad idea, I thought. A terrible idea. The management of the real estate firm I was working for in 2006 introduced the company policy for Facebook. From then on all the agents were to create two Facebook accounts: one personal and one professional. *What's the difference?* I thought to myself. *I am professional because I am personal. I am the person I am because I love my job.* Well, they explained, the company didn't want to be associated with images of us, their salespeople, drinking at a bar or half-dressed on a beach. And, according to the new policy, neither would our clients.

I immediately said, "No!" All heads turned. "I'm not going to be split into different people. You can't please everyone. I am who I am, and I am one person. I want my clients to see all the colors of my rainbow. We need to attract attention, not run from it."

And guess what? I convinced the company to drop their suggested new policy, and my decision paid off. My more than five hundred thousand followers have played a crucial role in me becoming number one.

Whether you're an obstetrician or an undertaker, you need to find someone who will pay you for what you do. You need an audience, and every day is an audition! But how do we find your audience? Come closer. I'm going to whisper something very important in your ear: *Stop wasting your time.* The days of door-to-door are over. Today you can open a lot of doors at the same time. It's time to score new business and attention the twenty-first-century way: through social media.

No matter your career, it's still important to build a network of contacts, and though there are certainly old-fashioned, Rolodexy kinds of ways to do this, social media is the easiest and most effective and lets you precisely target those you want. Let's say you are a writer working on your next book; with social media you can befriend and target readers, publishers, and journalists. A dentist, a contractor, or a landscaper can attract clients and referrals. A seller like me can grab buyers and bring attention to what I have to sell.

The instantaneousness of it all is refreshing, regardless of all the optional filters and guaranteed information overkill. A good picture with an inspiring caption of a very honest moment taken in the now and shared with your world is a hit, a giant billboard, a perfect pitch, and many times goes straight to the heart.

And this social media phenomenon is just beginning. The platforms will continue to change, evolve, and grow, and you (and your future empire) will with it. Your digital influence will only get bigger from here, and, if you work it well, the percentage of your sales sourced online will soar. Your followers, buyers, fans, high-kickers, friends, or whatever you want to call them are yours to keep and will be your digital capital in the bottomless bank vault that is social media.

So, let's get rich together. Let's invest some time and effort into social media. Let's talk about how to use these platforms to make The Sell—instantly, globally, and for *free*. Those are three powerful words, so remember them.

But saying you are good at social media makes some people uncomfortable. To them, it's like saying "I like getting attention" or "I'm vain, egotistical, and self-promotional." To other modern-day Luddites, social media seems like it's a user's personal billboard proclaiming, "I want to be popular." Well, I have some news for you, friends: To be successful in this life, you need to have a little bit of braggadocio. What we post on social media, and how people react to those posts, does, indeed, mirror our lives. The question is, are you good at it or bad at it?

Perhaps you feel overwhelmed with all the platforms, all the chatter, and are fearful that the ship has already sailed without you. Do you feel like social media is one giant, annoying competition? Do you think everyone online is pretending to live amazing lives, always on vacation, chasing beauty and perfection? Do you dread the task of staying updated, thinking there are already not enough hours in the day, and you just want to unplug, tune out, and turn it all off? Do you believe if you see one more hashtag you'll scream? Do you think if you have to check in at one more place, you'd rather just check out for good?

You do? Good! We all do at times. That is why this chapter is so important. That is why we need to talk about it and really break it down. Together we can figure this thing out.

One thing about signing on to film a reality show, especially doing the first season and then seeing it air and having people react to it, to *me*, has been freeing. Well, it wasn't at first. I was scared I would be judged, disliked, even hated by some, but I finally reached the realization that while *a lot* of people love watching and connecting with me on TV, I'm not going to please everyone. Ever. Sharing my life with millions of people has made me grow thick skin and believe in myself and my own path. And hopefully there can be a lesson for everyone in that. When it comes to social media, always be authentic to who you are and stay true to your real self. And don't be scared to share it with the world. That is not just my secret to social media success; it's my overall perspective on success at life itself. What's scary for most of us is that anyone with a keyboard is a critic, and believe me, they can and will find a way to say something mean, so you need to stay strong and not focus on the negativity, or the petty jealousy. The naysayers have always found—and always will find—a way to project their own misery onto you.

You absolutely can't let the fear of someone's disapproval limit your social media expansion. And that's what it is, expansion, and it has only begun. We are just ten years into it, and it has already transformed our lives, the way we communicate, and the way we make The Sell. Instead of seeing social media as a threat and something overwhelming, you need to see it as an opportunity. You don't need to conquer it all at once. Baby steps, little baby high-kicks, one post at a time.

Obviously, you'll need to know your company policy and think about what your clients and future job opportunities will see about your life. The way I do that is by keeping things positive. I don't put anything that's offensive or depressing. For me, the point of sharing is to inspire, make people happy, and make The Sell. Why would I post something that would run contrary to those three things? Yes, I write about my feelings and emotions, but I stay away from too political and polarizing issues. They don't make The Sell. Quite simply, if you post strong political views, you will lose half your audience (the lefties or righties), which could be half the potential buyers of your message, and if you post photos of yourself trimming your nose hair and messy homes, you're grossing people out.

Okay, you say. Perhaps your worry isn't about the critic with the mean comments or about what to post. Perhaps you are a good poster but you simply don't know how to grow your audience and expand your reach. The good news is that there are so many different platforms today, so finding your favorite is fairly easy, and then gaining momentum and followers there is then actually fun (and not a chore). And the key to social media—and this chapter—is to stop looking at social media as a little circle of friends and family and instead as a new global network of buyers of whatever it is you're selling. You have a few billion people that are interconnected to choose from, so let's get started.

If you aren't on YouTube, LinkedIn, Facebook, Twitter, and (my personal favorite) Instagram, you should not wait a second longer, and create accounts now. That is the first step. You don't have to post right away. Instead, you can establish an account on each platform so that you can follow the people that are really good at it and learn from them. That's right: Stop hiding from your high school arch nemesis and get social. Stop complaining that technology is upending your in-person social encounters, and stop thinking that the fad will die, because it won't. You need to join the rest of the planet.

And I am writing this to myself. I am behind, too. I think we all are, per definition, in this social media race. All I can do is take each day to get better at it. *Don't be hard on yourself, Fredrik. You are doing well; everything starts and ends with your next post. Treat each post as a little piece of art, and don't overthink the end goal, or how to reach millions of followers on all platforms at once. Just make a commitment to yourself, and your followers, that you will do your best—that's all.*

If the Greeks are known for drama and the Egyptians are known for their hieroglyphics, we in the twenty-first century are going to be remembered for our social media explosion. It's the modern way of expression, and for business, it's starting to become everything, for real.

Today social media accounts for more than a quarter of my business. It's not just important; it's crucial. Every developer, numerous journalists, and most of my top competitors follow me, and if they don't, I think they are missing out. Whenever I have a meeting with anyone, I look them up on various social media platforms and study their life. I invite them to follow me, to join my world, which is now our world to share. That's why it's both exhilarating and scary at the same time. Soon you really are connected to a lot of people, people that can make you very rich. I befriended Andy Cohen on Facebook before I was cast for *Million Dollar Listing New York*, Ivanka Trump before I sold Trump SoHo, and Bruce Littlefield before we met to discuss doing this book together.

Here's something I've realized. Ninety-three percent of the

THE SELL | 137

people using social media have no training in it. That's right. Only 7 percent of you holding this book have training in social media compared to 100 percent of you who were taught to read. I certainly don't have any training in social media. Almost all your friends on Facebook have no training in how to use it either. We speak English and do math, and we learned how to do that in school. We drive cars and ride bikes, and someone taught us, right? But in social media and its numerous platforms, nine out of ten of us have had no training in how to actually do it. Considering how many of us use it, and the amount of time we use it, that's kind of absurd, don't you agree?

I taught myself social media through years of homeschooling. I've studied it, analyzed it, dissected it, experimented with it, failed at it, and aced it. For now. It's continuing to evolve, and every day it gets more complicated or easier to use depending on how you look at it. To me, finally after all these years, it's all really fun; and like a flashing, spinning, winning Las Vegas slot machine, that has paid off. *Big!* In fact, I'm writing this sentence right now, and the book you're now holding is already sitting at the top of the sales charts on the two largest book sites in the world. I haven't even finished writing this line *and it's a bestseller!* How'd that happen? Two words: social media. Actually three words: *only* social media. I posted and promoted the cover of *The Sell* through my social media platforms and then engaged with my followers and watched the sales click. No magazine articles, no TV appearances or radio interviews, no print ads, no nothing. Just social media.

My book agent and publisher say they think this is the first time a nonfiction author has become number one in presales months before the book is even out—from a single social media post. Another somewhat historic example is when I launched sales of my new development in Tribeca, 11 North Moore, with one Instagram post (only) and sold $100 million of real estate in the building in one month. That Instagram post and the first weeks' sales were written about in *The Wall Street Journal*, *The New York Times*, and *The Real Deal*.

You can do this, too. I'm going to try to teach you how. I'm going to keep it as simple as I can, because I hate those hideous textbooks on social media you find at airport bookstores, five hundred pages long and written by someone neither of us have anything in common with. I mean, how can it be that the authors of those books are the most uninteresting people to follow on social media?

Professor Freddy has two questions for you: Do you have a life? Do you have a smartphone? That's how easy it is to enroll in Freddy's School of Social Media. You don't need anything besides those two things. Congrats, you are breathing! That's amazing, because your life is the script for your future top-rated reality show on Twitter, Facebook, and Instagram. So, grab that smartphone and thank Steve Jobs for inventing it or the Koreans for copying it, and let us emphasize these two simple facts: It has (1) a camera and (2) access to every social media application.

Now pay attention, class. You in the back, get off your phone and look at me! I've already told you that 25 percent of my business comes from social media. (For reference, my Eklund real estate brands pulled in $20 million last year in commissions. That's $5 million worth of "likes.") Thumb up? I heart it!

I recently sold an $11 million listing direct, without a cobroker, through a Facebook post in twenty-four hours at a 6 percent commission. That commission check was $660,000, and I didn't need any media consultants, graphic designers, or ad buyers. There were no meetings, no conference calls; there was no planning. I didn't need to meet any deadline, because it was instantaneous, at the push of a button, and it was global, so I wasn't dependent upon some archaic distribution schedule. I posted it, and the world was my customer. Best of all, it was totally free. High-kick! Actually, no, the best of all was that we filmed that transaction on the third season of *Million Dollar Listing*, and because we filmed me taking photos of myself and posting it on Instagram to promote the listing, I got thirty-five thousand new followers the night the episode aired in the United States.

The first trick to start attracting followers is being active in your postings. It doesn't come without effort, and it will take time, but that is okay. Success does not happen overnight. Your posts need to be integrated with who you are on a daily basis (which is why the people that are good at it take so much pride in it). It doesn't matter whether you're an account manager, a yoga teacher, or a salesperson, you always want to be giving something to your followers—a laugh, a piece of good information, or an intimate peek at your life.

The secret of sharing: It's not just one way; it goes both ways. Someone is following you, and in return you need to try to *give* them something. If you give them more than your competition, your follower will start talking about you, and, like a fertilized garden, your followers will grow. So, for every instance you brag about business or a new record, it better be inspirational and have a good photo attached to it—and then for the next five posts you only offer interesting things that aren't bragging.

I see social media as the way we define ourselves in the modern world. As crazy as it seems, it's our time's real religion. It is the final and ultimate individualization, the creation of self within a large group: the one united digital world we now live in. Whatever we put out there is a demonstration of how we see ourselves, a self-portrait of our lives.

You can tell a lot about a person online. What someone posts says so much about who he or she is, but also about how he or she wants to be perceived (which is usually two different things). How many times have we met a new person, perhaps before or after a first date or a party, and scrolled through his or her social media profiles to judge and ultimately decide—in twenty-two seconds—how compatible we really are?

I love watching Swedish slalom skiers zoom down a mountain, zipping between the series of gates. They move fast and make a lot of turns. That's how I look at social media. I see each post—from the outrageously spontaneous to the carefully planned—as one of those gates, a benchmark of my life. Yes, to repeat myself, all the colors of my rainbow. My social media—@FredrikEklundNY—is the official record of where I've been and where I'm going. My first tip to you is to have the same account name on all platforms, and also keep the content the same or very similar on all by reposting from one to another. It's really the only way to be able to manage it all while simultaneously expanding.

One might call your social media profile a modern and more colorful autobiography, with juicy contributors offering their likes and comments, most positive and some negative. Those posts are our markers for the zigs and the zags of our lives as we plow through them, our validations and insecurities, our queries, our search for beauty, our overcompensation, and an immediate gauge of other people's interest. With all that comes our ability to make The Sell, to engage others in what we have to offer. My social media is my single best lure for business, and we're going to make it yours, too.

And, by the way, why is it *my* social media? Because I do it myself, and I believe that is another secret to its success: I've never let anyone touch it. Though I've been offered many services, in which I could pay people to do my social media, I've always proudly done it myself. And I want you to as well. Why? Because only then is it authentic, and if we want to make The Sell, we must always be authentic. People can smell a fake.

These "social media experts" told me, and they will tell you, that doing it yourself is going to drive you nuts and that you won't have time. Only they can help you build a big following. I considered it, and then I turned them all down. This goes back to you being *you*: *Be who you are and don't try to hide.* If you are going to hide, don't post anything, but hiding behind someone else pretending to be you is the weirdest kind of hiding.

Several of my top competitors have bought followers. It's getting more common, and I find it tacky. Although I don't support it, I understand why they are doing it. In a competitive industry like mine, which is so numbers driven, they got on the social media wagon perhaps too late and now want to inject a bit of steroids to win the game. Did you know you can do this? Increase your online followers by five thousand for $9.95? There are these programmers sitting in their pajamas munching Doritos who will, for a fee, play shenanigans with the Internet and increase your number of followers. You can even buy likes on individual posts. They use "bots," web robots that act like people on an assembly line and will over and over again do an automated task . . . like vote for you! Those bots aren't real *bods*, and if they aren't real bods, they aren't real eyeballs. And if they aren't real eyeballs, they aren't real friends buying what you're selling.

How can you tell if someone is faking it and buying followers or likes? Their numbers jump magically in an hour or overnight. The one thing no one can buy, at least so far, is a comment, and by looking at the number of comments you can see who is fake or not. I've come up with a formula for the average Instagram post: 2 to 5 percent of your followers like your post depending on how good it is, and 30 percent of those who like will comment. It's almost an exact formula; check for yourself. Therefore, the problem for the faker who has five hundred real followers and buys fifty thousand followers is that he only gets sixteen likes (then pays to bump the sixteen to 3,016 likes) and still only has three comments on the post. And there is no way he can increase that, except maybe by paying his five hundred real followers to post.

Let's move on from the fakers. You, my social media student, are going to be a star because you're authentic. On that note, no one wants an autograph these days. They want a selfie so they can post it on social media. I've never been asked for an autograph, but I've been asked for a thousand selfies. That's the new autograph. (Maybe you have a photo of you and a celeb? Show it to me by posting it with #TheSellfie.)

In a column she wrote for *The Wall Street Journal* on the future of music, singer Taylor Swift (Hi, @TaylorSwift13 #callme for that new #penthouse I know you want!) said that in the near future singers aren't going to be getting record deals based on their ability to sing; they are going to get them based on the number of followers they have. To that point, one of the reasons I got a *big* advance for this book was because of the number of actively engaged social media followers I have (and love!). This next line is for my competitors who are reading this book: In the future the seller of a home will pick the real estate agent with the most followers. But it's not just a numbers game. It's that my followers and I are engaged in an ongoing dialogue, a two-way street.

If people follow you, they trust you. If you have followers who love you, it's a measure of credibility. Yelp is an example that operates on the same idea. If someone's looking for a good place to eat, they'll pick a place others say is good. Social media is the new word of mouth, which used to be all the rage in sales.

Let me get spiritual for a moment in all this digital hashtagging. My parents and the older generation are living in the "real" world. My mom feels most alive when she paints, my dad when he is writing at his horse farm. They are in their element. Time stops; they are *there*. Yes, they have online personas and check them occasionally to see pictures of me or share this or that painting or a photo of the farm. Let's jump to the *now* generation, like my nine-year-old nephew who lives in the online world. That's where everything happens. That's where he passes notes in class. That's where time stops, where he is in *his* element. And it doesn't mean he doesn't like to play football or fish or ride his bike, but if he had to choose, he would choose to do those things on his iPad.

I don't think it's sad that kids today would rather play computer games than play outside. I don't see it as the real world versus the digital world. I think it's sad when people, old or young, live *only* in one of the two extremes. The two worlds can coexist and need to for anyone in business today and in the future.

I am actually fifty-fifty, precisely, and I love it. Let me explain: When the offline and the online worlds collide in the exact same moment, I'm in heaven. That's when I lose myself in time, in my element. I do that by connecting the old world with the new world, through my smartphone. Let's say I'm in Paris. It's 6:05 P.M., and Derek and I have walked all day. I'm holding his hand. It's all so romantic, that local red wine is getting me closer to it all, and everything is colorful and seductive. I hear French chatter from a group of people eating outside a brasserie. The stress of New York is far away; the emotions of being *one* with the old city feels real, there and then. We cross one of the stone bridges, and I put my palm on it, still warm from the day's golden sun, now setting. Are you with me? Do you also smell how sweet this old City of Light is tonight? Well, there I kiss Derek and then grab my camera, snap a photo of us in the sunset that can only look this passionate in Paris. I increase the colors ever so slightly, and write down my emotions, like a love letter to life, into the piece of metal, glass, and plastic in my hand. I pay tribute to this very moment by making it forever. I hit the share button and channel the love to my five hundred thousand followers, and exactly there, at that moment, somewhere between the offline and online worlds, as the thousands of likes and comments come in, I am in my true element.

Here are some of the trends I see in social media right now:

1. **Social media investment is becoming a necessity, not a luxury.** Traditional forms of selling, marketing, and prospecting are becoming secondary to social media tactics. The results speak for themselves.

2. **A continuum of social engagement is vital.** The first step to success in the crazy social world is to get by the one-and-done

hump. You need to change the paradigm of thinking from single-shot activity to a continuum of ongoing engagements.

3. **You need to be everywhere your customer or influencer is.** Don't think about a single network. Your prospect is social everywhere on the web, and your social activity must behave in the same way. The experience should be consistent and the data synchronized across all web platforms.

4. **Multimedia and visual storytelling is key.** Start thinking like a storyteller! Turn your life or agenda into a personal story with heroes and villains from your personal or professional position. Smart content is powerful and grabs eyeballs.

5. **Content must be mobile friendly.** It's important to go the extra mile when thinking about the content and how people experience it. It should come as no surprise that mobile is king when it comes to social media. Be thoughtful and strategic as you engage and participate on social media with the mobile user in mind.

6. **Response/engagement is crucial.** Get to know your audience and understand both their business and personal interests. Offer content that entertains as well as helps them meet the challenges of life. We live in the era of instant everything! Success belongs to the quick and the nimble.

But which platform is the best one to help *you* make The Sell? I'm glad you asked. Let's discuss the biggest: LinkedIn, YouTube, Twitter, Facebook, and Instagram.

LINKEDIN

LinkedIn is the social network of choice for professionals networking and making connections. It was designed specifically for the business community and is the modern-day resume and referral service. LinkedIn represents your professional expertise and experience and is an incredible facilitator of new professional relationships. The idea is that you build your profile on this platform to document and highlight your employment and education history, and then you connect with people you know and trust professionally. But the added benefit is that you get to network with the people you've worked with professionally or gone to school with and can make connections and get introduced by one of your contacts to someone within LinkedIn's network of three hundred million members from two hundred countries who might help your career.

On LinkedIn you can showcase your experience, control your positioning and messaging, generate targeted leads, showcase credibility through professional endorsements, connect with professional influencers and like-minded people (both colleagues and potential customers), and make The Sell.

Most of us have trouble keeping track of all the people we know who might help us in our career. LinkedIn makes the network of people we know visible and shows us who we know and *who they know*. It will, for example, show you that your favorite boss from your first job knows someone at the company you want to get a meeting with.

Let me show you how that can work to your advantage. A big rule of business revolves around who you know. Let's say you're an accountant looking to get new clients. LinkedIn helps you keep track of the network of people you know and have worked with, and you can directly offer them your services, but you can also use LinkedIn's recommendations feature to have your previous customers boost your credibility by providing quick praise for your work and abilities.

LinkedIn gives you the ability to look outside your own network to find the best person to help you. The platform lets you see the connections of your connections and who in their circles might need your services. You can ask your friend (your shared connection) for an introduction. It's that simple.

Let's say you're looking for a job at Apple or want to get advice from someone at Apple on how to let the world know about the new app you're developing. You might think you don't know anyone at Apple, so you either give up or go the old-fashioned route and cold-call their human-resources department. With LinkedIn, you do a search for the HR manager at Apple. The result is that you find the name of the person in the position and any of your connections who know the person. Next step? You talk to your shared contact and ask for an introduction.

Further, LinkedIn allows you to search for people in any industry that might help you personally and professionally. The LinkedIn Influencer feature lets you follow professionals who blog about topics related to your business. Remember our discussion about learning from a superstar in your career? This gives you the opportunity to see what an expert in your industry knows and to benefit from that wisdom by applying it to your own career. Sending them notes to say thanks simply and instantly puts you on their radar screens.

LinkedIn is the perfect way to interact with your customers. From messaging people directly to taking surveys, you show that you care. People appreciate knowing their thoughts matter to you, and by listening you not only learn a lot, you also achieve the highest satisfaction level among those who know and work with you.

YOUTUBE

When most people think of social media, they probably think Twitter and Facebook. Before we discuss those, I should also mention that YouTube can serve as an outstanding learning tool, and creating video content can increase your profile and audience to bring attention to what you have to offer or sell. People are building entire careers by posting YouTube videos.

There are more than four billion daily views on YouTube. That's the equivalent of more than half the world's population watching a video every day. Yes, many are viewed for strictly entertainment purposes (Lady Gaga, I'm watching you!), but a substantial number of the videos watched each day are for people seeking information or help. In fact, more than thirty-five million searches each month are for how-to videos. So, how can you use this to your advantage in making The Sell?

If you're a plumber and create a video on "How to Fix a Leaky Toilet," you're not just helping someone solve his problem, you are also setting yourself up as an expert and, for the people near you, as the one to call when there's a burst pipe. If you're a New York City veterinarian who provides a video on "How to Recognize the Symptoms of Lyme Disease," you could be the one I call if Mousey is exhibiting those signs. If you're a real estate agent who provides video tours of your properties, you're not just showcasing your properties; you're highlighting yourself as a professional in the marketplace. If you're a bestselling lifestyle expert who creates a video on "How to Reupholster a Dining Chair," you're not just helping someone solve her dilemma; you're also bringing attention to your books. (Just ask my coauthor, Bruce Littlefield, whose video on the subject is quite popular!)

According to a recent survey, videos have proven five times more beneficial for reaching new customers than traditional content, and 90 percent of customers viewing a video online will make a purchasing decision based on that clip. So make yourself the expert in your field by creating engaging content that appeals to our visual nature. Share information about your product or service that establishes a following. If it's clever, you might even go viral, and that will bring you a bottomless pool of clients and buyers.

TWITTER

Twitter calls itself the "global town square" and suggests that the revolution will not be televised; it will be tweeted. Twitter is today's real-time water-cooler conversation. Call me a twat, but I don't really like Twitter that much, although it's changing, so I have promised myself to try again to like it. This book is about how to sell yourself, right? To that end, I think Twitter has three tragic flaws: (1) It's 140 characters makes it very limited, even for an elevator pitch between two floors. (2) It's too noisy since the majority is just text. (3) Most people have no idea how many people read your tweets.

A hundred and forty characters? As I'm writing this line, I'm already at more than 450,000 characters into this book, and I'm not even half done with it. If you're a journalist, a rock star, or enjoy watching basketball with millions of other people in the palm of your hand, Twitter can be important. Yes, it's fast; yes, it's where people can get news when there is an earth-moving event; and yes, it's a good place to announce things. But with the limited character count it's a limited sales tool.

On top of that, the traffic rushes by at NASCAR speed on Twitter's informational highway, so unless you're only following one person, you have to basically be logged in 24/7 (and reading a screen!) in order to see it all. We follow more people on Twitter than we ever have time to read in this lifetime. This translated means that if you send out a tweet, perhaps only 5–15 percent of your followers might actually see it.

There are 190 million tweets a day. It's like you're holding a megaphone and yelling in a crowd of other people who have megaphones and are yelling. And, to make it even more teeth gritting, everyone with a megaphone thinks she's the funniest or wisest person on the planet and doesn't realize she actually just has Tourrette's syndrome. Ugh. Watch Twitter when there's a big world event and everyone is vying to say the cleverest thing. There were one billion Twitter impressions during the telecast of *Sharknado 2*. How many of those biting tweets do you think you'd be able to catch while simultaneously watching the movie?

I have tried to get actual sales from Twitter, and tracked the lack of them. When I tweeted repeatedly to my almost ninety thousand followers about this book, with a direct link to preorder it, I only got a dozen sales. When I posted about it on Instagram and Facebook, it shot up on the top-ten lists worldwide. But then again, perhaps my mediocre performance has to do with my lack of enthusiasm over the Twitter platform itself. I would love to hear your success with Twitter as a sales tool.

In Twitter's defense, it has recently changed significantly in several key areas: Tweet sponsorship (equivalent of Facebook post boosting) exists in a helpful way. The new platform allows users to get their content in front of an extremely specific and targeted audience *or* an incredibly large audience for relatively low cost. A big potential ROI. Also they have changed their impressions: Twitter now has the equivalent of Facebook insights, allowing the user to see exactly how many impressions each post receives. And lastly Twitter has call-to-action cards: a tool for business development and engaging with a targeted audience.

Twitter, more so than any other platform, can be a platform for discoverability, and this is something I enjoy. Sometimes I search for #MDLNY and can see every tweet ever tweeted about my television show, or #TheSell and see what people are saying about my book. In fact, this platform is very driven by the ability to discover conversations about specific topics. Twitter invented the hashtag after all! Being strategic on Twitter allows more people to find you. You can participate in a larger dialogue within a very targeted community.

Yes, I am going to give Twitter a second chance. It is a text jungle, where I think I'm going to get strangled by an @ and hit with a #. But one really nice thing about Twitter, besides honing your cleverness skills, is that you can get retweeted. Your witty 140-character message is cloned and has the chance to reach a lot of people. Going viral on Twitter is possible if executed properly. Consider this my homework assignment to myself—try to become a master of the Twitterverse.

FACEBOOK

Pretty much everyone you know is on Facebook. If I'm a little snarky, I look at it like a big high school reunion where you get to see old friends and a few relatives, and everyone is telling one another how great his or her life is. If I'm a little smart, I look at it as a genius sales tool.

At times, Facebook might make you feel inadequate, like

your life isn't adding up to the hype of other people's lives. But here's the reality: Everyone has good and bad days. Some post about the bad ones, but really almost everyone posts exclusively about the good ones. What started out as a way for college students to connect has now become the worldwide go-to spot to brag about a vacation, announce your engagement, show off your new house, new puppy, new job. But get over any feelings of inadequacy and get yourself in the game. You have to be on Facebook, and you have to grow an audience there. Let's look at the numbers according to StatisticBrain.com:

- Facebook has 1.2 billion users.
- Seven hundred billion minutes are spent on Facebook each month.
- The average person spends fifteen hours and thirty-three minutes a month on Facebook.

Now that you see the importance, how do you reach the most people?

Facebook uses a complicated algorithm that they have rewritten a thousand times to choose its "Top Stories" amid anyone's feed. Basically, the algorithm controls what you are seeing and not seeing. No one really knows the exact formula of how you get listed the highest—Facebook keeps it guarded more closely than Coca-Cola with its recipe or me with my secrets of success until I wrote this book—but I've done some reconnaissance and learned a few things.

Every seven minutes Facebook measures how many likes one of your posts has gotten. It also measures how many comments you have, as well as *who* is commenting and *who* is liking. The first seven minutes, your post will come pretty high up in basically everyone's feed, and then it starts either dying or growing. Every post is therefore exponential—it builds or it dies. I, for example, have more than two hundred thousand followers. When I post something, the likes will either build and become fourteen thousand, or peter out at three hundred or so, depending on how engaging (early on) my post is.

There are many theories regarding what time of day (or night) one should post to get the best traction on Facebook. I've found the ideal time is around 11:00 A.M. in New York, because it's around 5:00 P.M. in Europe, 11:00 P.M. in Asia, and 8:00 A.M. in Los Angeles—basically everyone in the world is online. It's a weird game of Russian roulette, though, and that is why Facebook can get so addictive: You never know why some posts become successful and some don't. You think you know, and then you realize you really don't. Just like a slot machine, it's rather unpredictable, but I will share with you my secrets to make it less so.

Why is Facebook's algorithm so complicated? Duh. They want to make money. How do they do that? You can pay to "boost" a post or "promote" a page to basically force the post to accelerate in the algorithm and go higher. This is fairly inexpensive and fun because it takes out some of the unpredictability.

Before we go into advertising on Facebook, let me explain the difference between a profile and a page. A profile is what most people have. It's where it all started: your personal portal with your name. Your profile is great to keep connected with your friends and family, but since you have a copy of *The Sell* in your hand and realize that you are your business, you should definitely have a page. The page gives you a wider range of options; it makes it easier to grow a larger audience and advertise, and, most important, it gives you statistics on how you are doing with it all.

Facebook will give you the numbers. With a simple click of a button, you can view your page's "Insight"—statistics on your most successful post, your number of likes, the reach of your content, number of new followers, clicks, and shares, really all the data about your page. There are nice graphs to see these numbers over time. Basically, you get to see what's working and what's not. In sales, that is a *valuable* tool.

Historically (ten years is a *loooong* time in social media's evolution) it was complicated to advertise on Facebook, but since becoming a publicly traded commodity, they've been forced to put programming and design muscle behind their platform so the common man can easily advertise there. I do it more and more, because you can make it super precise and targeted and then follow up on its success with Insights. And you should, too.

YouTube has some great video tutorials on how to advertise on Facebook. Take them. When you figure it out, it's a powerful promotional tool.

When you're marketing something, selling something, or even talking about your Swedish meatballs, you want as many people to see the post as possible. And the right people. You'd be lying (or not thinking clearly) if you said otherwise. Facebook makes this possible, and you can choose if you want to pay for views (impressions) or actions (clicks and/or likes).

The more people you reach, the more people will share your posts on Facebook, which takes your reach one step further. Sharing, much like retweeting, is the act of somebody reposting what you've posted. Instantly your post will show up—as you— in the feeds of people who aren't even following you.

It is all silent, digital, and instant, but so, so important. Call it gawking, gossiping, bragging, educating, or what you will, but it feels nice to have something *you* posted talked about by a lot of people. The initial post about *The Sell* showing the cover and saying "preorder now" had fourteen thousand likes and was shared more than a thousand times. It reached a total of 989,000 people, according to my Insights. That is one heck of a post!

To buy a spot on TV that would reach a million people would cost a lot, and still, until Apple invents their own TV, one can't click on a commercial for a product (or a book) and instantly buy it. Facebook allows active engagement. To buy a full-page ad in a newspaper that is actually read by a million people and not thrown out or flipped through would cost a fortune, too. And don't even get me started on how long it would take to go knock on a million doors.

INSTAGRAM

My favorite! My little, colorful square jewel. You are so cute; you are so modern; you are so hip. You are perfect the way you are, and I want to thank you so much for helping me both professionally and personally. Yes, Instagram is the newest kid on the block. This pretty little sister of Facebook was specifically set up as a mobile photo-sharing and (later) video-sharing social network. It is simple: You get to take a picture, make it look good with a dozen easy-to-use digital filters, and then write a caption for it. Then that photo goes into the feed to your followers, and there are no ads (yet!), no noise, and no distractions.

Here are six things I love about Instagram:

1. **Unlike Facebook, the posts are completely linear.** I follow 852 people, and each time I look at Instagram, their posts are

in the order of when they were posted. It is sorted by time, not anything else. This means if you scroll back far enough, you can see each picture of all the people you follow. I never miss one photo, and each time I post one, there are close to three hundred thousand people following me who will see it.

2. **It's fresh and hip.** Most of the more than three hundred million users have signed up for it in the last two years. People on Instagram are engaged and pay attention. There are fewer inactive users, and the people who use it use it a lot. It's highly addictive and fun, and users go into the app more times a day than any other social network. The brand is cooler, more stylish, and grabs more attention. Instagram is where everything is going, I think. In a way, it's the new Twitter, and most people are now turning their creativity and attention away from Twitter and onto Instagram.

    And with it, Instagram is creating digital celebrities like Swedish @Yoga_Girl, who is worshipped for her online persona and poses. That is much more difficult on Twitter. When @Yoga_Girl posts a photo on Instagram, she instantly has ten thousand comments from people on how much they *love* her. Some people would call it an obsession. I call it The Sell. Because guess what? She's got a bestselling book, too!

3. **An image is the perfect sales tool.** Instagram is just you looking at one image at a time. One square of color. A perfectly framed Instagram photo says more than a thousand words or 140,000 characters. My Instagram feed of the people I follow has great contrasts, from the world's greatest outdoor photographers to intimate selfies of Madonna, and every-

thing in between. Trust me on the importance of *imagery* for you and what you have to sell.

4. **The software is genius in its simplicity.** The scroll of Instagram was modeled after slot machines, making it addictive to flip through the square photos with your fingers touching the screen. Its easy-to-use filters can make each photo look artistic, as if taken by the great photographer you always dreamed to be but without all the heavy and expensive equipment.

5. **The likes are inspiring.** Instagram is like-driven, and creates a competition with yourself (or perhaps your competitors). In my early days using Instagram, I'd get so excited when a photo would get a hundred likes. Now I'm disappointed if I don't reach ten thousand likes on a favorite photo. It's all relative. That is why I believe in the game of it and why I think it is here to stay. For Beyoncé a hundred thousand likes is a success (she is actually very good at Instagram and the only one I know that never, ever writes a caption to her photos, which somehow seems to make them more important). The emotional high I get when I reach ten thousand likes on a post is the same as when my business partner, John, reaches a hundred.

6. **It's easy to be spontaneous and see the spontaneity in others.** If used correctly, Instagram opens a little door to who you are. It reveals the artistic side of yourself, what's in your heart, and how you see the world. Beauty is in the eye of the beholder, and two people will photograph one object completely differently. It's *you* in a moment, a true picture of where you are right now without worrying so much that

so-and-so is going to see it, and there is something freeing, and at the same time uniting, in that. I can feel really connected to people on Instagram whom I have never met, and probably will never meet, but because I follow them, I see their lives unfold, their travels, their dreams, their intimate moments. And I don't just "like" it; I love it.

POP QUIZ!

Do we acknowledge that social media is here to stay? Yes or No.

Do we think it's going to become more and more of who we are? Yes or No.

Did you believe me when I said my book became a bestseller off of one social media post? Yes or No.

If you answered yes to any of the above, you must start or enhance your social media empire now. You must use social media as the incredible sales tool it is to forge your own path to the top in whatever endeavor you're pursuing.

THE SECRETS TO GETTING MORE FOLLOWERS

Now that we have some basic knowledge on the most popular platforms, let's talk about some universal secrets of mine to grab attention, find more followers, and get the most likes:

1. **Always use a photo. A photo says more than a thousand words, and it hits you in a millisecond.** Always, always use a photo! Even if it isn't on Instagram, include a photo. A

simple text post is really boring—and simply isn't as engaging and results in fewer likes. The clearer and more beautiful the photo, the better. Since everyone always asks how I get such beautiful photos, I'll tell you. I use the Camera+ app for my iPhone 6 Plus, then use 20 percent HDR, increase contrasts slightly, and sometimes add the filter Sierra. Even if I'm only posting "High-kick! I just set a record in SoHo," I'm going to include a picture, perhaps of a high-kick, but usually of the streetscape or fabric of SoHo.

2. **Know what attracts eyeballs. Animals, babies, and nature grab attention, as do sunsets, sunrises, skyscrapers, ocean waves, and half-naked photos.** In one of the posts about this book, which was essentially what I call a "bragging post," with the targeted purpose of selling more books, I used a photo of me kissing a giant Great Dane named Titan, and it was one of the most successful posts in my social media history. Everyone loves a top dog.

My post that got more than 20,000 likes: "Woke up this morning to see that my book was TOP 10 on Barnes & Noble global sales out of 30 million book titles! So I dressed up in my favorite suit, went for breakfast at the Crosby Hotel in SoHo and kissed this dog named Titan. Reserve your own copy of #TheSell at www.bn.com. And if no one told you they love you today, I do. And Titan does too."

3. **Obey the five-hour rule.** Never post more than two things in five hours. People get turned off. And it's certain death if you're posting a variation of the same thing. Let's say you've gotten engaged. A "He asked me" post gets a lot of likes. A half hour later you do an "I'm in shock" post, followed shortly thereafter by a photo of you, again, smiling and saying, "I'm so happy." Look, girl, I've already given you a like. How many times in a day can I say I like you about the same thing?

4. **Make your followers cocreators.** Yes, social media can be about bragging, selling, and promoting, but there are very subtle ways to do it right. My trick is to make the follower feel that he or she is a part of it. The classic no-no is posting a photo of fifteen people at a long table and saying, "Amazing night with my friends." Now your followers feel left out. They are obviously not invited to the party. They aren't sitting at the table. There's nothing you're sharing with them. They sit in their dark rooms by themselves staring at their computer screens while you say, "Look at my fab life!"

●●●●○ Verizon LTE   2:29 PM   59% 🔋⚡

←   **PHOTO**   ↻

fredrikeklundny   🕐 10w

♥ 7457 likes

fredrikeklundny I came home from a long day at work, only to find Fritzy sitting up in the couch reading #TheSell. Did you order your copy yet?

You don't want to rub something in people's computer-screen-lit-up faces. If you want to include your follower, make him or her a cocreator by saying something like "With all life's ups and downs, I feel blessed to have great people in my life." That's a little humbler. It adds a different dimension, and it's also true. But then add a question at the end: "Don't you agree it makes all the difference?" *Boom! I like that!* I've made the emotion transferable. We are in this together. And why is this important? Remember, we agreed earlier that there's no use posting anything if it's not going to be seen and shoot to the top of the feed.

6. **Play with contrast.** In social media, repetitiveness is death. People have a very good memory, and if you repeat yourself, followers' eyeballs move on. I consciously go back and forth between five themes:

- something sales related—a record, a new listing, the $100 million in sales in a month, a promotion of this book, etc.

- a really beautiful photo of New York City, or where I am right now on my travels, attached to a dreamy text describing how I feel in the moment

- my dogs, Fritzy and Mousey, or some other really cute animal

- a selfie, occasionally half-undressed, outside, like on a run or on a mountain hike (never in the mirror at the gym or in the bathroom)

162 | FREDRIK EKLUND

- people with me having fun, and I try to keep it to two or three people in a photo *or* a group shot of lots of people

If you go to a small island in the Maldives, where there isn't so much variety in what to shoot, post a photo of a palm tree with the white beach in the background. Only the first post is going to get a lot of likes. Don't post ten photos of the same beach until you're saying "Good-bye, Maldives." You will turn people off gradually by posting too many of the same theme with lunch at the beach, swimming at that same beach, the selfie under the umbrella, the massage under the cabana, dinner in the sunset with so-and-so. Unless you are an incredible photographer and shoot undeniably beautiful photos, less is always more.

7. **Be outrageous.** Social media is a numbers game. You want as many people seeing your stuff as possible. You want people talking. That doesn't mean you have to post a video of you twerking with your boss at your company Christmas party, but if you do, do it with style and make sure to own it, because it will certainly set tongues wagging. It's okay every now and then to step outside your comfort zone a little. It grabs attention, and although the post itself might not get as many likes as you hoped, it will certainly separate you from the crowd. Remember when everyone thought Miley Cyrus twerking was going to be the end of her career? There was a wave of hatred against her, an immediate uproar about her taking it too far. She certainly did! For the first time in the history of social media, she gained two million followers. Overnight. And she is now the best selling artist in the world.

8. **Engage with others.** I like people's posts, like actually like them with my thumbs up. I like the comments people make on my posts, each and every one, even though sometimes there are thousands of comments on my post. It might take half an hour, but I acknowledge that I've read their comment with my like. When I have time, I try to reply to people's comments. Social media is one big monologue sometimes, where we all stand in a corner of the room looking at one another but talking to ourselves. Go to the middle of the room and talk *to* everyone; connect with your followers. So few people realize that this can and should be a dialogue. Everyone wants to be heard, validated, and to have a connection. That's making The Sell!

Don't make the mistake that some salespeople do and expect buyers to walk in the door and hand over their money. Why are you on social media? If it's to keep your parents updated on your whereabouts and what you're doing in life, then perhaps call them instead? I'm quite sure your mom will like that more. Tell her I said hi. But if you want to sell your cupcakes, your advertising space, your book, yourself, you need to learn how to play this game and do it with style. You must start building your followers before your competition does. As social media evolves, the correlation between your follower engagement and your bottom-line results will become even clearer. There will be a direct correlation between how well you engage your followers and your bottom-line results. To me, social media is The Sell.

But, perhaps most important, those slalom gates (my posts on social media) that I place in front of me and have left on the trail behind me do two rewarding things for my life at the same time, one on the surface and one deeper down at the spiritual core. The pendulum swings between the two.

1. **Social media helps me look forward.** In some weird way, social media actually helps me make decisions that will lead to a happier life. I know that some people won't like the idea of making their choices based on what a bunch of faceless strangers say, but the reality is that your followers like what you like. That's why they like you. Therefore, if you can figure out what they like, you will probably like it, too.

   I have friends who pick out clothes based on what they like to be photographed in. The question is, "Would I want to stare at a photo of myself in this outfit for the rest of my life?" If the answer is yes, they know they are buying something that will make them look good and feel good.

   I sometimes choose my travel destinations based on where I think I'll get the most likes. Hawaii or Ohio? *Hmmmm?* Why? Because my followers are my second family, and they know me and where I should go. When I am on the romantic medieval bridge in the sunset, I'm there in that moment, that particular moment, but it will become really special when I post it, write a caption that perfectly describes it, share it, and create the map of where I should go next. An extreme example would be Fredrik at a bar equals not so many likes. Fredrik kissing his grandma equals a thousand likes. Grandma *always* wins over cocktails. Given that social media is about connection and engagement, it makes us steer our lives toward the positive, the truly important things in life.

2. **Social media helps me look back.** In the unlucky, and hopefully unlikely, event I get into a car accident and I'm in a wheelchair, I'll have a lot of material to go back and relive. I've captured some truly amazing moments and lived life fully. My social media is proof of that. Life is a series of heartbeats. Every beat, every second, is soon in the past and flashes by us so quickly that all these photos, these captions, these comments and likes compose a personal journal. It's yours. No one can take it away from you. There's no way to get the past back, but I have lots of heartbeats to look back on. The posts are of the most important events of my life. Yes, I post three to five things a day, and usually the three to five most important parts of my day. In a wild world, where everything moves so fast and we all consume so much information, if nothing else, I feel that I have this vault of my wonderful moments.

If nothing else, there's one thing that makes your social media effort worthwhile: Look at it as your colorful diary, which also can make you money. Now, go post something and tag me in it.

CHAPTER 8

PITCH PERFECT

Learn to Accentuate the Positive
(about Yourself and What You Have to Offer)

I was in the elevator on the way up to the biggest pitch of my life, the grande dame of all pitches. It bothered me that there was no mirror in the elevator. I had to check my hair in the unfocused reflection of the door's metal frame. I had picked my outfit carefully for my audience, not wanting to look too fancy or too preppy. I had skipped a tie to appear casual, calm, and confident. But I felt everything but calm and confident. I was nervous, as I knew this pitch would alter the course of my life.

As the elevator door opened, I saw the door to the room in front of me. I could hear my heartbeat. I went over the questions in my head. *Why do you deserve this? Why are you better than anyone else? Why do you think this will work? Are you sure you won't disappoint us? Do you understand that what you are asking from us cannot be taken back?* I was so nervous that for a split second I couldn't remember any of the answers, even though I had thought about it for days. I moved my hand toward the door handle and momentarily hesitated. Either this pitch was going to work out and I was going to leave the room as the happiest man in the world, or I was going to walk out the same door I was about to enter as a failure, and for the rest of my life I would look back and wish I had pitched myself better.

I lifted my chin, smiled my biggest smile, and opened the door to say "Hi!" to Derek's mother and father.

SELLING THE DREAM

There are many definitions of what a pitch is. My definition of a pitch when it comes to selling is what happens in the first ten minutes of the initial meeting. Although a pitch meeting can sometimes take hours, more often than not the outcome is decided in the first ten minutes, no matter how long it is. In the eleventh minute or so, the pitch is turning into something slightly different, more of a negotiation, because the buyer, seller, or whoever your counterpart is has already made a decision (in his or her head) and has started looking for the best terms in the transaction.

On the first page of this book, I wrote that a lot in life can be sold, negotiated, and transacted but that some things are sacred and priceless. Like love. That's true, but we do pitch ourselves to our loved ones every day. And sometimes to our loved ones' parents. I knew that the first ten minutes with Derek's parents would be the most important ten minutes of my life. Not only was I going to ask them if I could marry their son, but I also wanted to have him move from them in the United Kingdom to be with me in New York.

Asking someone for what you want or telling someone what you have to offer can be scary. But if we want to be successful in this world, we all have to do it. And do it well, many times a day. Because pitching is offering something in hopes of an investment in money, time, and/or emotions by the other party, and it's often an anxiety fest that requires a lot of finesse, forethought, nerve, and skill. Our ability to obtain the things we want and achieve great success is directly correlated with our ability to influence others to like us, our ideas, and our products or services.

I've pitched my selling skills to Donald Trump, my on-screen services to Andy Cohen, and a future with Derek to his parents, and I've found that there is one common thread. Whether you're asking your boss for a raise, proposing your skills to a new client, showing a buyer a $10 million apartment, or convincing your wife to hire a housekeeper, the number one goal of a pitch is to get someone else excited enough to say yes.

If you're looking to pitch anything to anyone, first get your counterpart to acknowledge the need you're going to fulfill. *Everyone would rather know what you can do for them than what you've done for someone else.* There is a big difference between those two things. So, let me repeat it: Everyone you meet wants to know how you can benefit them, which needs you are fulfilling.

Some might say that I'm being cynical. But my view is exactly the opposite of pessimism. It's actually very positive. Every person on the planet you have an encounter with—whether you're pitching to him, talking to him, or just looking at him—wants to leave the meeting feeling better, not worse. Never forget that. And you have an opportunity to do exactly that, encounter by encounter, making this world a better place. If you're making people feel better, they're not only buying what you're selling; they will be happier doing so.

The same is true for any pitch scenario. A pitch is your opportunity to introduce yourself, your idea, or your product to someone with scarce time and/or money. When you're pitching, your job is to communicate to the other person: *I'm going to make your life better. You need what I've got. You will hire me, buy from me, say you want to date me again, just be with me, build a future with me. And all that before I walk out that door. Why? Because I've shown you that I have* our *ladder up. It's yours and mine—it's our ladder together—and we are now going to use it to climb up above the clouds, where there is always sunshine. I want to solve your problems, be a part of helping your life grow, help you be better. You see the possibilities. So do I. Let's do that. Now.*

Now I want to take this one step further (up our ladder). Anyone can describe why a tasty cupcake, a new home, car, watch, or massage is great (or why they themselves are great). Anybody can describe how a product or service is high quality and well priced in the marketplace. That's the easy part. The real secret to the perfect pitch is to sell the counterpart on the 2.0 versions of themselves—a new life, a new opportunity, a new luxury—which allows them to leave the older 1.0 versions behind. Change is good, especially the change that you are bringing. When a woman turns her nose up at a property because her old furniture won't fit the style of the new apartment, I consider it a grand opportunity. My task, and my pitch, is to remind her that this is a new start. She's trading up. She is moving forward, not sideways or backward. I paint the picture of how a new kitchen table, with new guests and better food, will look in that *new* spectacular apartment. "I'll even come for dinner!" She smiles and doesn't know whether I'm kidding. Then I put my arms up in the air, very animated and slightly theatrical: "Look at your guests sitting there! I can see you there with lots of guests. I can smell the food. Wow, I didn't know you were such a good cook! I can hear you pouring the wine into the glasses, good choice of merlot! *Mmmmmm*, now I'm thirsty. I think we should go and have a glass of wine and celebrate!"

If I were pitching you to buy a used car because you couldn't afford a new one, I might say, "It looks brand new at a third less cost! It won't depreciate a dime when you drive it off the lot! That's very smart of you."

I recently had a client who was downsizing, and I knew it was because he needed cash, but if I'd said that to him, he would have never wanted me to help him. For anyone, downsizing because you're out of money would be hugely disappointing. Instead, my objective was to take the situation and make it positive, to point out the good without mentioning the bad.

My pitch to him was to let me sell his big house and help him buy a smaller one, not because he *had* to but because it was going to be *good* for him on several levels. I told him, "You never needed all that space anyway. You haven't even completely furnished it yet because you travel so much. Yes, you love traveling more than anything, right? Now you will be able to travel even more and not feel guilty about leaving that big apartment sitting empty. You'll have a smaller apartment, but we'll find one with a terrace. You always wanted outdoor space. This new neighborhood is a lot closer to all the restaurants and to the waterfront. You are done with that stuffy old area anyway. This is a fresh start in your life. I'm so excited for you. This is amazing! I'm getting goosie goosies just thinking about your new life. My grandmother always said you have to get rid of the old thing to receive the new. Yes, there you are, the new you; you are finally smiling! I knew you would be happy."

I promised Derek's parents in that room that day that I would make him the happiest man in the world, which is the most important thing to them. And I think I am still keeping that promise.

In real estate, I always try to remember to make the buyer or seller love not only the apartment or townhouse, but also the journey with me to get there. Of course the property itself will improve the customer's life, but what I also need to pitch—in the pitch itself—is the decision itself. The *process* to actually *hire* me needs to be amazing. It all needs to be enjoyable, so I try to pitch in glamorous environments, nice restaurants, beautiful hotel lobbies, or at a picnic in Central Park on a sunny day. Remember, you've got competition nipping at your heels, trying for the same thing, whether it's the coworker in the cubicle next to you, a rival seller at a competing firm, or another paramour in a dating scenario. So even *dealing* with you needs to be a step up in the counterparty's world. Just watching and listening to you do your thing should be something they want to pay for. And when you are done, they need to want you to come back, just to be around you and have you pitch to them all day long (like a first date who wants a second!). Regardless of the situation, you need to feel sincere excitement in your heart about the possibilities, improvements, and new opportunities, and project that onto the person you're trying to convince to buy what you're selling. Trust me, even in the toughest situation, there is always a bright side.

It's all about optimism. You want to sing like a little bird, even when it's raining.

What did I recently say to the frowning clients who couldn't afford an $11 million townhouse on the Upper West Side of Manhattan and had to consider Brooklyn? I said, "You're getting a better house for $4 million. This is a mansion! It's only twenty-five minutes from Manhattan. With the money you save, you could take a car service every night the rest of your life and still have enough money to buy that condo in Miami. Besides, Brooklyn is where everyone wants to be right now anyway."

You can always find the positive, even when a situation isn't 100 percent peaches and cream. Just like life itself, there is something good even in the worst of situations. It's my job to focus on the warm, not the cold. And you know what? It's the best way to live life anyway. To always look at the glass half-full, not half-empty. And then share that glass with whomever is with you.

LOVE AT FIRST SIGHT

Set your egg timer. If you're sitting down with a first date, your boss to ask for a raise, or with a client to sell an apartment or your thingamajig, you've got ten minutes in a pitch to wow 'em and woo 'em. If you don't, you're cooked. Within that short time—from hello to the tenth minute—they've decided whether they are interested enough to move further. If, after those ten minutes, they're wanting more, you're already on to the next step: the negotiation (which is our next chapter).

Have you ever been on a first date? I'm betting you have at least once and that you remember it as a tricky operation that ended up in either great success or heartbreaking failure. On a first date, you second-guess your every move. You catch yourself fidgeting. You notice the deafening silence in your conversation. Your head fills with questions of *Should I?* or *Shouldn't I?* The event, like a pitch, is a beginning or an end.

Let's go on a date, you and me.

What has to happen first? I have to reach out and ask you on the date. How I go about that will hopefully elicit an enthusiastic yes because the other result is kind of a fiasco. . . . And there can be a noticeable bruising on the heart when someone tells you he or she isn't interested.

Rather than calling you and asking, "Would you like to go out?" I'm calling you with a definitive idea, a plan. "Hi! How about some Pinot Noir at ABC Kitchen (my favorite restaurant in New York) at eight P.M. tomorrow?" I've offered you something specific that says something about me, shows I'm confident, but still with a question mark at the end.

"Yes!" you say.

That's so much more effective, proactive, and certain than the deadly back-and-forth dancing of "When are you available?" Heads up: If someone does ask you this, be definitive. Make the decision. Don't be wishy-washy. People appreciate and respect someone who can quickly make up his or her mind.

"Great, and I have something to tell you," I say.

Bang! That's the starter pistol. We're set. You and I have a date. And I've dangled a carrot. You're dying to know what I have to tell you, aren't you?

Here's the big secret about any kind of deal making: Every baby step you take is one move closer to making The Sell. It starts the moment you first make contact. So, when you want something from someone, your opening salvo better be alluring and tight because any pitch starts at hello. I didn't just invite you for dinner. I strategically invited you to my *favorite* restaurant, argu-ably *the best* in New York, and I also created anticipation with my *secret* something to tell you. Similarly, if I were asking my boss for a raise, I'd suggest to her, "Could you meet with me Tuesday at two P.M. for ten minutes? I have an idea to improve our profit-ability." That gets her attention and gets you the ten minutes.

Here's how I use that same, simple technique to sell someone on a great apartment and investment. A buyer e-mails me to see one of my listings: "Can I see your apartment on Sullivan Street tomorrow morning?" I immediately e-mail back, "Calling you shortly." Just like that. I don't say yes or no. I leave the buyer waiting for my call.

First baby step: *Establish credibility.*

The pitch has already begun. I leave a few minutes, just enough for the buyer to be drawn into my little world. My e-mail signature provides a link to look at all my listings and social media pages and to see my latest press men-tions. Before I call, the buyer hopefully has picked up from my e-mail signature that I am "The number one agent in New York by *The Real Deal* magazine." The future close has therefore already started—before we have ever spoken and before the buyer has even seen the property.

Second baby step: *Create urgency while saying positive things.*

I then call up the buyer and open up with great energy. "Hiiiiiiiiiiiiiiiiiiiiiiiiii. Oh my God, the weather is gor-geous today, don't you think?"

"Ehhh . . . Yes, it sure is. Yes, love the weather."

I tell him I can't believe he already knows about the property, as I just listed it. He must be at the top of his game, too, since he is so quick, and he'll be able to see the loft before the first open house, before anyone else. I sometimes even say, "I like you." (I can hopefully tell that it makes the buyer smile.)

We talk about when to see the loft, and I mention I have three showings there the day after tomorrow for fellow brokers in my office who have been dying to get their clients in. He'll definitely want to get in before them.

Third baby step: *Instill confidence in a dialogue, not monologue.* We meet the next day outside the loft, and in the elevator up to the apartment I speak about the market in general. This is my opportunity to say that the market is on fire (if true) and how I closed $138 million in deals in less than three weeks, my best month ever! I might add there are a lot of Europeans, all cash buyers, lately, and I ask the buyer why he thinks that is.

Fourth baby step: *Establish a friendly dream while creating a little more urgency.*

I open the door to the loft and start showing him around, talking about the seller's attention to detail. I make the seller, who happens to be in Paris right now with Beyoncé on her European tour, seem personal and fabulous, and name-drop just the right amount. No gimmicks or falsehoods, just facts. I explain how much love has gone into the home and how difficult it is for the seller to now part with it and this amazing area. I mean, after all, this is the hottest location in the world right now. Sometimes I even go to such lengths to say that I am afraid the seller might change his mind if I believe this might actually be true.

Here I also ask the buyer a lot of questions. Everyone loves being asked for his opinion. It's important he feels I'm interested in him, but I am also fishing for information for a later negotiation. "Where do you live now? How big is that apartment? I see. Good, okay. Hmmm . . . How was your summer? Really? Oh, I love Greece, too." I have one goal: to get the buyer not only comfortable, but also obsessed with the neighborhood, the apartment, and me. We are friends now. We like each other. You must do this with whatever you're selling.

So, The Sell doesn't start and end where it is obvious: It starts with *you* at the very first point of contact, whatever that is. From the first seconds of our contact (via e-mail), he was able to see he's in the hands of someone at the top of his game (and if you are not, you can still add something fabulous in your e-mail signature, or if nothing else your favorite quote that makes people share your view of the world). In our two-minute phone call, I let him know I'm impressed that he's on his game and he's going to get to see the apartment before anyone else. In the thirty-second elevator ride up to the apartment, we covered that the market is hot and we fired him up. If he liked the apartment, he should move fast. As we walked in the door, I began immediately pointing out details and the seller's amazing taste. I asked questions, made him feel at home, and at the same time collected information. I clinched his active interest by minute ten by suggesting I was scared the seller liked the apartment so much that he wouldn't sell it. Everybody wants what everybody wants. He started talking numbers. (And we never discussed a single other apartment.)

Now you and I are going back to our date! OMG. OMG. OMG. I'm so excited. What to wear? Should I bring flowers? Will we drink champagne and eat filet mignon? Will tonight be the night we *seal the deal*? And what is it that I am going to tell you?

I've got a plan for the night, but I am not going to force anything. I'm confident in who I am, but I am even more confident in the universe's bigger plan for you and me. Something great will come out of tonight. I already know how to dress for the occasion and how to be charming. It's time to set The Sell in motion.

On our first date, I'd of course bring my happiest self, make eye contact, smile, and listen. You start the night by saying, "Okay, so what is it that you want to tell me?"

I look down and then up. And in a cute way, I say: "That you are incredibly beautiful. That's all. Stunning. Everything about you is beautiful."

Many first dates, interviews, and presentations start with the oldest, most boring scenario in the book: "Tell me about yourself." Ugh! Don't fall for it! Don't make the mistake: "I was born in Stockholm. . . ." Even if the person you're with has asked you about yourself, it's a trap. He doesn't really want to know your bio. That will all come later, not now. In these early moments of any relationship or presentation, it doesn't matter that you were the chess champion at twelve. What matters is how you can positively affect his life (or simply the time you're together).

During my first ten minutes with anyone, I never speak in the negative. If we were on our first date, I also wouldn't use big words or corny come-on lines or mention marriage. Doing so would immediately cause you to put up walls. Instead, I might tell you a story about my favorite meatball recipe that I made last week for the million-dollar commission earners on my team. That kind of story accomplishes many things at once: It says I can cook. It says I'm a good boss. And it lets you know I'm making money because my team members under me are. The best part is you make that conclusion yourself. I didn't brag once; I only kind of bragged for my colleagues.

Ding! The egg timer has gone off. Our first ten minutes are up. Do you want more? Because you have already made the decision, and we both know it.

FREDRIK'S PITCH PERFECT

Let's make it happen for you! Whether you're selling vacuums door-to-door, selling yourself for a bigger position in your company, or selling apartments, let's make you pitch perfect.

Remember your first job interview? That's a pitch. I remember mine very well. I was seventeen and was vying for a summer internship at the Salomon Brothers office in London—my dream job. That morning I dressed in the only suit I owned, off the racks of H&M, and in the pants pocket I concealed a napkin, which I was using to dry my sweaty palms. I was so nervous walking onto the cavernous trading floor, which was once a train station. I had been up half the night. I remember my heart beating so loudly I thought people could hear it. Looking back, I realize I made the mistake pretty much everyone makes before any big meeting or interview. I built it up the night before to be this huge, monumental thing. That's not the mistake. The mistake, I now realize, was that I was going it alone!

Here's what I've realized happens to most people before a big meeting: They isolate themselves. They close the world out and run things over and over through their heads. This is very similar to my first week of filming the original season of *Million Dollar Listing*. I got myself so worked up in my head about each day's shoot that I ended up looking like a stiff in front of the camera. I've now learned to do something with someone before my shoots and pitches. It leaves me more liquid and helps me make a seamless transition.

Have you ever been on a date, pitched something, or tried to sell something, and it didn't go so well? You look back and wonder, *Why in the world was I so boring?* I'm *never* boring when I am with my best friend; that's when I am fun, relaxed, and myself. Well, that's the point: You want to be exactly like you are with your best friend. So one of my secrets is to bring my best friend and business partner, John Gomes, to any pitches I do. More on that later. If you can't, for all the obvious reasons, bring your best friend into the meeting, bring him or her *to* the meeting and leave him or her at the door.

If your friend can't tag along, speak to him or her on the way there. Laugh, pretend he is tickling you. Have her say how amazing you are. Sound crazy? It's not. You are making The Sell if you walk into a pitch with a puff of happiness beneath your wings. That's why John and I rarely lose a pitch, and if we do, we lose it together, and that allows us to dust ourselves off from the failure quickly, and we can afford to laugh at it and move on.

Further, if you know your friend is standing by, your fear isn't going to overtake you. Someone has your back. While you're in the interview, you know the worst thing that can happen is that if it doesn't go well, you'll have a shoulder to cry on, and then go eat some Swedish Fish together.

In any interview setting, it's an audition. *You* want that role! No one wants ordinary. Remember what sets you apart and play that up because anyone you're meeting with—interviewer, home buyer, tax assessor, your boss—is hearing from people all day long. So what sets you apart? I'll walk in the room backward and wear flashy socks if it makes 'em laugh. My theory is that if you entertain yourself, your charisma will be so appealing that you'll get the part. If you don't get the part, it wasn't the right thing for you anyway, and you had fun losing it to someone boring.

Now to the specific logistics of that ten-minute window:

1. **Give a nice handshake and a real smile with eye contact.**
    Let your customer or client take her eyes off you before you do the same to her. When Fritzy looks me in the eye so long I have to look down, I know he is the boss in the house. (I'm afraid this is starting to happen more and more. . . .) Also, you're definitely judged on your handshake, and you want it to say confident and friendly. Your handshake should be firm but not bone crushing and should last two to five seconds. And your smile should be so warm it's hot. I have a phobia of cold and sweaty hands. It's like you are squeezing a piece of cold, raw chicken fillet. And what does that say about the person?

    Practice your handshake with someone you trust, and get feedback. I have my team members practice with one another. Most bodybuilders talk about how to connect to a muscle, to put focus *in* it with your brain. The bodybuilder working his biceps will concentrate all his brainpower on the bicep and become the bicep, be one with it. Do the same next time you shake somebody's hand: Become one with the person, really become your warm hand; send your mental, silent, but perfect pitch through the nerves of your arm, out to your hand, and then into your buyer's body. It's shocking how it works. Try it. I'm writing this very sentence doing it from my fingertips and into your brain. Feel it tickle in there?

2. **Exude positive energy.** Before the meeting starts, act like it's already over and that you've won your client's business. Humble and confident at the *same* time. Immediately tell the person how great it is to see them, using his or her name. Nothing is sweeter to someone than the sound of his own name. Make sure you use it both in your hello and your good-bye. (And as a general practice, say people's names more. They like it, and if you're meeting someone for the first time, it helps you remember it.)

   How do I give off good vibes? I visualize success, and I make sure I'm really enjoying myself. I mean, I really do enjoy myself. I crack myself up. I love dressing up; I enjoy my own image in the mirror (almost every day). I am proud of the challenges that I have overcome and will continue to overcome in the future. You must know in your heart that you will succeed—or even more important, that you have *already* succeeded but can always be better.

   My technique is to immediately identify the positive traits of the person with whom I'm speaking. Give *genuine* compliments. If she has nice eyes, I say so. That makes me happy; that makes her happy. If he's sharply dressed, I say so. That makes me happy; that makes him happy. If a couple's kid is the cutest thing in the world, I say so. That makes me happy; that makes them happy. If they have a puppy, I forget everyone and cuddle with it on the floor. That makes me happy and the puppy happy, and I don't care what anyone else thinks.

I also always look around people's apartments for personal items and comment on them. If I see a family photo from Rome, and I've been there, too, then we have something in common, something emotional perhaps, and that is a good thing. If you're meeting with your boss and see the photo of her kids on her desk, it never hurts to ask about her kids. It's a bond, a *genuine* conversation not involving work or the issues at hand, and I've never met a mom who doesn't like to brag about her kids. I love to find common, personal ground. Every point of connection is a check in the winner column, especially early on.

When you're making The Sell, you want the other person to know you're on the same team. You are family. I actually say that to my clients and even to my conservative developers: "We are family now."

3. **Take control of the conversation.** In any discussion of anything with anyone, you have the power to choose what you want to talk about. Yes, you might be asked questions, but you can steer those questions into the points you want to make. Politicians have this mastered.

    You must know precisely what you want from your interactions with others, and you must also know what you don't want. Without knowing these parameters, you have no agenda, and without an agenda, you have no direction. Our true goals and intentions are often what's said between the words.

    After my agent, Todd, sent out the proposal for this book, ten publishers were interested in buying it. I went around and met all of them. By the third meeting, I was adept at steering the conversation away from them asking the stinky old "Why do you want to do a book?" question and toward me exclaiming, "We're going to be a number one international bestseller!" I took control from the moment I stepped in the door. I was selling *The Sell*. And the result? *A bidding war!*

4. **Use the competition to brag about yourself.** A little bit of bragging has never hurt anyone, and it is important to brag when pitching, but there must be finesse to it. Brag the correct way. I have a secret to my bragging. It's genius (if I do say so myself), and it will make you want to brag more, and people will want to hear you brag. It works like this: Brag only by connecting yourself to your competition in a backhanded, humble way. Know your competitors' strengths and weaknesses and use them to your advantage. I proactively tell people they should meet with six or seven of the city's other top salespeople so that they can educate themselves. I slip in that I'm number one and that it only helps me if you will meet more brokers. "There are thirty thousand agents on the island of Manhattan, and you should definitely meet more people," I say with a huge smile. They don't know if I'm serious or not because it is exactly the opposite of what other brokers would say.

Sooner or later, most people will say, "We need to see all our options." Therefore, I say it to them *before* they have a chance to say it to *me*. Car shoppers or TV buyers are going to say, "We're going to test-drive a few others" or "We're going to look at what the guy at the mall has in high definition." Right? So, the trick is to suggest the competition before anyone else does. It's about taking charge and show-ing confidence. And slip in some bragging. Yes, it's the ulti-mate brag because it does the trick and goes by pretty much unnoticed. It helps them trust you because you're not scared of the competition. By you recommending it first, the likeli-hood of them actually meeting anyone else is greatly dimin-ished, if not completely eradicated.

5. **Avoid negative remarks about others.** If you start talking trash about others, people won't want to work with you. It's just tacky, and being negative turns you negative. They'll just wonder why you're so defensive. I never disparage. It never works and always catches up to you. You become what you say, and if you utter negativity, you will eventually be pulled down by it. You can see it in negative people's eyes, the grumpy old man on the park bench mumbling about losing to the world. I read about this experiment in which if you cut an apple in half, separate them, and every hour whispered that you love one half and screamed "You are an ugly piece of sh*t" to the other half, the latter will rot much faster. That's what talking bad about someone does. It's just rotten. In-stead of saying my competitors are terrible sellers or unin-formed about the market, I'll say Competitor X is a really good company with a great platform. "I would work for them if I hadn't chosen Douglas Elliman, which is the city's larg-est." Boom!

About a rival salesperson whose name comes up as com-petition for a downtown loft, I'll say, "I love her! She's actually a friend of mine! She's one of the best." And then I quickly add as an afterthought: "Last night at dinner, we talked

186 | FREDRIK EKLUND

about her and how well she is doing. She's got some great listings uptown. . . ." You see what I am doing here? I only gave praise to my competitor, but the message was clear: Your apartment is downtown. I didn't have to mention that I did $400 million in sales downtown last year. All I did was speak positively.

If it appeared I was trying to undermine someone, it wouldn't work. The compliment wouldn't be genuine. I take charge and gain the upper hand in a situation by saying nice things about the competition while at the same time sneaking in a tiny punch. I disarm the situation. I deliver my version about the competition in a pretty package. "They offer some great deals at X Cars! I know they're working to get their crash-test performance higher." Key point: If you're going to offer a criticism, make sure it's accurate! You don't want to be accused of spreading false rumors.

Yes, it's a tough game, but you can play tough *and* be professional and—most important—almost always win. Never bad-mouth the competition; leave the bad-mouthing to them. Oh yes, they will bad-mouth you, but you should only worry if they stop. It means you're doing something wrong, because they no longer think you're a threat.

6. **Lead with the positives.** There will always be positives and negatives about the product or service you're selling. In business, a common rule of thumb is that 80 percent of your sales come from 20 percent of your clients. I have a theory, which I practice when pitching, and it's my own take on the 80/20 rule. In the span of the pitch, I point out the positive 80

percent of the time and the negative 20 percent of the time on my *own* product or service. Inherently, with anything, there will be something negative. Why even mention my own negatives? Because it reinforces the positive, and you will be answering their unspoken questions and therefore gaining their trust. Like yin and yang, positive and negative can't exist without each other. If all you do is go on and on about how incredible this product or service is or how wonderful you are, the buyer will eventually think you are covering something up. Buyers are jaded, they are sophisticated, and they can smell a rotten Swedish *lax*, or "salmon" as we say in English, from around the block.

When you are done, you do not want them to have to ask, "So, what's wrong with it?" because it means they were thinking about that all along and didn't really listen to all the amazing things you were saying. Before they even get a chance to think about asking that question, I'll say, "The only real negative with this apartment is that the cabinets in the kitchen need to be changed, but that is a fun project and not a lot of money." Or: "I love what I do. It's amazingly rewarding, but it is a lot of work. Sometimes I think I am not going to be able to set yet another record, because it can get exhausting always striving to stay number one. But then I meet someone like you and see an apartment like this, and I know I will."

It is all about helping the customer feel what it's like to have this thing, in its entirety, all the good (and the little bit of bad). To give both creates trust. And once you get the negatives out of the way, you then shine the spotlight on everything wonderful.

Ding! The egg timer has gone off. Listen up! Ten minutes have passed. When *they* begin discussing numbers, you're done pitching.

And here you are. You have gotten to the point in the pitch where the little light flickers in your buyer's, seller's, investor's, boss's, date's, husband's, wife's, dog's eyes. You've grabbed their attention. In this very second, the pitch is done—congratulations! You are getting closer to making The Sell! A relationship is starting to form, but the terms are not yet set. So now the next phase starts: the negotiation.

Oh, but one last thing before we start negotiating: Check your zipper and your teeth before any big meeting. The only thing worse than leaving a pitch without making The Sell is leaving it with your fly down and a piece of broccoli stuck in your big smile. Don't laugh. It has happened to me, and the only thing I won was weird looks.

CHAPTER 9

MAKE THE SELL

Align the Hopes and Needs of
All Parties and Close the Deal

In kindergarten, the girls and the boys had this game where three of the bigger boys would sit on one side of the seesaw and the girls would pile on, one by one, on the other side until they found balance. Three bigger boys equaled five smaller girls. If one of the boys hopped off, the girls' side would slam to the ground. The whole schoolyard would laugh. I wasn't laughing. I was studying the scene. The word *equilibrium* is not something you understand at that age in a schoolyard, but observing the scene made me aware of something I've been using my entire life: Negotiating is a delicate balance.

For any deal to happen—especially in a business transaction— the two sides need to get in balance. A negotiation can only lead to a deal when there is a final acceptance of the happy middle. If you removed one of the boys from that seesaw, the deal was off. And that, by definition, is a negotiation—getting two sides in balance.

You might not think about it, but you negotiate all day long. We all do. At work with our colleagues, at home with our parents or children, husband or wife, and even at IKEA regarding the delivery of our furniture. I even negotiate with Fritzy: "Come here, boy. . . . Please . . . Look, a bone!" I always say life is one long negotiation. Every point of contact with *anyone* in life, not only in business, is part of the dance. Negotiating, and doing it well, is simply the way to get what you want out of life.

Whether you define it as reaching an agreement or compromise, or finding balance, or a way over or around obstacles, at the end of the day, negotiation is making a deal for yourself. So, let's be good at it. No, let's be *amazing* at it!

Earlier in my career, when I was a bit of a dummy about negotiation, I read books such as *Negotiating for Dummies*, *Selling for Dummies*, and *Success as a Real Estate Agent for Dummies*. As useful as those books were at the time, my firsthand experience negotiating billions of dollars in deals has taught me what works and what doesn't. And now I'm going to share what I've learned with you. Whether you're a mom negotiating with your toddler to eat his peas or a CEO negotiating your salary before a hostile board, mastering the give-and-take is everything.

Welcome to Sergeant Eklund's Negotiation Boot Camp.

Listen up, recruit! I will give you my secrets, and you will give me your full attention. That's nonnegotiable. Now, let's get to the exercises:

1.   **Put your foot down.** I looked down at my feet and back up at my trainer. He said, "Give me ten more push-ups." I said, "I don't have any more in me." He said, "Okay. Five more." I said, "I told you I don't have any more in me." I fell to the floor, exhausted. This negotiation was over because I had reached my floor, literally.

Look down now at your feet. That's where it all starts. With your feet, you can walk away, and you need to know that if necessary, you're going to use those feet to do exactly that. Before getting into any conversation about something serious where time, money, talent, or your self-respect is involved, always identify where your floor is. The floor is your bottom line, the absolute worst deal you'd be willing to make. That way, if the deal falls through the floor, you know exactly when to walk away.

In negotiating properties, the seller's floor is usually reached when he's losing money on the deal. In negotiating a salary, the floor is usually not getting any kind of raise at all. In negotiating in a personal relationship, the floor is usually reached when we simply give up and want to move on.

There are other things to consider than just an ideal number or an exact scenario. There are nuances to every deal. I've seen many deals where a buyer has paid over the asking price and asked for something like the antique chandelier or Persian rug to be included. And for everything you're selling, there are other factors. For example, when I was selling this book to a publisher, I considered the size of the advance, but I considered other aspects to the deal, like the market power of the house and the editor and publicist I'd be working with.

Regardless of what the floor is, getting close to it should send off a warning signal in your head. Beep, beep, beep! When that happens, you could pretend you are going to walk away from the table. Some call that bluffing. Or gambling. I call it dancing close to the edge, and it excites me.

The suggestion of walking away brings the negotiation to a screeching halt. Here's how I sometimes do it: I stand up, thank everyone involved for playing the game, pick up my papers and phone, put on my suit jacket, and slowly walk away from the table. My hope is that they will call me back or suggest another idea. If they do, my dance has paid off. If they don't, I walk from the room, leave the meeting, and consider another strategy to keep the negotiation from actually hitting the floor.

If you need proof this works, the next time you're looking at cars, get to the lowest price you can, and then walk away from the car dealership. I promise you'll get a call with a lower price, even if you have to wait until the end of the month.

2. **Keep 'em waiting.** I had come back from Mykonos after meeting Derek. He had gone back to London, and I was dying to hear from him and tell him that I knew he was the one. I really wanted to take the relationship to the next level. At the same time, I knew that timing is everything, and I had to make it work for me. I didn't want to seem desperate or too eager so I waited a little bit of time. After all, we lived on two different sides of the Atlantic Ocean, and we had just met. But after two days, I couldn't take it anymore. I texted him, "I miss you," and he texted back, "See you in New York next Friday." High-kick!

When someone wants something from you, use time to your advantage by delaying it all a bit. Tick tock, tick tock. Give the negotiation some breathing room. The trick is not letting too much time pass, which leads to frustration and anger, but just enough for the other party to wonder what you're thinking. Some professions take this to the extreme.

This is extra important between the pitch and the negotiation. The two often seamlessly overlap, but you can take control and create an advantage by separating them with time. When I'm on a listing pitch, I *never* give my clients the price right there and then. This is my secret. They want to know what I think. They ask, and I smile, pause, and wait a brief second. I then tell them I'll send it in a few hours. "Look out for it. It's coming tonight." Let the person that you're trying to convince of something get a little frustrated that you aren't giving her the hard sell. Let her come closer by metaphorically turning your back to her for a short while. People want what they can't have. Hermès's most expensive bags are always out of stock, and Apple's newly released iPhone sells out in hours because the company makes showy announcements about them weeks before anyone can actually buy them. Your job is to make people want something before they know they can have it.

This is a very common negotiating tactic in the high-end art world. Someone is strolling through a gallery and stops for a while in front of a painting. The gallerist sees this but pretends he doesn't. The buyer tries to get his attention, but the gallerist's attention is elsewhere. When the buyer does finally grab the gallerist's attention, the gallerist offers her the price on three paintings he knows she passed on her way to the one she wanted. That's his backhanded pitch. She kindly declines and points to the one she is interested in. "Oh, that one?" the gallerist asks, grimacing. "Unfortunately, it's not for sale." Guess what? The buyer wants it even more. She'll pay *anything.*

Or have you ever gone jewelry shopping? Do you see that bauble beneath the glass? You want to touch it, right? Well, you can't. Point to something in the case that you want to see. Watch how the salesperson will proclaim his love for it, pick it up, fondle it, polish it, and admire it before handing it over. Pausing . . . tick tock, tick tock. Every second counts, because it works. You practically want to snatch it out of his hands, but then the alarm will go off, so you keep quiet, wanting it even more.

Mark my words: The *delay* is crucial. The person with the information is in control, and the person waiting is wanting and pining, *When is it going to come? I want to know!* As long as the waiting is whetting the appetite and not starving them to death, it strengthens your position.

When making The Sell, you want a potential buyer 10 percent frustrated because he or she isn't getting *all* the information, just enough to want it all: What's the price? Is it available? When can I get it?

When, rather than blurting it out right away, I (finally!) send a potential seller the price a few hours after the pitch, it accomplishes three things: (1) It has made them want it, and therefore my services, more. (2) It is in writing, which makes it more solid, and in our world more true, like there is nothing else really to discuss. Putting it in writing basically says,

This is the price, and I'm not asking for your thoughts on it. And (3) since it took so long, the impression is that there must be a lot of thought, knowledge, and research behind it—which there is!

3. **Make it face-to-face.** I've always liked discussing things in person. In fact, during my first month at the Stockholm School of Economics, I was writing a paper about language in e-mails. There was a lot of research at the time that suggested the majority of all e-mails were misunderstood. This was way before emojis. E-mail was still in its infancy. My radical middle-of-the night idea was that I should stop writing the paper. I had a better idea. The following morning I asked my professor if I could instead do a speech on the subject in front of the whole class, to save time and to make a better impression—and perhaps most important, have no one misunderstand me. I did and got an A+.

   If any deal or life situation isn't going the way you'd like it, the best damage control you can do is to get in a room with the person and talk it out. This might not always be possible, but if it is, make it happen. If I've been communicating with someone through e-mail, and my price isn't being accepted, or the contract isn't getting signed, or negotiations are turning sour and that celebratory high-kick is slipping away, I immediately ask to meet face-to-face. I'll write "CALL ME!" in the subject line and nothing else. That's how I get the other party's attention. Then, when I get the call, I say, "We need to meet. I'm coming over. I'll be there in ten."

In today's society, where all of us have our brains connected to our phones and e-mails all day long, this is often easier said than done. But try to make it happen. Why? Because a great negotiator, when needed, uses his emotions, family heritage, spirituality, body language, fashion, sexuality (oh yes!), humor, and everything else in between to win, to make a deal happen. How can you ever use those skill sets in an e-mail? More than 70 percent of our communication is expressed without words—yes, that's right! Seventy percent! Your emotions, excitement, and mood are all communicated with your body. No number of emojis or exclamation points can make up for that.

Also, it's much more difficult to say no to someone sitting in front of you, but very easy to type "No" in an e-mail or avoid someone's phone call.

When the phone is your only option, always have an agenda. Know what you want out of a phone call before making it. Keep the calls short. The best phone negotiators use few words, where every word is important and means something. Speak clearly and with weight. Rid yourself of verbal tics. When someone says "uh" and "you know" repeatedly in any conversation, it makes me cringe. If it's during a negotiation, it puts that person in the awkward position of looking dumb or insecure. Pause between your counterpart's talking and your answer. Speak like it's final, without question marks.

Further, try to speak on a landline if possible. There's nothing worse in a serious conversation or negotiation than "You're breaking up," unless you want to hang up on someone and blame it on the bad reception. And, please, don't negotiate on the phone outside on a windy street next to a construction site. Nothing irritates someone more than having to repeat something five times because you can't hear them.

4. **Listen closely!** It was my birthday, and I was hoping my grandfather had planned to take me to Liseberg, the largest amusement park in Sweden, but it came with a price, a price I didn't really mind. Before our outing, my grandfather wanted me to come over to his apartment in old Stockholm. I knew that what he really wanted was for me to sit and listen to his stories about his days acting and filming with the legendary director Ingmar Bergman. It was a birthday present for him. Everyone wants a chance to be heard.

   Listening is one of the most important skills you can use when there is something you are trying to achieve. Whether you're negotiating your salary, the purchase of a car, or resolving a dispute with a coworker, active listening is critical for your success.

   Negotiations are often emotional. Taking time to acknowledge your counterpart's feelings, rather than minimizing them, can help bring things into balance. Experts suggest such techniques as paraphrasing, which is repeating what the other person has said in your own words; reflecting, which is repeating the last few words someone has spoken to you; asking open-ended questions, which provides you further insight; and encouraging, which might be a head nod, an "I see," or an "Okay."

   Here's what I say about listening, and to me it's simple: Try to listen more than you speak; utilize silence and pausing; and build rapport and trust, which can lead to a great outcome: agreement! By the way, have you ever noticed how good of a listener Santa Claus is?

5. **Speak with your body.** My first three or four live TV interviews didn't go so well. I had these nervous tics. I thought I said really smart things, but I looked like a weirdo. Fortunately, a friend told me that I needed to watch the tapes of myself because I was twitching too much and licking my lips. It embarrassed me terribly, but I knew I needed to work on hiding my nervousness. No one was listening to what I was saying; they were watching what I was doing. That's when I realized it's more *how* you say than *what* you say.

    When you're in a room with someone, discussing something important, realize that you're talking with both your words and your body, and make sure that the two are in alignment. If you want him to come up to your demands, be open with your arms and be convincing, smile, and sit closer. If you are disappointed with the terms and situation, cross your arms and sit farther away.

    I realized by the time I graduated kindergarten that our body language tells a story, and our faces sometimes reveal all. You are in control of a conversation, if you are smiling sincerely and making eye contact. When you start looking away or squinting, or biting your lip or clenching your jaw, you are revealing that it isn't going the way you want. That's all fine—if your *intention* is to show the other party you think their offer is disgustingly low or their terms aren't anywhere near doable. Since most people haven't watched themselves negotiate, they don't even realize they are reveal-ing these signals.

When I'm talking with people, I try to keep my arms and hands relaxed and often in my lap. I almost never cross my arms, and the only time I'd clench my fists would be un-der the table. When I used to bite my nails, the worst was getting caught doing so while negotiating. I might as well have sent up a flare telling the other party they were getting to me. Remember, negotiating is like poker. You don't ever want to let the other side know what your next move will be, so don't let your face reveal your cards.

Watch your legs and feet, too. That means stop shaking your legs or tapping your feet under the table. My move if I'm standing up while negotiating is to open my suit jacket and lean in to the person I'm with, putting my energy on his or her face.

I often like zigzagging between two opposites to inten-tionally create a little confusion. This takes a little practice, but it generally works for me. I *say* very aggressively something like "This offer sucks" while *looking* cute and boyish, and by doing that the information is more easily absorbed. It's like I'm dressing up the negative information in a cute outfit. It signals that I'm unhappy but willing to keep talking.

I love scanning the other person's body language when I'm negotiating because I can learn so much. Watch for the other person's tells, subtle giveaways as to what he's thinking. Sometimes I realize a guy is trying to be tough and in con-trol, refusing to improve his offer, but I can see his jaw clenching and, if I listen carefully, I can hear his foot tapping against his chair. If he truly was comfortable in his position and not ever coming up to my price, he would be relaxed. Or, if he really was at the highest he could go, he might start to look sad as he slowly acknowledges the deal isn't happening.

6. **Take unexpected turns.** I often simultaneously send out opposite energies with my words and body. I recently had a big negotiation for a townhouse that I had worked on for three months. I then got an extremely lowball offer from the buyer's broker. I was *angry* over the insulting offer, so I *smiled* really big and said with wide-eyed enthusiasm, "Thank you!" My contrariness told her she was never getting anywhere with that stinky offer and gave me the upper hand in the negotiation. Similarly, if I'm super *excited* over a high offer, I stay completely *neutral* and say, "Mmmmm . . ." Why? So I don't make the buyer feel he is overpaying.

I always tell my team that negotiating is a game of upside downs. Everything can be the opposite of what it really is, and that's when the real fun starts. You need to be ready to bluff, and as you do, know you are risking more by bluffing. But with more risk, comes a greater potential reward.

If your counterpart knows what waits around the corner, he or she will be prepared, and you want to keep the other side *unprepared*, on his or her toes. I have invented an emotionally dramatic curve that I want you to consider. I always start off the negotiation at a happy place, being nice, smiling, and laughing like a little bird.

I enter the room with great energy. First impression lasts. I establish confidence and control. Arms open, perhaps even a hug. And I make the other side feel at ease with me, thinking, *This guy is so pleasant. I'm sure I can control him—this will be easy.*

But they are in for a big surprise.

All of a sudden, I let the energy fall to a bad place where there is darkness. I'll blurt out, "There is no way this will work out!" The other side suddenly thinks, *This guy is a lunatic. He was happy five minutes ago, and now he is a real bitch.* The point is that I start killing the deal, turning the situation sour quickly and unexpectedly, so the other side is taken off guard. They feel they need to stop the crash. I pretend I'm offended. The other side is fearing the deal is dead; then I resuscitate it, not a lot, just a little hope for life. I open the door slightly to let some light in. I pause, give him or her a long look, and perhaps say, "Okay . . . Let me think here." I give just enough hope, and from there, more positivism until the deal closes.

Do I sound crazy? Good! That's the point. It makes me in control by grabbing the emotional wheel in the car and throwing my counterpart into the backseat. It also puts things in perspective: As human beings we are driven by emotions, and emotions by definition are relative.

You can only see the sunrays coming in through the window because the room is dark. Remember that one.

7. **Step away from the deal.** Sometimes during a tough negotiation or when we've hit a bump, I look down at my iPhone and exclaim: "Oh my! My mother just e-mailed me. Hold on." Twenty-five seconds of silence as I read an imaginary e-mail. My counterpart is caught off guard and perplexed. I've unexpectedly taken the attention off the deal. I look up at him: "She is coming to New York to visit! I'm sorry, but this just makes me so happy. Hold on. . . . I need five

minutes. I will be right back." The other side fumbles for words as I stand up and walk out of the room (or hang up if we are negotiating over the telephone).

After five minutes I'm back and talk about my mother and her upcoming trip. I ask about the other side's mother. I make the other side forget about the deal for a few minutes. I take the conversation to a place far away from real estate and to a happy place. Then, all of a sudden without any notice, I bring it back to the negotiation. "Now, let's get back to the deal. Not a dollar above two million!"

Why? By forcing a pause in the negotiation, and elevating the energy away from the deal, by making it seem small in comparison to our mothers, I'm lifting the lid off the pot of boiling water. This is especially good when the negotiation isn't moving in the direction you want or when things get too heated or you're having trouble convincing the other side you are right. By suddenly talking about your family and the other side's family, your background, or something else highly personal, you can go back to the deal and come in from a new angle, with newly won control and energy. Trust me: The chances that you will get what you want are much greater.

8. **Throw it in neutral.** I sometimes like to throw a negotiation into what I call *neutral* gear. Instead of being upset or unhappy over the other side's input, I go completely neutral like that robot from *Prometheus*. Robots don't feel or show human emotions, and that can make them great negotiators. It's very effective because it forces the other side to continue along working hard to get a response.

My classic response when I'm throwing it into neutral gear is a long "Mmmmmm . . ." with simply a blank stare across the table. As seen on *Million Dollar Listing New York*, I do this a lot, and people think it's funny. I think it's effective. It goes something like this:

The other side might say, "I know you are bluffing. I know your client wants this apartment and can pay more!"

Me (calmly and with the neutral robot voice, thinking my blood is made of liquid plastic): "Mmmmmm . . ." without taking my eyes away from the other person.

It is impossible to read what I am saying. Am I agreeing or disagreeing? Or do I simply not know what I want? Am I even really listening to him? Do I need to go to the bathroom because I'm constipated? Am I human, or a robot? The other side isn't sure. The other side is completely confused and at the same time annoyed. We are both quiet.

The key here is not to say anything.

The other person: "Mmmmm *what*? Why are you mmmmmm-ing me?"

Me (keeping the neutral mask and the voice from outer space): "Mmmmmm . . ."

Now the other person is upset, and it's amusing, but don't smile here. Robots don't smile. When somebody is upset, they show their true colors. They lose control.

Try it. It *always* works and is actually a lot of fun.

9. **Play good cop, bad cop.** When it comes to dealing with Mousey and Fritzy, I'm usually the good cop and Derek is the bad cop. Most negotiations can benefit from a good cop/ bad cop routine, and I use it often. We are trying to reinforce

the same message, to not poop inside the house, but we use different methods. I praise them when they poop outside, while Derek shouts when they poop inside.

To use good cop, bad cop with the other side, you need someone who knows you and works well with you. My business partner, John, is that person for me. We almost always negotiate in tandem. The good cop exists only with the bad cop, and they seem to be working separately, but it is an illusion. After all, they are on the same team.

It's always good for a customer to hear the same message from *two* different people, from two different perspectives. Telling someone to buy an apartment can sound completely different depending on whether the good or the bad cop says it, but the core message is the same: *Buy* the damn thing.

Good cop: "It's such a beautiful apartment, but don't stress it—if you don't get it, I'm sure there'll be another one coming along soon. . . ."

Bad cop: "You need to act now! You're going to lose it, and I can't imagine there will be another one like it on the market for years!"

Two different people say the same thing using two very different tones, two different approaches, one easy and nice, the other pushy and aggressive. The client will always like one over the other, the nicer probably, and that's the point really. The bad cop is there to reinforce the message of the good cop. Regardless, the client will listen and buy.

When stressful situations arise, the client sometimes needs to ventilate/consult with the good cop as much as he or she needs to be pushed/forced by the bad cop. What I am saying is that a lot of clients do better when they hear from *both* the bad and the good cop.

Furthermore, not all people will connect with and like you. It is human nature: We all click better with some people than others. Therefore, it is always good to have a negotiating partner that can come in, and sometimes even take over, when it gets rough.

10. **Always have a Mr. Kim.** The Korean developer I was working for was a pain. With every question we'd present, he'd say, "I have to ask Mr. Kim." (His boss fourteen time zones away.) We worked with him for several years before I eventually realized there was no Mr. Kim. Genius! The developer just needed someone to hide behind in order to make and stand behind his own decisions.

This is easy to do whether you work for yourself or for an organization. You're creating someone to take the heat off you, like when you were a kid and said, "I have to ask my mom." When someone asks me to negotiate on my commission, I always say, "I have to ask my manager." That gives me an escape hatch. I can certainly negotiate my commission if I want to, but I don't want to. I deserve my commission. I'm not discounting myself! Twenty-four hours later, I simply call the client and say my manager said no. It provides me with an untouchable authority. Thank you, Mr. Kim.

CLOSE IT!

Many studies on selling show that more than 50 percent of people who don't make The Sell fail to do one simple thing: They don't ask for what they want! Therefore, let me remind you of this simple thought: In order to be married, one of you has to ask and the other has to say, "I do."

And when you're brave enough to ask, you make The Sell!

Congratulations! You have closed the deal! It's time to pop the cork on the champagne.

We can all make The Sell every day. Whether small or large, success takes effort, diligence, and commitment to our dreams. My thought is that each of our sells presents us with an opportunity for celebration, for acknowledging this great life and the active role we play in it.

I've made a lot of deals in my day, but none will I cherish more than my wedding, my ultimate sell.

I remember it this way: The sun was dropping like an orange ball into the blue ocean at the exact time we exchanged rings. All our family, friends, and loved ones were sitting on the beach, all dressed in white, and there wasn't a dry eye around. Even Mousey and Fritzy were howling in happiness.

I recall thinking that this was a huge victory, an end to all those years spent being single, the lonesomeness, the sadness and suffering, the worry about not ever meeting my soul mate and having to travel the world by myself, forever falling asleep and

After our ceremony, Derek and I stood out in the water, our white pants rolled up, and watched the sun drop into the ocean and the sky light up in layers of red, orange, and blue. Then the sky burst with fireworks and we celebrated making life's ultimate sell.

waking up alone. As the sun sank into the water, I realized how the years of struggle and difficulty—our long-distance relationship, the hundreds of e-mailed love letters, the battle to be able to legally get married and live together in the United States—was now behind us. And, like any great sell, all that work only made it sweeter. All my deals are sweet, but this was the happiest, biggest, best closing of my life.

Derek looked so happy. I cried way too much. There were cameras there, but I didn't even think of them; all I thought was that I wanted the moment to last forever. And now I don't want it to ever end.

Here's to your big deal!

PART
THREE

My brother, Sigge, and his two sons and I were at an amusement park in Stockholm staring down at a wrinkled little white napkin on an outdoor restaurant table. It had stains of ketchup on it from the hot dog it had just wrapped, and my brother ironed it down with his fingers so it didn't fly away in the wind. He took out his pen and wrote, "Eklund . . . Stockholm . . . New York . . . ," and said, "I want to connect those three words, equally powerful in different ways." My nephews grew frustrated that their dad and uncle were now more interested in words on a napkin than seats on a roller coaster. But that napkin was a life changer, more exciting than hitting the crest of a coaster's highest hill, because the words on that napkin would help me climb even higher. That napkin was the first step to my multinational luxury real estate brokerage that would become highly profitable and set records in every market it would enter.

Have you ever heard the phrase "rest on your laurels"? It means you're satisfied with your achievements and can stop trying for a little while. The etymology of the phrase is based on the ring of laurel leaves worn on the head in ancient times as a symbol of victory. You know what happens when you rest on your laurels? You lose your crown. Your competitors take your business, and your success dries up faster than a crown of laurel leaves.

The Sell is a lifestyle. And you, my high-kicker, are going to get big results because you're looking to continue growing your best-selling life. What I've found is that once you start getting results, you see the world differently. You recognize opportunities everywhere because you believe in yourself. What I know is that when we begin achieving success, that's not the time to coast; that's the time to amp it up, to build on those triumphs and to create more opportunities. Nothing, after all, succeeds like success.

That's why I started to look for my next big thing before I even reached the top of the New York real estate market: my own company in Scandinavia.

So, what's next for you?

This third part of the book is going to tell you how to build a team, find a business partner, start building *your* empire, promote yourself in the press, and learn to deal with failure, and perhaps most important, we are going to discuss how to best enjoy your life. It's time to *live large*!

Together we're now going to master how to:

- get people to work with you;
- grab attention;

- grow your business;
- turn failures into victories; and
- enjoy your success!

And then I'm going to send you onward by giving you a lucky charm.

CHAPTER 10

HOW TO WIN FRIENDS AND INFLUENCE PEOPLE TO *WANT* TO WORK WITH *YOU*

Find, Hire, and Manage Great People

People in the real estate business and the press were noticing my success. They said they had never seen anyone so young come into real estate and quickly grab so much business. How, my competitors wondered, was this kid getting all these listings and now selling out his first building, the Onyx on Twenty-Eighth Street and Eighth Avenue?

I'll tell you how. Since my first open house at that two-bedroom on West Twentieth Street, I worked every client, every showing, every open house like a showman under the big top. I made the experience exciting and fun, and then I followed up with *every single person* who attended and made many of them my friends, customers, and referral base. I also marketed myself heavily to the other owners of apartments in the buildings in which I was selling, and the number of other apartments I got to sell expanded exponentially. Every day my client list grew. I had gotten so big so quickly that it was a lot for me to juggle.

The Onyx was my first entry into new development and an intense project that I oversaw for two years. I programmed the building with the architect and developer—perfected unit sizes, layouts, finishes, and amenities. Then I priced all the apartments while working on the collateral material such as the brochure, website, and sales gallery. It was nonstop work, but the financial payoff was big.

We only had four apartments left at the Onyx, and I decided to invite every other cobroker who had brought their buyers and done deals in the building to a fancy lunch at the Four Seasons. The idea was that they knew the building and were likely to do a second deal in it. A broker named John Gomes had sold an apartment in the building and was one of the dozen or so brokers attending my luncheon.

I never thought I'd have a business partner. Though I was a little stretched (and stressed), I was doing fine on my own and figured I'd always go at it alone. John changed that. I vividly remember the moment we first shook hands, and I remember the great conversation we had at lunch. He says he remembers the moment, too, but like any great yin-and-yang partnership, he remembers it a little differently.

John says his impression of me was that deals were falling off my desk because I had so much going on. He said he "could pick up those deals and make *us* a lot of money." I didn't realize he was making a business proposal because I didn't realize I was looking for one.

Shortly thereafter, I made him an offer. I had another building I'd been working on for a very long time, 52 East Fourth
Street. I knew people liked John. He's very charismatic and a
dynamic shower—someone who gives clients a tour of an apartment. A great shower walks into an apartment and, like a model
on a game show, points out, showcases, and fondles every feature, all while entertaining the clients. I said I'd give him a flat
$10,000 fee for every apartment sold at 52 East Fourth. He ac-
cepted, and, with his help, we quickly sold that building out.
While he was showing those listings, it freed up a lot of time for
me to pitch new properties and more development projects.

John and I then began tiptoeing into a more serious business
relationship, and I must admit I was uncertain it would work. I
mean, split the money? Have two people involved in every decision? Share the spotlight on my way to the top? But I followed
my gut that two of us were far better than one. I acknowledged
that I had weaknesses—including limited time—that would be
complemented by his strengths. I realized that one plus one could
equal a lot more than two. We discussed splits between us for a
while, and at first we couldn't agree. I mean why would I split
everything with him fifty-fifty when I had worked so hard to get
where I was? But he told me, "You will not get half of X; you will
be getting fifty percent of Y, where Y is five times as great as X.
Y is what you *and* me will create together."

He frustrated me at times. (He'd definitely say I was doing
my best to drive him crazy, too.) I was working days, nights, and
weekends and felt a little resentful because he was working
mostly "normal" hours and spending the summer weekends relaxing on the beach at Fire Island. I also felt tasked with teach-
ing him the development end of the business. To put it mildly,

we had lots of disagreements in the beginning. But, as in any great relationship, we were figuring it out. John was a quick learner and started producing incredible results and could sell the unsellable.

My job was (and still is) to bring in new business and get the development deals and John's was to go out and show them. When it came time to negotiate, we tag teamed. We moved closer and closer to a fifty-fifty relationship, which in the end we both realized was the best thing for us. When it came to money and time, we split fifty-fifty, but something far more important happened that neither one of us ever expected: We became best friends! We started enjoying each other's company outside work, and when we finally took time off to go to Europe or Asia, we traveled together. We made each other laugh, we picked each other up, we completed each other's sentences—and we started building what was to become the number one real estate team in the nation.

Then the Great Recession hit. The economy came crashing down, and with it, the real estate market screeched to a sudden halt. I told John (and myself) that this was the best thing that could happen to us. We would grow stronger, be humbled, work even harder, and come out of this even better.

That was easier said than done. During the downturn, my bills were higher than high and my income was lower than low. As an example, I was the *only* broker that made a deal in SoHo during the first quarter of 2009. (It was a loft on Greene Street, and I convinced my buyer to purchase the apartment even though she had fears she was overpaying because of the terrible economy. Since then, she has tripled her investment.) Deals were scarce, and no one knew how far the market was going to drop.

But guess what happened? John came through for me. And I

for him. Instead of splitting up like many other real estate teams, we both did everything a real partnership should do. We, like a good married couple, became *equal* partners.

Now, why does it work? John loves showing apartments. It's not that I don't like showing them; it's just that my talents are better used somewhere else: programming new buildings and pitching new business. In economics, this is known as core competencies: You might be really good at lots of things, but to be efficient you need to do the most of what you do best and the least of what other people do better than you. John's strength, like no one else's, is sitting with people who are thinking of selling and buying and connecting with them about their wealth, needs, deceased husbands, dueling families, fabulous dogs and kids, and penchant for purple. And I love sitting with developers and fantasizing about floor plans, finishes, and amenities of their soon-to-be-built skyscrapers.

Those of you who watch *Million Dollar Listing New York* are probably confused as to why John isn't on the show. John used to be on HGTV's *Selling New York*, but now he doesn't want to do reality TV.

Why Finding a Partner in Business Is a Genius Move:

1. One plus one is, in fact, not two. It's actually three or four or five, perhaps even ten if you find your perfect match. Two heads are better than one. Your strengths and abilities are greatly amplified when you combine talents and skill sets with another dynamo. Even the best can't do everything, and we all lack certain talents and abilities. If you can recognize that and acknowledge both your weaknesses and your

strengths and find someone to complement both, you will be unstoppable. Plus, when you add a partner to the mix, you add a new perspective, a whole new set of personality traits, experiences, and talents that can help you come up with ideas or solutions to problems you might not see yourself.

2. Not everyone is going to like you (and you're not going to like everyone), but if you have a partner, you've doubled your chances that everyone you meet will enjoy working with at least one of you.

3. When you want to give up, there's someone to stop you. There's someone who has your back. Plus, when you're a team, you don't want to let your partner down, so you will naturally work harder even if you start to feel disillusioned. John and I work together, travel together, laugh together, and truly enjoy each other's company. When we found Jordan, our team's flight control, it became what I like to think is a trifecta. We each take care of our respective points. That's real success. To become a number one team in New York City (or anywhere on anything), you not only have to be good at pitching or pricing or developing—and working incredibly hard—but beyond the amazing numbers, you also have to be there for one another at those pivotal moments—those crises in which you are both faced with difficult dilemmas and decisions—and you need to know that you will be there for one another even outside the workplace.

4. If you can have *fun* while working, you have won the lottery. Work is no longer "work," but just part of your amazing, rich, and yes, demanding, life.

In short, success is more fun (and, I believe, more easily attained!) when shared. In my opinion, the real reason people get married is that humans need partnership, someone to be our complement, to be by our side in good and bad times, and to be the missing piece of our puzzle. Marriage requires a "we're in this together for a lifetime" mentality, and that, more than any religious reason, is a highly motivational incentive to pair up. In psychobabble this is called "transformation of motivation." What this means to me is that I'm much more inspired to do well when I have someone with whom to dream a bigger dream.

That brings me to another point—when I talk about finding the right partner, I don't just mean a business partner. I mean that person who will help you on your way to achieving your dream of mastering The Sell. A business partner is certainly important, but your personal life has a tremendous impact on your professional life. If you don't have someone waiting for you at home at the end of a long day to tell you how much he or she loves you and how proud of you he or she is, someone to support your crazed rise to the top, you will have a much harder time succeeding.

Derek is a painter. I'm a businessman. Our careers are quite different, but our life together motivates both of us to be better people and to work toward our mutual goal of finding life's happiness. That he is six foot five and the most handsome man I have ever seen doesn't hurt. It's like we're running an exciting race together, and I will not let him fall, nor he me, as we gun it to the finish line.

The other day I actually read Derek the chapter from this book about my day to explain to him who I am (and what I'm going through) when he doesn't see me. It helped me communicate the differences in our day without trying to sound like a "my life is harder than yours" battle like the ones I used to have with John about how many hours we worked. Our days are different, but we're working together toward a unified goal: our happiness. You and your partner, or friend or family members, probably have opposite careers, too. Why don't each of you write down the details of your day—whom you see, the things you do, the struggles you face, and triumphs you make—and share them with each other? That exercise might be the best advice I could ever give you. (Yours free with purchase!)

Regardless of your career, I believe two heads are better than one, and I know many couples who support and encourage each other in their pursuits, whether with ideas or enthusiasm. The same must be true in friendships and in work relationships. We want to feel that the people around us are on the same team, running with us in the three-legged race. I certainly don't want to ever feel that someone is dragging me down, or worse, intentionally working against me.

FINDING GOOD PEOPLE

In case no one's ever told you this, you're a combination of the five people you spend the most time with. Translation: Your success depends on connecting with other people who are everything you want to be. Humans are wired to try and fit in, to belong. That means we imitate the people who make up our inner circles, because if we don't, we're worried we'll be rejected from the group. You know this. Think about it: When you're around someone who is ambitious, hardworking, and wildly successful, doesn't it make you want to work harder? Likewise, if you're around lazy people, you end up spending more time on the couch. Think through the people you have in your life. What are they like? Hopefully, you're hanging around other successes! Do they love what they do? Do they work hard? Are they kind? Are they smart? Do they make you laugh? Do you enjoy life more when they're around?

I don't know about you, but I want to be around people who are:

Genuine. I'm looking for people who are authentic, real, and true blue. They might be outrageous characters, but at least they say what they think and break it down to what is authentic.

Accepting. I like people who like me for me and who, if I sometimes act goofy or weird, will laugh and applaud, not judge and snarl.

Trustworthy. That's someone who keeps a secret and is always true to his or her word.

Forgiving. We all make mistakes. I like people who are compassionate and willing to graciously accept my apology and let go of wrongs.

Capable of laughing. This is perhaps the most important trait, because life, our world, and all that buzzzzzzzziness out there can be an absurd and truly hilarious ride, if you let it be and share it with people.

Prepare ye, high-kicker. Now that you know The Sell, you're going to have a meteoric rise over the next few years. Some harsh realizations will come along with that. There will be people who will try to hold you back. These naysayers will tell you all the reasons why you can't, why you shouldn't, why they wouldn't. . . . I love naysayers! When I hear from this choir, I *know* I'm succeeding. Listen to Gandhi: "First they ignore you. Then they laugh at you. Then they fight you. Then you win." Don't be afraid of the naysayers; just prove them wrong. That is one of the greatest feelings in life.

Over the years, I've had friends who have tried to hold me back. There were friends and colleagues who did not want to see me succeed. They told me no, No, NO, NOOOO! When I told them I would move to the United States, they told me it was stupid to leave everyone and everything I knew. When I decided to go into real estate without a salary, they said I was going to be poor forever. When I decided to start my own company, they said it would bankrupt me. When I signed with Bravo to do a television show, they said it was going to ruin my life and career. When I decided to get married on that same show, they said it would end badly. When I said I was going to write this book, they said I didn't have enough to say.

Now I can see the truth. They were dreaming of being brave or chasing success like that for themselves, and whether they realized it or not, they didn't want me to achieve something big before they did. They were jealous. It actually probably had nothing to do with me; it was just more convenient if everyone in their lives stayed at their level because that would mean they weren't failures—or at least weren't alone. They were holding down my little balloon like a big, heavy weight. So I cut the string.

The only role a naysayer should have in your life is as a tour guide. They provide you with a road map telling you exactly what you should avoid. My brother, Sigge, once told me, "Don't worry about the people talking behind your back. They are behind your back for a reason."

How about trying this little exercise? Draw a line down the center of a piece of paper. On the left side, write a plus sign and on the right side, write a minus sign. Beneath the plus sign, list the people who make your life better, who truly and I mean *truly* want you to do well regardless of what that might be. Beneath the minus sign, list the people who are dragging you down or holding you back from achieving your dreams. I know it isn't an easy task—life and friendship aren't always black or white—but try! Now you're going to spend as much time as possible with anyone on the positive side. Those on the negative side, you're going to avoid. What? That's not harsh! That's self-protection. (Give those negatives this book as a good-bye gift. Perhaps they'll find their better selves.)

Forget worrying about letting them down and forget the guilt of letting them go. Say good-bye to anyone who, rather than encouraging you, always finds a way to discourage you. At work, find the colleagues who cheer you on. Socially, be with friends who make you feel good. At home, don't engage with family members who belittle your dreams.

Now that we've dumped Debbie Downer, Negative Ned, and Pessimistic Polly, there are five people all successes *must* have in their lives:

1. **The family representative.** This is the person from your family who helps you think through and sort out any familial dramas. This relative (or it could be a best and oldest friend) knows you from your earliest days and will listen to you

during the latest of nights, and is always willing to give you honest, yet supportive, advice. For me, that's my brother, Sigge. My big brother provided guidance and a shoulder to lean on during my parents' divorce, encouraged me when I said I wanted to move to New York, and always has my back.

2. **A love.** This is the person you want to lie down next to at night and wake up with in the morning. This is your special someone who is willing to celebrate you at your best and deal with you at your worst. It's not about finding someone who is the answer to all your problems. It's about finding someone who will not let you deal with them alone. This is the person you've found that makes your life happy. That's my Derek.

3. **The aspiration.** We all need someone to look up to, a person we can learn from and want to become more like. This is a person much more successful than you, someone who has achieved greatness and is willing to share a little of that shine with you. For me, I am lucky to have three: Urban Edenström, one of Sweden's most successful real estate entrepreneurs, and a board member and investor in Eklund Stockholm New York; Dottie Herman, CEO of Douglas Elliman and one of the most successful female entrepreneurs in the United States; and Andy Cohen, executive at Bravo, TV host and personality, bestselling author, and God of everything pop culture.

4. **The equal.** This is a person on the same level as you, a confidant who happily exchanges ideas with you without judgment. This person questions you, laughs with you, and challenges

you to keep up or be left behind. In some circles, the equal is known as a BFF. My business partner, John, fills this role in my life.

5. **The student.** This person is below you on the ladder rungs of life and presents you with an opportunity to teach, inspire, and encourage. In addition to allowing you to give back, this ward will give you a reminder of where you've come from and energize you to go further. For me, it was writing this book for you.

Bonus. The dog! (Fritzy and Mousey wanted me to say that.)

BACK TO BUSINESS

Once you're in the game and the snowball of your success is accelerating down that steep hill, you have only one enemy: lack of time. To give the day more hours you need manpower. Manpower equals man-hours. Your day is limited, but with more bodies you have more brains to get more done, thereby capturing more money. But how do you know it's time for a new hire? Will hiring someone new help you focus on growing your business? Much like having children, there's no perfect time to start a family and bring on a new hire, but if you wait too long, you'll lose lots of business to your competition. Are you missing opportunities because you don't have time to pursue them? If the answer is yes, it's time to have "kids"! Assistants help push your ball down the hill, but also start their own smaller balls running parallel to your big one. Soon, you can create an avalanche of meatballs and no one will be able to keep up with your success.

Let me give you some advice on how to find and team up

with the best people and how to train and compensate them appropriately! Here's a start:

1. Realize that no one is quite like you, so you'll have to accept an almost perfect imitation.

2. Know that your best teammate might currently be your competition.

3. Recognize each member of your team's greatest gift, whether it's charm or book smarts.

4. Learn to allow people to make a few mistakes without having their heads handed to them.

5. Pay people enough to keep them happy and make it worthwhile for your business.

I hired almost everyone at my former brokerage when I was there, all of the salespeople in my company in Sweden and Norway, and of course all the people on my team in New York. So I've hired a lot of people, and here are two tricks I learned in finding excellent teammates:

Put out a finder's fee to your current people. Let's say I have ten people on my team but I need another person, a top producer, and my time is scarce. Finding that person, trusting that new person and her skills, and then on top of that coaching her and integrating her into the team is time consuming. So, instead, I open my Monday morning team meeting and tell the current people on my team that we need one more person. "I want you to find me that person." As an incentive, offer 10 percent of your share of the new hire's first year of commission to the person who finds the right newbie. What's genius about this is that you now have ten headhunters working for you, and you can almost be guaranteed that their recommendations will be great, because their bonus depends on how much business the new hire can produce. Furthermore, once hired, the current team member brings the new team member on pitches, getting them up to speed and taking them under their wing—automatic training.

Let someone else be your reference. My second secret to hiring the right people, and actually getting them to want to work with us when I do like them, is to do the exact opposite of what you might expect. Meeting me is important if they want to be on my team. It is the same with any boss or leader, but there is always distrust when I am selling myself to a potential new team member. It's important to meet me the first time so I can spread my gold dust. Then I have that person go into the conference room without me. Instead, my five top team members are there, ready to be truthful and friendly. The prospective new team member can sit down without me in the room and interview my current team members about how our organization works. They can ask anything: "What has been your experience?" "Is he nice to work with?" "What's he like on a bad day?" Trust me, nothing is as strong as having the potential new team member hear from your top people that you're great to work with. You will win the new person over.

The reason for this extra step is that the new team member assumes that I (the leader or boss) will paint a perfect vision of what it's like working with me. Any workplace is not just champagne and roses; it has its ups and downs. This is especially true at a younger company, a start-up perhaps, which can be messy and chaotic. It is also hard for me to sit there and talk about those negative sides. Let your prospective teammate hear it from the other people, your top people who are already successful. There's nothing more convincing to a prospect than hearing a current employee say, "Despite X, Y, or Z, we would never want to work anywhere else."

And the best part? This doesn't cost me anything.

HOW TO LEAD (AND BE A PART OF) A HAPPY WORKPLACE

I became a boss at an early age. At twenty-three, I was leading a tech start-up with forty-five employees, and I wasn't the real me. I was acting how I thought the boss should act: strict, boring, old. Because I was responsible for a bunch of people's output, I thought that was the only thing I could worry about. I assumed that if I was too fun or too friendly, my employees wouldn't take me seriously. I had my priorities askew. I hadn't yet realized a very essential concept for success in the twenty-first century: the importance of a happy workplace. When people are working happy, they are giving you their best, their all. Today I use the carrot, not the stick. I see myself as a team mascot.

I always say to my team members that we need to have fun and that we need to create something memorable in all that we do, which will attract more business. I see my team as a family, and a happy family is one based on love. A person who feels appreciated will always do more than what is expected. The business world is so demanding and can at times be incredibly stressful. So I treat my team well. We celebrate our success together and we treat people like people—with hopes, dreams, interests, and personal lives—not just cogs in a wheel.

I realize you might not be the boss yet. You might be a part of a team. That's great. Help inspire your boss and you're moving up. I love when my team brings me great ideas. Those who do are happily rewarded. Here are some of the things we have put in place that seem to work to keep people happy and help motivate them to succeed:

After-work drinks and parties. My team tries to go out for drinks or dinner every other week and have a big blowout party twice a year at Christmas and during the summer. These outings provide an opportunity to get out of the conservative office mentality and let our hair down a bit. In the United Kingdom, people head out to a pub every day after work. It's a chance to be social, to see the person behind the job title, and to find out about everyone's lives. Most important, it provides an opportunity to have some laughs together, which always lifts the lid off the pressure cooker.

Prizes, competitions, and trips. The unexpected surprise or luxury is a huge credit in building loyalty. I recently surprised my team by taking all of them to Mexico for my birthday, but your gift doesn't have to be that expensive. From flowers to dinner gift certificates, people just want to be noticed and feel appreciated. For my brokers in Sweden and Norway, we have quarterly competitions based on a point system. If you get in the press, you earn points. If you make a sell, you earn points. At the end of the quarter, the highest point getters receive prizes, from spa treatments to a luxury trip to New York. These treats create top producers and long-term job satisfaction and make people happy to work harder.

Office treats. No one wants to feel like a corporate drone. Offer them little luxuries that make them feel appreciated. Google really has this down, offering its employees a lot of perks aimed at keeping them happy and healthy, from delicious food to being able to bring their dogs to work! I try to provide my team with as many office sweeteners as possible. Dinners with tequila and dancing on the table in a Mexican joint (the alcohol and warm, red cheeks are an important part of the team building), everyone bringing their dogs, or their neighbor's dog, to a picnic in Central Park, and weekly team meetings where we remember to just thank one another for one another's existence.

Everyone should have a voice. People want to be heard. All members of your team need to feel as if they can speak their minds. With my teams in Europe, we have a weekly call in which everyone is represented, from the receptionist to the brokers.

A shared dream. As in a marriage, your entire team should know where the company is headed. Where are we going, and what do we want to accomplish? The management better know not just the financial goals, but also which ten key words represent the company's values. You want people to be emotionally invested. It's much more interesting and gratifying to work in a place where everyone is working toward a common goal. In my team, it's simple: Double our sales every year.

Bonuses and commissions. There should be a dangling carrot for people to want to do better, achieve more. You should have a structure in place that rewards and encourages success. Just as sales is about motivating clients to buy, so, too, does the boss have to motivate the team so each is inspired to go big.

MY PEOPLE PHILOSOPHY

Every human being is beautiful. And good at something. Whether we're talking about your coworker, your team member, or your spouse, everyone wants to feel appreciated. Your goal as a successful human being is to be interested and encouraging and to let each person close to you know that he or she is important. Call attention to triumphs; be forgiving of mistakes. Offer apologies as generously as you accept them. Praise wholeheartedly; criticize sparingly. Listen, learn, and love. Happiness never decreases by being shared. Spread joy to the people you encounter each day, and it will be returned in your life tenfold. You will win friends and influence people to want to work with you.

CHAPTER 11

F*CK! STOP THE PRESS

Learn How to Use the Media to Get Attention

The first time I showed Leonardo DiCaprio an apartment, the Swedish media—yes, the *paparazzien*—happened to be there. *How did they know?!* At first I was annoyed; then I felt intruded upon. But, in the end, I was happy—because I realized the attention was a gift, an opportunity. Fortunately, I had on my best suit. I waited on the curb for Leo's black SUV to roll up in front of the SoHo apartment building I was about to show him. I pretended the flock of long lenses pointed in my direction from across the street weren't there. What happened? He rolled up, got out of his car, and I immediately grabbed his hand to shake it. Click. Click. Click click click click click click click. It was front-page news in Sweden. What did millions of eyeballs see? "Fredrik Eklund: broker to the stars."

The truth is I never sold anything to Leonardo, but at that

point it didn't really matter. People connected my name with his and either assumed I did, or didn't care as long as I was seen with him.

I love getting attention, as should every great seller and anyone in the business world. Why? A third-party endorsement says you're tops at what you do. Yep, I know what some of you might be thinking. *Why would anyone want to do a story on me? What would anyone have to say about my life, my business? I'm not important enough.* Stop! That is not how a successful person thinks. You are important, destined for great things and big money, but you have to help bring it on.

As I told you in the social media chapter, I've sold many apartments for more than the asking price by creating a word-of-mouth frenzy among my followers. That is certainly the least expensive tool to sell yourself and what you have to offer, but there is also another inexpensive tool in your toolbox. It's called the press, and you can use it to help you get *your* name out there. It's yours for the taking; all you have to do is ask.

Publicity is worth its weight in gold. It creates visibility that translates into clients knowing who you are and what you have to offer. These mentions (and people talking about you) attract what everyone needs: people to know about the service you provide. Your name bragged about by a friend, in the paper, or in your thirty-second interview on TV, says to a potential customer, *This high-kicker is the expert.* Getting something like *The New York Times* to say you're the expert at doing what you do is a better endorsement than you could ever buy. In fact, a Harvard study showed that PR is up to twenty times more efficient than good old advertising. That means ten dollars spent on a regular ad compared to the same money spent on public relations can get you $200 more of a return on your investment. You could put a PR wiz on retainer or work out an arrangement to pay one on a per-placement basis. But you must do something every day to get yourself noticed. It is the key to big business. A rave by someone about your goods or services on Yelp can be worth thousands of dollars. A profile in a prominent newspaper can directly lead to *millions* of dollars in increased sales. (Trust me, I know.)

THE BILLION-DOLLAR BROKER

I gulped as I stood in a Miami Starbucks and stared at the front page of *The New York Times* Sunday Styles section. There, below an article on Oprah, was the eye-popping headline about me. I was on the cover!

How that happened is really the story of how I became a number one success story and really the story of how you have this book in your hand.

In 2006, the year I aimed to do $1 billion in sales, I decided that instead of spending money on advertising, I'd spend $10,000 to hire a video crew and create a video pilot called *Billion Dollar Broker.* Clever, right? Remember my first listing on Twentieth Street? After my record-breaking deal there, that building continued to feed me clients, and a producer was one of them. He was around my age, right out of college, and was forming his own little production company, and we became friends.

Here was my train of thought: The sales business is a numbers game. You have to get noticed, and every appointment is like an actor going to an audition. I needed to flip that on its head and have people lining up to use my services. I knew from experience that if I sent out a thousand mailers, I might (if lucky) land one new client out of the effort. I realized there's not enough paper in the rainforest to get a hundred new clients out of a mailing. If I wanted to, indeed, become the number one broker in New York City, I couldn't rely on a piece of paper touting my credentials that most likely was going from mailbox to trash can. My goal was big, so I had to think big to get there. I needed to have hours and hours with each potential buyer and seller, to have my name seared into their heads, but I only had the same twenty-four hours in my day as all my competitors. The only way that seemed possible was if I somehow got myself in their homes . . . perhaps on their televisions.

At the time, I noticed that there were two shifts in culture. Reality TV was becoming the must-see TV and the real estate business was changing dramatically. The old-guard real estate agents put the property ahead of themselves, or they were hiding behind their properties, depending on how you looked at it. The property was the star and they were merely the way in. Meanwhile, the new stars were making *themselves* the stars, and the really vibrant ones with great PR skills were becoming brands. These individuals would be so fabulous—and talented, of course—that people wanted to work specifically with them, and the properties would follow suit.

People were calling me because they'd heard I was fun and the best, but I knew that if I wanted to be the biggest brand in New York City I needed to do something spectacular. Calling, faxing, knocking on people's doors was just farting in the wind. Those days were over. The attention getters were the ones getting all the business and hitting all the sales records. I asked myself how I could get the most attention for my business. And the answer was reality TV. Not just any kind of reality TV show, which could be hurtful for business. I needed a show that showcased my record-breaking deals, my obsession with real estate, my tenacity, my anything-is-possible approach with clients, and my superior deal-making skills.

Shooting the pilot was hard for me. It was my first, and to this day last, pilot. We did it all on our own as a promo video to get the attention of the decision makers at Bravo. We had no producers or experts advise us on what to do or say. I wasn't a big consumer of TV, but I knew the basic arc of good storytelling. We needed a journey. People like to hate you in the beginning and love you by the end. So we came up with some ideas we thought Bravo would like. After all, Bravo was—and is—the number one network in the world for this kind of television. It also has a more affluent viewership than other reality TV networks, with a wealthy bicoastal audience, the same people I wanted to reach. Furthermore, after doing some research, I learned that some of their more successful franchises were sold to more than 150 countries around the globe.

I flew in a helicopter over New York because reality TV loves glamour. I fought with my team because reality TV likes some conflict. I went to a gay club looking for love because reality TV needs love. And I showed property because that's what a billion-dollar broker does. We showed I was really successful in real estate and that I was a bit crazy and really fun. The hook was simple: Can this guy sell $1 billion in real estate in one year? I still have that DVD in my drawer at home, and I watch it every now and then to get a good laugh.

My brother had an agent contact in Los Angeles who got a meeting with Bravo during their pitch season, in which the network meets with all these production companies about the ideas they have to offer. I was excited. Nervous, but excited. A few days before the appointment, the agent decided it was best if I wasn't in the meeting, saying the executives could talk more freely about me if I wasn't there. I thought that was the dumbest thing I'd ever heard, but acquiesced. After all, I knew nothing about high-stakes TV pitching. I flew my brother in from Sweden and sent him as my representative.

They watched the tape and loved it. Then Andy Cohen asked the billion-dollar question: "So where is he? Bring Fredrik in! Is he outside waiting?" The agent stumbled a bit on his answer, "Well . . . We thought it was better if he wasn't here." The meeting ended with Bravo saying with certainty, "We'll call Fredrik if we decide to do a New York real estate show. We love that guy."

It was a fiasco and a huge disappointment.

Meanwhile, back at the brokerage I was working for at the time, the owners watched my pilot, laughed hysterically, and promptly told me I was smart but crazy. "What a fun idea," they said. A few weeks later, I walked into the office and there was a meeting going on in the boardroom. Every top agent was in there, except me. I asked the receptionist what was going on and she said, "There's a meeting with HGTV about a new show they want to do with us called *Selling New York*."

My heart sank. I called a meeting with management. "What's up?" I asked. "Why wasn't I included in that meeting? You know I'm interested in doing a real estate show."

He said, "HGTV didn't pick you." I was crushed, and even more crushed when they started filming and I had to go to work and hide from the cameras. I felt like it was an active *un*picking, and I took it personally.

I kept contact with Bravo, who was moving toward a New York real estate show but at a snail's pace.

I went to Greece to clear my head, and, the day before I met Derek, I got the contract to star in *Million Dollar Listing New York*. I had to run and borrow paper from other hotels in order to feed it into my hotel's fax machine. On the very same day, *The New York Times* called and said they wanted to do a cover story on me for the Styles section.

Within those twenty-four hours, a lot of things happened: I met the man who would become my husband, I secured a front-page profile in *The New York Times*, and I signed a contract to star in a Bravo show. And because of all of it, I became the number one broker in New York City.

How is this relevant to you? You don't have to have a Bravo show, but you *do* have to tell your story to someone. You have to get the message of *you* out into the world.

If you don't have a big budget, there are plenty of ways to bring attention to yourself without breaking the bank. Let me give you some ideas.

How to Get People to Know Your Name

1. **Be friendly.** Start with the people you know already. Use the contacts in your smartphone to compile a list of all the fabulous people you know. Whether you're selling pet clothes or cupcakes, that list is your initial client base. This is whom you'll tell about your product, service, and happenings. You want this group to be your fan base, so you'll want to keep them informed as to what you're doing by sending them clever announcements, throwing a fun party, or hosting a few rounds of drinks at a local trendy bar. A small investment of time and money in your immediate social circle can lead to big contacts. Early in my

career, I regularly hosted parties, which always landed me clients, referrals, and cash in my pocket. Why? Those people are your word-of-mouthers, your back-pocket PR reps. They will talk you up to their contacts (and social media).

2. **Help a reporter out.** Sign up at HelpAReporter.com to have direct access to journalists, editors, and producers who need sources for their stories. HARO gets you on the radio, TV, and in print. Here's how it works: Three times a day, you receive an e-mail with queries from media outlets. If your field of knowledge matches their needs, you simply e-mail the contact and pitch yourself. Then, after the interview, you sit back and get ready for your star turn as the "expert."

3. **Send out a press release.** If you haven't already started building an e-mail list of all your contacts, start one today. The easiest way to begin your e-mail list is to mine the e-mail addresses in your e-correspondence and merge that with the contacts from your address book. In the old days, press releases were written targeting the media. Today they are often used to communicate directly with the consumer, your audience, your buyer. A great press release starts with an attention-getting headline, such as "The Market's Meteoric Rise," and gets right to the point in the first paragraph with hard facts and numbers and the all-important attribution: "according to Fredrik Eklund, leader of New York City's number one real estate team."

4. **Write a newsletter.** Every company and everyone in business should have a newsletter or blog to communicate with their audience and promote their goods, services, and ideas. My

accountant sends out a newsletter each month highlighting changes in the law and things I can do to save money on taxes. I look forward to it, and I know it's gotten her referrals.

5. **Respond to breaking news.** It's not just CNN that responds to breaking news these days. You can, too. Get in on a trend story. My industry is real estate, so if there is a breaking story in my marketplace, I quickly comment on it through social media and e-mail blasts and by calling my media contacts. Market just jumped 20 percent? I release a "Why You Must Buy Now" statement to my followers and to producers and reporters in my database. A developer just sold a megamultimillion-dollar apartment? I send out information on how my megamultimillion-dollar apartment is a shinier trophy and a better investment. This works for any industry.

6. **Contact a reporter.** Attached to any article written anywhere these days is a direct link to the journalist. When you click on his or her name, usually you get the e-mail address. It's that simple. Why are people so skittish about e-mailing a journalist for *The New York Times*, *The Wall Street Journal*, or your hometown paper? Well, I'm not. I have the top reporters on my speed dial. I call and e-mail them on a weekly basis. I flood them with stories and always include myself in them. If you find a story you like, call or write the reporter and rave about how you loved the story he did on so-and-so, and say at the end, "I might have a story for you. . . . But I can't really talk about it yet." Journalists *love* getting a scoop, so they love being let in on information they're not supposed to hear. Then wait a few days and pitch him your idea. You're

doing him a favor. Reporters need ideas, and whatever your business, there's a story on you. "As quoted in *The New York Times*" is a line you can spin for gold. I now spin it a little further: "As featured on six front-page stories in *The New York Times!*" High-kick!

7. **Make your own news.** Figure out how you can billboard your product or your services. It may literally be a clever billboard, a short video on YouTube, or a contest you create to find a hidden treasure, but cleverness counts. You can also offer to be a guest on local radio shows or to do an editorial in the local newspaper.

If you don't get noticed, you can't make The Sell. Your job is to tell us—your audience and your potential customers—what you've got, what you can do for us, and how we can get it. You don't have to get your own TV show or sit in the middle of Fifth

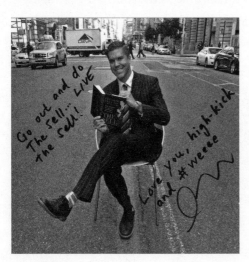

Stop traffic! In order to grab some attention for *The Sell*, I actually took an office chair and sat in the middle of Fifth Avenue signing books. Upside: I posted it on social media, and we sold all the signed copies. Downside: I almost got hit by a bus.

Avenue to get attention, but if you do (and you think it's fun), I say go for it.

Now, before you do anything else, set a Google Alert for your name. If you implement the ideas in this chapter, you're going to get noticed, and Google will happily remind you that your bold-faced efforts are working.

CHAPTER 12

WHAT TO EXPECT WHEN YOU'RE EXPANDING

Get Bigger, Better, and More Efficient

Remember that poster I told you about that was on the wall in my parents' bedroom when I was growing up? The one of the duck that was swimming beautifully across placid water, but beneath the surface he was paddling like crazy? That's what life was (and still is) often like for me, and I'm pretty sure for you, too. Life is busy. It's how we manage it that makes the difference between chaos and achievement.

As I mentioned, my first development project was a building called the Onyx Chelsea on Twenty-Eighth Street and Eighth Avenue in New York. I won that business my third year in real estate. I was so excited—and scared. What did I know about programming an entire twelve-story building with just the right mix of units at the right sizes? What did I know about designing kitchens and bathrooms, maximizing light and air, placing walk-in closets, or programming amenities like gyms, roof decks, and lobbies? I didn't know the first thing about creating a brand for the building; identifying the ideal buyer long before the concrete is poured; commissioning someone to build a website; seting up an off-site sales office; designing a marketing brochure; and pricing the building to sell the sucker out—at numbers that would not only make the developer happy, but also build respect in the industry and garner press. It was daunting, and very exciting.

I had to go into those first new-development meetings calm and not let anyone see how inexperienced I was. I was trying to get big but still felt small. My face was calm as I diligently took notes, but out of view of those hotshots my little duck feet were under the table paddling like crazy.

Here's what I've realized about those kinds of moments when we're taking a leap forward: If you're wholeheartedly and enthusiastically invested in any project and delivering good ideas, no one cares what you have or haven't done before. They want to know what you can do for them, *right now*. Everyone loves enthusiasm, hunger, drive, and sharing a vision of success, much more so than experience, pessimism, and mind-numbing dullness.

So, as you expand in life and business, here's my advice:

Be passionate. Enthusiasm is infectious. The people I want to be around are excited about the day and the days that lie ahead. If you're the one who brings the fire, you're the one who everyone wants to work with, newbie or not.

Take chances. I've taken some crazy chances in my career—quitting Stockholm School of Economics, moving to New York without knowing a soul, taping the *Billion Dollar Broker* pilot, filming *Million Dollar Listing New York*, leaving firms for other firms. Playing it safe doesn't get you anywhere. It hardly gets you out of bed in the morning.

Act now. There's no time like this very moment to take action on a good idea. Actually the best time was yesterday, so the only thing you've got is today. Many people don't trust their gut, and spend time sending their good ideas out to committee, hoping for approval from others. If you wait, it dies. Jump on opportunity. As they say, it doesn't knock twice.

Know that procrastination is a deal killer. Putting things off is the equivalent of erecting a giant billboard that reads, "I'm not really excited about this." That is a confidence killer. Get out of bed in the morning with a plan. Fill your plate. The busier you are, the more you'll get done. Make sure your calendar is always filled, in one way or another. Time off? Hit the gym. Weekend calm? Be actively resting, writing, or planning, or just soak up some sun on a beach somewhere. Play hard, work hard, but just do it.

Realize that balance is for zombies. Forget finding the happy middle. That's where the dullness lives. Instead, fully invest in two extremes: Work hard when you're working and play hard when you're playing. In both instances, be involved, invested, and into it, and people will want to join you.

525,600 Minutes

There's a song in the musical *Rent* called "Seasons of Love." It asks how you measure a year in the life. What are you going to do with those 525,600 minutes? Forget money or your grandmother's heirloom diamond ring; time is your most valuable possession. Many people waste it or let others steal it from them. Don't. Time management is everything. To flourish, you must have a lot of balls in the air at any given moment, and to accomplish that, you must put systems in place that map out how you'll use your time in a day. You can't control traffic, a snowstorm, a bomb threat, or other people's time, but you can manage your scheduling such that when you run up against those things, your day doesn't crumble.

To Do

Do you have a to-do list? You should. At the end of the day, I like to review my accomplishments but set my new goals for tomorrow to be bigger and better. As Ingvar Kamprad, the founder of IKEA, said, "The most dangerous poison is the feeling of achievement. The antidote is to every evening think what can be done better tomorrow." Success, to me, comes by being merciless about what matters. As we've discussed, my top priorities are sleep, eating well, exercise, and nurturing my intimate relationships. If those currently don't have priority, I want to change that. I need to put them back at the top of my to-do list. Without paying attention to those first, the rest doesn't matter. Once those are set, I follow with my toughest task first. Then, once that hurdle is jumped, I carry on with the other action items of my next day. There's nothing like the satisfaction of checking something off as "done." It's addictive and makes me want to accomplish more.

The Phone

I'll be the first to say it: I hate the phone. Though I use it all day, way too much, I consider it a necessary evil. But chitchat for the sake of chitchat is an aggravation. Let's call that a time waster. Skype and FaceTime are even worse. Not only do you have to be attached to a device; you also have to have clothes on and your hair combed and sit in good lighting. It makes me really uncomfortable. The phone can suck the life out of me, especially when I'm coming home to Derek and it just keeps ringing. Which is why I don't call my mother three times a week or Derek three times a day. I take my mother on trips where we can have great fun and good talks. I write Derek love texts, knowing his time is limited, too, and he just wants to know I'm thinking of him.

Limit phone calls to things that have to be talked out or when you're trapped in a car, but the best is always the real face-to-face, regardless of all this new technology.

E-mail

There are many different theories on how to deal with e-mail. As I've told you, during my workday, I try to deal with mine in real time for two reasons: First, I love not having anything piling up. Second, it's very impressive for the person asking something of you to hear back from you right away. It says that you're on your game.

If you're answering in real time, you'll find that you put out fires before they start and that you eliminate the need for storytelling and long explications. I'd say nine out of ten of my e-mails can be answered in a line or two. Let me give you a few examples of my answers to e-mails from my day today:

Q: Is this penthouse available to be seen?
A: Yes. Jordan will be in touch to set up. [cc'd my assistant in]

Q: When can you talk about the last chapter of the book?
A: Tonight at 7.

Q: Where do you want to eat tonight?
A: Someplace healthy. You pick.

Q: My client wants to reduce her offer.
A: Call me.

Now, there's a lot of discussion as to when to stop answering e-mails in your day. Is it when you leave work? Is it when you get home? Is it a few minutes before you go to bed? I generally stop answering when I'm home, settled in, and Derek is ready to have our time together.

I look forward to the day that Siri reads e-mails for me and can interpret if there's an issue I need to address. Unfortunately, until then, I have to handle it myself, so I've figured out what works for me.

Friends and Family

Let me be blunt: Some people have nothing in common with you except that you went to the same high school. People change and, therefore, so do relationships. What worked when you were seven or seventeen or twenty-seven probably doesn't work for you at thirty-seven. Plus, you only have a limited amount of time to spend with people. As you meet new friends, you have to cut some of the old ones. You do not have to feel obligated to take every person up on his or her social invitation. I don't hang out just to hang out. I evaluate who makes me happy and cares for me now, today, and not who did yesterday. Find amazing people that you trust and admire, and work with people you like; then love them, too, and make an effort for quality time with only a handful of nearest and dearest. I take great trips with my parents and my friends, and we make the time to really enjoy one another.

Once, when I was fretting about my friendships, a therapist told me, "Fredrik, you are looking for the wrong thing. What you need is four to five strong connection points in your life, not five hundred, five thousand, or five million." His words stayed with me. I stopped thinking that the more acquaintances I had, the happier I would be and no longer felt the need to keep in touch with every single person I've ever met. I now concentrate on real, strong love and trust with a handful of intimate friends.

Getting There

My dad, a leading economist in Europe, taught me an important term when I was a little boy: *alternative cost*. The alternative cost of something is the value of what you would have made doing something else. That brings me to my car and driver.

Getting a driver was a huge fight between John and me. As I've told you, John really likes to hold on to his money, so it took a lot of convincing. Not having a driver cost me millions of dollars, I told him. Before I got my car and driver, I spent a lot of time trying to find an electricity source to plug my phone in. If it dies, my day dies. My car is my mobile office, my charging station; it gives me comfort from wear and tear and pollution, saves a small fortune in dry cleaning, saves a big fortune in taxis, and is a rolling billboard of cachet, which has brought in millions of dollars in business. Plus, it saves me a ton of moneymaking time by moving me around all day, every day, every year, come rain, snow, sleet, or hail. Most of all, a car is a business expense! I can write it off my taxes.

Now we have two cars and two drivers. It sets us apart. Our business has quadrupled with our cars. John has taken this car thing to a whole other level. His car is washed almost daily, his dog Zoey Mama gets transported in the car to Boston for the summer, and he has a special caramel scent imported from Germany for the interior (which gives me light nausea). You should see John's routine when he pulls up to a building in his Mercedes where people are waiting for him to show them an apartment. He lowers his tinted window and points to the gold phone he has hooked up to his iPhone, pushed against his ear and mouth: "One second. Finishing up." Then he rolls up the tinted window. It always causes a bit of a scene, but he's communicated, *I've arrived. I'm in control.* (Or to some people it says, *I'm insane,* and that's okay, too, because he will be remembered and he is not boring.) When we leave a meeting and each walk out to the drivers who open the doors on his Mercedes and my Land Rover side by side . . . You can call it pretentious, but it makes The Sell!

A top seller like me saying he can't afford a private car is like a CEO saying he can't afford an assistant, or a chef who can't afford a sous chef. The point here is time efficiency, or as my dad says, "alternative cost." The cost of the car is far outweighed by what I can do in the time it saves me.

Now, you might be saying, "I can't afford a driver and a car." Then what can you do today to take some of the pressure off your life? You'll make more money if you can do more work, more efficiently. Test it out by taking a car and driver (or even a taxi) one day a week and scheduling all your important appointments on that day. You'll see the success it manifests. I want Instagram proof!

Delegation

The speed of the team is the speed of the lead horse, but good delegation can translate to a 20 percent increase in profitability. Any task done almost as well as you could do it is a job done well enough. In sales, for example, especially in the beginning, 40 percent of your time is spent selling and 60 percent of your time is office paperwork. The goal of a salesperson is to get from 40 percent of his time being spent selling to 100 percent of his time. The office is not where I should put my time. Think about why. If I'm making $400,000 out meeting people while utilizing 40 percent of my time, hiring someone to cover 60 percent of the back-office minutiae can increase my earnings to $1 million. That's why I found Jordan. He loves the office paper pushing—for now—and is much more adept than I am at making the office run like a well-oiled machine.

The same can be said for things at home. Think "alternative cost" there, too. How much could you accomplish with the time you're now spending on the mundane tasks like housecleaning or dog walking? Hiring someone to do those chores might help you double your income. Further, I paid someone to organize my closet, my kitchen cabinets, and my home office to make them work more efficiently. You're headed for big success; prepare your home environment for the busy life that is about to come.

In planning vacations, I choose where to go depending on the time it takes to get there. I map it from my apartment until the time I can be on the beach with a cold Corona in my hand. I mean, really. If any of you readers work for Expedia or Travelocity, the first one of you that develops a button that can map out the exact time it takes to get from home base to beach chair will see your stock skyrocket! I'm not interested in whether the flight is two or four hours if the arrival airport is two hours away from the hotel, the check-in takes forty-five minutes, my room isn't even cleaned, and there is a thirty-minute walk to the beach. I want to know exactly how long it takes me to get from here to there. It's all about efficiency, because time is money.

TIME IS FREE, BUT PRICELESS

Time is your scarcest resource. Use it wisely.

Do you have any of those "Hey, do you have a minute?" people in your life? I call them time thieves. Did you know it takes ten minutes or more to recover lost concentration? Don't allow someone to steal your time. Simply say, "I'm in the middle of something. Make a note of what you need to talk about and let's discuss later." I'll also answer a phone call and say, "I see that it's you and want to say hi. So, hi! Now, gotta go. Let's catch up later." Keeps it sweet, to the point, and results in no dead time.

I like to think of it this way: If I can squeeze 20 percent more time out of my day being efficient, the implications for success are enormous. If you gross $1 million a year, that's $200,000 more! If you gross $10 million a year, that's $2 million more! But it's also not just about money. Any minute you spend on one thing cannot be spent on something else. You'll never get it back. Why spend your time doing things that you hate or that don't benefit your future? Once you master the art of reminding yourself of this inarguable fact, you will free yourself to have a happier, more productive life.

CHAPTER 13

FAIL UP!

Handle the Ups and Downs of Life (and Business)

I'm going to teach you a word: *pronoia*. It's the opposite of *paranoia*. Paranoia is when you think the world is against you in some shape or form. Pronoia is the happy opposite: having the sense that there is a conspiracy that exists to *help* you. I just decided that's how it is, because I said so. I run my life on pronoia, and I want you to start, too. Right now. Did you know there's actually a great conspiracy that exists to help you? It's called the universe. Step a little closer. Let me whisper it in your ear. *I'm telling you that the world is set up to secretly benefit you!*

Think about that one for a moment.

When something really bad happens, you can choose to think of yourself as a victim and whine, "Oh, poor me! Why is this happening to me?" Or you can choose to see it as exactly the opposite. It's the best kind of 'noia there is.

Tell yourself that the reason your flight is delayed is that the universe told the airline you needed a few minutes to finally call your grandmother or deal with your accountant's questions or write that childhood friend you haven't spoken to in two years. You have been feeling guilty for not getting those things done, and now you can get them off your back. The delay is a gift for you. You can now take care of the little things you've not been able to give priority.

Tell yourself that the person in front of you in the express lane, who is suddenly backing up the line with her credit card that won't work, is giving you a minute to flip through a tabloid and get a laugh at some of the preposterous stories and pictures. See how pronoia can make that frustrating moment a gift?

Tell yourself that your dog pooped on your expensive rug because it was divine intervention. You were becoming so materialistic, and this reminds you that possessions aren't the most important things in your life. Besides, he did you a favor. That rug was full of dust mites and had to get out of your house!

Failures and frustrations are parts of life. Problems are as important to your life as food, water, and love. Why? Because problems give you the opportunity to find answers, and finding answers is inspiring, liberating, and uplifting. You feel accomplished when you're finding solutions, ways over and through life's obstacles.

But the best part of pronoia? It's highly contagious! You've just caught it from me. So, guess what? Now the world *does* revolve around you!

THE SEVEN DEADLY SUCCESS STOPPERS

There's a saying in Sweden, "En lugnt hav har aldrig skapat en skicklig sjöman." Translated it means "A smooth sea never made a skilled sailor." Any journey to your dream destination will be filled with waves, squalls, wind, and maybe the occasional shark.

Here's what I see as the obstacles standing in our way to success: self-doubt, jealousy, not succeeding as fast as you'd like, disappointment in others, loving someone who doesn't love you back, money issues, and sickness. How well you deal with these annoyances is an indicator of both how fast you get to the top and how much you enjoy the climb.

Let's face it: The hard work it takes to succeed in any career worth having can make you go crazy. In my business, in addition to my own emotional life, I have to deal with greedy sellers, cheap buyers, deal-breaking attorneys, ridiculously conservative bank appraisals, unethical cobrokers, and the damn economy. It sometimes seems everything is out to get me, that everywhere I turn there's a fire to be put out. Sound scary? It is. And that's where people often fail. Rather than facing the fire and putting it out, they run from it and let it burn down the house.

It does get better with experience, but the uncertainty of business (or life, for that matter) does not change: It's an erratic ride. You will fall to the ground. I'll say it again: You *will*, and furthermore, you *should*. We all will and should. The trick is how fast you get up, dust off, hop back on the saddle, and start again. And again. And again. Sometimes the fall hurts, sometimes the embarrassment of failure is humiliating, and sometimes the fiasco can even cost you money. But you know what? Dealing with flops gets easier with experience.

Life's roller-coaster ride can be extremely scary for all of us. The highs are high and the lows are low. The high when you succeed is incredible, and you feel like the master of the universe. Let me give you an example. Last week, I had a huge contract signed by a buyer—*yay!* I told everyone I talked to about it and got big applause in my office. The next day I got a text message from my seller with his change of plans. He decided to stay in New York and take the property off the market. Boom! Like that, a black cloud over a sunny day. I could have easily fallen into a frustrated sadness, but I now realize that gets me nowhere. Dwelling in that failure leads to more failure. Instead, I reminded myself that there will be other deals. I move along and start climbing again.

Now, let's take on the Seven Deadly Success Stoppers.

Self-Doubt

I like a little self-doubt, the nagging voice that says I can't do better or achieve more. That's normal and healthy, but being your own worst critic is taking it too far. There's enough noise trying to kill our dreams and no reason to join that chorus, to be overly self-critical, to compare ourselves to others and think we'll never measure up. *You're old. You're dumb. You're never going to be successful.* You can't let self-doubt sabotage your path to achievement.

Are you afraid to take on a project or act on one of your ideas because you're afraid to fail, worried you'll look bad? That's self-doubt you need to shake, because it's paralyzing. Was I worried about moving to New York from Sweden with no contacts and no idea of what career path I might take? Of course! That's why I *had* to do it! If I hadn't, I'd have forever been mired in what could have been. When my nasty self-doubt voice speaks up, it's almost like a map to where I have to go, to what I have to do. I became excited for creating my job. I made the mountain and then set out to climb it.

Figure out if there are specific triggers that bring on the cloud of self-doubt. If, for example, you're worried about speaking in front of other people, get some coaching to help you deal with that performance anxiety. If you always need to ask other people for approval before making a decision, try to go it alone a few times and see how that works. If you're starting to think your clothes are feeling tight or your face is looking saggy, hire a trainer or find yourself a dermatologist. There's no reason to live with things that you know set off a bout of self-criticism and suffering.

I often try to visualize the self-doubt as a wall. Then I imagine myself as the Flash superhero and walk through that wall by vibrating my molecules. Just walk through that damn wall! Or climb over it if you can't get your molecules to vibrate.

We each have a choice. Either we can believe in ourselves or we can allow ourselves to wallow in self-pity. Imperfection is part of the human experience. Relish your imperfections. Let doubt be a background noise, not your theme song. Separate your consciousness from ego and realize the special person you are. If all else fails, get outside. I put on my favorite music and walk toward the sun.

Jealousy

As my career soared, my income quadrupled, my fame increased, and I fell in love, the jealousy others had toward me also increased. I think jealousy is the greatest human flaw. We all have it to some extent, but some people are consumed by it. It eats them; they see you flying like a bird while they feel heavy like a stone. This person is dark and dangerous, because he or she is like your antimatter. You are bright, happy, aggressively pursuing your goals and dreams, while the jealous person is usually unhappy, frustrated, and angered that you're achieving your goals and dreams.

The difference between the jealous person and the previously discussed naysayer is that the jealous person doesn't say no to your face, but instead to everyone else's—about you. He or she doesn't stop there; the jealous person will try to create a revolt against you, spread the "truth" about you. Sadly, in some deranged way he or she probably actually believes it. His or her goal is to expose the lies of your success to the world. Only then can he or she get some rest.

Jealous people are all over. We all have a small jealous person somewhere within. After all, we are all human. But by acknowledging we are human, and therefore flawed, we can better ourselves. By identifying that little jealous spot within us, we can contain it and disconnect from it.

Try this exercise: A friend of yours, somebody you actually like a lot, wins $10 million in the lottery. You see the post on Facebook or read about it in the newspaper. The ego will instantly kick-start and react: Why wasn't that me? But you have a choice; you always have a choice. Realize that's the little jealous spot within you talking, not the whole you. Remind yourself that you *want* good for the world and especially for the people around you. You also know all the good your friend is going to get to do with that money. If it helps, think about it a little selfishly—if you are supportive of others' success, they will want you to be a part of their lives. And, remember, you want to surround yourself with successful people. If you help them, they might help you. Jealousy won't get you anywhere but alone. Letting go of it frees you to be the best person you can be.

Now that we accept the flicker of jealousy left inside, let's go back to the real jealous person out there trying to destroy our success.

Let me tell you a little fairy tale. Once upon a time in a village far, far away called Manhattan, there was a Swedish prince in a castle. And there was another prince, who was number one. He was often in the press, the people loved him, and he made millions of dollars. He seemed to have it all. Then the Swedish prince came along and got a TV show that everyone watched and had a thumbs-up or thumbs-down opinion about, but it helped the Swedish prince take the number one spot. In short, one prince stole the other prince's thunder.

The dethroned prince started talking badly about the newly crowned prince and told everyone he could that the new prince was a phony. The Swedish prince was hurt. Not his business, but him on the inside. He was saddened. He kept it inside and started feeling sick. He never wanted to upset anyone or do any harm.

Rather than work harder, the envious prince forgot his own incredible talent and experience, and instead made his mission to take down the Swedish prince. Then the Swedish prince's mother gave him a piece of advice: "Framgång är den bästa hämnden." ("Success is the best revenge.")

Okay, in case you haven't figured it out, the Swedish prince is me. The day after I talked to my mother, the universe gave me a sign. I was sitting at lunch, still fretting with friends over my hurt, when an e-mail came in from the executive producer of *Million Dollar Listing* reading: "OMG! OMG! OMG!" Everyone around the table asked me what was happening, but the e-mail ended there. Ryan and Luis were addressed in the e-mail, too, plus all the other producers of our show, so it was obviously show related. I replied, "What am I missing?" Then I got a tweet from Andy Cohen announcing that *Million Dollar Listing New York* had been nominated for an Emmy! In capital letters it read, "WAY TO GOOOOOOOOOOOOOOO."

I was nominated for an Emmy! The nominated episode was the one in which I married Derek. I got tears in my eyes: *This is your sign!* And I decided then and there to never look back, to never let the jealous people be a black cloud on my sunny day.

I write this for you, too. You might have somebody in your life hoping you fail. If you don't, you probably will in your future. The more successful you become, the more likely it is. Don't strike back. Take the higher road. Keep doing your own thing. People will hate, and that's okay. They're not really hating you; they are projecting their own issues on the success that is you. Let yourself soar above.

I now know to wish jealous people the best. I also realize the real lesson, which is to stay humble and kind. Why? I'll have my time at the top, but I will not be number one forever. Someone else will one day take my place. Maybe it will be you! Life is about change, about being liquid. Don't fall prey to anyone else's jealousy. Moral of this fairy tale: Success is the best revenge.

Not Succeeding as Fast as You'd Like

This is probably the deadly success stopper with which I have had the most difficulty. It comes with the territory. Many successful people are impatient. I'm impatient with a capital *I*. When things aren't happening fast enough, it feels to me like a failure. The truth is I'm probably successful because I'm impatient. Impatience pushes me forward. I want things to happen quicker than most. I don't like to wait. I want everything to happen overnight.

The dark side of my own impatience is that I become annoyed when the next thing isn't coming fast enough. I'm not pretty when I'm annoyed. Most people aren't. Fortunately, with age and experience, I've finally (almost) realized that success only comes with patience. It's about planting a bunch of seeds and waiting. Like trees, successes take a while to grow. You can't force a tree to suddenly get tall. As much as you scream for it to grow faster, it won't. It can't. You can give it encouragement, make way for more sunlight, water it, fertilize it, prune its branches, but it's still growing in its own time.

With my success, the process of getting there—the crazy wild ride—has been the true thrill. I'm realizing it's not the goal but the process of getting there that is the real joy. The steps, the setbacks, the momentary failures are part of the adventure. The satisfaction really isn't the arrival; it's the journey. That's the philosophical part.

After I invested $10,000 to film my pilot, *Billion Dollar Broker*, it took four years to land *Million Dollar Listing New York*. Four years! Do you know how many sacrifices I made in that time? Can you see how jealous I was to watch other people at my firm star in *Selling New York*? I waited. I worked. I pushed the sadness to the back of my mind. Instead of asking myself, *Why me?* I kept thinking, *Why not me? It's going to happen.*

Every successful person will tell you that he or she made huge sacrifices along the way. Just take the first step, then the next, then the one after that. Remember, I started with my first deal. But before that I got in the cab at JFK Airport, and before that, I got on that plane in Sweden, and before that I quit the Stockholm School of Economics. . . .

Disappointment in Others

The problem with a lot of relationships is our own high expectations. I'll give you this, if you give me this back. My love and commitment to you is contingent on you giving me something back. If you go around expecting things from others, you're setting yourself up for failure. Here's my advice: Just give the people you care about love without expecting anything back. I know, easy to say and hard to do. But trust me, it's a good way to live life. Why? It gets rid of all disappointment.

Now, let's apply that to business. If you work with people you admire and love, you don't expect anything. I truly love John Gomes. If one day he decides he's leaving New York for Paris and is going to be a fashion designer, I'd congratulate him and support his decision. I would not try to stop him. I'd still love him even after he left me.

I've said to every employee I've ever hired, "I know one day you're going to leave me, and on that day, I'll congratulate you. Hopefully, you'll love me so much you'll let me be a part of that." If I tried to control them, that would be a failure, a setup for disappointment and sadness. Further, if they do leave, as some of them have, the door is always open for them to come back like a boomerang.

I don't expect anything from my clients. I don't expect them to buy or sell. When you think this way, every deal then is a bonus, a celebration, a success. And really takes the desperation away. As I'm writing this, I have a $30 million property on the market that the client is getting ready to pull from me. She simply wants too much for the apartment, and I can't find a buyer who will pay her price. I said to her, "First and foremost, I'm your friend. I support you in everything you want to do." As soon as I said that, which is the opposite of what other brokers might say, she began having second thoughts and rethinking her resolve. "I don't know what I want to do," she said. I'm betting I still sell it.

On a deeper level, I'm not in the business to keep anyone as my hostage. People who don't want to work with me are free to go. I approach any relationship this way. Let's enjoy the time we have together. People are going to come in and out of our lives. I want to be like a piece of sea grass on the bottom of the ocean floor and move with the waves, swaying left, then right, going with the flow. Fighting is too exhausting and, in my opinion, not worth the struggle.

In the end, we really can't control anyone. Even if we try by wielding our power or authority, we can only do so temporarily. And that would be a failure.

Loving Someone Who Doesn't Love You Back

In my opinion, you either love someone or you don't. I have shared my heart with people over the years, and there have been people who have crushed it. Indeed, it was sad. But I couldn't look at those times as failures. My love was pure, even if there wasn't love in return.

If Derek said that he didn't love me anymore and was moving back to Zimbabwe, I'd be incredibly sad, but I could not look at it as a failure, as crazy as that seems. I love him with all my heart, but if I try to control him, make him stay if he's not happy with New York or me, I'm just setting myself up for bigger disappointment later. I'd still love him, but I'd have to let him go and hope he would come back like that boomerang.

Don't spend your time trying to make someone see that you're special. It only leads to failure and a broken heart. I'll leave you with this relationship advice a friend gave me once: "Loving someone who doesn't love you back is like waiting for a ship at the airport. It's not going to come in."

Just know that you deserve to be loved.

Money Issues

It would be ridiculous for me to say don't worry about money, because you'd say, "Easy for you to say! You don't have to worry about money because you have plenty of it." But I haven't always had money.

Though money has never been my driving force, I do remember the moment I realized that going through life without money would be a failure I didn't want to face. It was the spring of 1992. I was fifteen years old. My brother and I left the snowed-in Alps resort in northern Italy where we were skiing with our dad and took the train south to Venice. It was magical to us, a much needed brotherly adventure escaping from the snow.

In Venice, we walked along the beautiful passages lined with name-brand stores that we hadn't heard of in Sweden. My brother bought a pair of expensive sunglasses, and, with the money I had saved working at an amusement park and chopping onions in a Stockholm restaurant, I bought a long, black coat. I still remember touching the fabric, putting it on right there and then, and walking out of the store in it. This was the very first time both my brother and I had ever bought luxury items. As we wandered through the cobblestone alleys, I remember thinking, this is how it feels to be rich, or more precisely, poor but with the hope of one day becoming rich. We were not poor in any way—in fact, we were okay—but the fancy and expensive stores of Venice made us feel poor compared to the Italian ladies and businessmen. It is all relative and is—in the end, I suppose—about how you feel. I decided then I'd work hard so that I'd be able to shop for whatever I wanted, buy the finest Italian-quality clothing, and try to help others who were feeling poor and wanted to become rich. I remember my brother and me standing in Saint Mark's Square with our purchases and looking at each other and deciding we wanted to start making real money.

Over the course of my career, I've had money problems more than once. My Internet start-up ran out of money, and we had to go back to investors several times and beg for more. When I moved to New York, I didn't have enough money to buy new sneakers. More recently, I ran out of money the first year getting my company off the ground in Sweden and Norway before the offices became profitable.

If you look at money the wrong way, it can lead to failure. Money comes and goes. You come into this world without it, and you certainly can't take it with you when you leave. When you have money issues, acknowledge that everyone has them at some point in life. Not everyone is going to be a millionaire. So think beyond the money in your bank account (or the cash stuffed in your mattress!) and focus on the things you have that make you feel rich. Remember those priceless things we discussed on page one? Loved ones, children, pets, values, beliefs, spirituality. These are the things that make us truly wealthy, and they are not for sale.

If money makes you happy, more power to you, but realize that not having it does not mean you're a failure. Money certainly provides a certain freedom. Today I could go into one of those stores in Venice and buy whatever I want, and now I don't have to constantly obsess about checking my bank account to see if

I'm overdrawn. But it's not the money that makes me happy. Success makes me happy. And all those priceless things—*experiences*—that I have that can't be bought or sold.

If you write a list of the top ten things in your life, you will probably notice that none of them are material. If they are, maybe you should reprioritize. Material things shouldn't be on anyone's true top-ten list.

Sickness

Millions and millions of people face illness every day. It's a harsh fact of life. But I can't go through life worrying about a potential health failure. When the diagnosis does come—and it will because it always does—I won't stop living each day fully (until I'm actually dead!). Sound crazy? It isn't. My goal then would be the same as my goal now: to squeeze every last drop of juice out of this delicious day, to live my life to its fullest potential.

My grandmother is a cancer survivor. Instead of running from it, she went into it, walked through that fire, and came out the other side even more alive. She told me for her it was a restart. She now appreciates every day to the fullest and the people who are in her life more. Don't wait to go through that war; start today. Make a pact with yourself to come out the other side of this day and live life big and bold. You'll never look back.

When someone dies, a lot of people feel guilt about what they should have done, should have said. That's why we mourn. I've accepted the very undeniable fact that, like everyone else on this planet, I am going to one day die, and I am determined to do all the things I can while I'm alive. When my clock stops ticking, I want to know that in my allotted time, I did all I could do. And I look forward to the next adventure. I'll meet you there.

NOW, FAIL UP!

Thomas Edison said, "I'm successful because I've had thousands of failures." I feel the same way. In life and business I've found you must have some trust in the universe. Call it flower power or whatever you'd like, but you have to believe that there is a plan for you. There is a journey you're on, and you're supposed to learn certain things, experience certain things, and go through certain things.

Yes, I know you have your difficulties. I have them, too. I know you have your pain. I have mine, too. I know, though, that if I put my problems in a pile with other people, I'd scramble to claim mine back. I'm betting you would, too. There are certainly lots of people with much bigger problems and obstacles than yours and mine. All you need to remember is that failure and frustration are stepping-stones to success. Together, let's find the opportunities in our struggles. In each of these seven scenarios, accept; don't fight; be liquid. If you think you can control these things, you are insane. My theory is that the more thankful I am, the more I attract things to be thankful for.

As I was once told, "Failure is like salt. It makes success taste delicious."

I agree. Let's eat.

CHAPTER 14

EAT, PRAY, CASH IN

Relish the Best in Life and Generate Even More Business

Imagine you're standing in the middle of a big casino in Las Vegas. I'm standing beside you. There's palpable excitement all around us. Dice are being rolled. Cards are being shuffled. Wheels are spinning. Lights are blinking. There's dinging, ringing, and bursts of applause. Big money is changing hands. Everyone is captivated by the moment.

"Let's play," I whisper, taking your hand and leading you over to a colorful slot machine. You look at me with that face of yours. You know the one. And shake your head. "I think your luck has changed. How much money do you have in your pocket?"

"Twenty-six dollars," you say. (Wow! That's coincidentally the price of this book.)

"Bet it all." I watch as you hesitantly feed the machine your money. "Great! Now, pull the lever."

You do. The reels begin spinning. See them? The first reel stops, revealing a dollar sign. The second reel stops . . . on a dollar sign! Your eyes widen. I let out a little "*Eek.*" Your heart is racing as the third reel continues to spin . . .

Could it? Will it?

Then *boom*!

Jackpot! The alarm goes off. Flashing lights and a waterfall of money! *You're a winner!* You bet it all, and look at the payoff!

Guess what, high-kicker? That's you *right now*.

You have aligned your own fortune and your future. You know who you are, you know The Sell, and we both know you're on your way to big things.

Now what? I think it's time to reap the rewards, to shower in the waterfall of your success.

What if, instead of waiting for everything to be perfect, you start living your dreams this week, *now*, making an investment in your own happiness? That's what I've always done. Remember me treating myself to a fancy Mexican dinner out and a new pair of shoes with my first commission check? That's how I believe life should be lived, marking our hard work and our achievements by finding ways to celebrate our success.

I surveyed my wealthy clients, investors in my company, and accomplished friends on what they've treated themselves to for all their hard work. So, let's talk about some ideas for fun.

LITTLE LUXURIES

I think it's total lunacy when I hear someone say they are going to cut out their daily cappuccino in order to save money. What a load of beans! We absolutely need little luxuries as an affirmation that our hard work is paying off. If you begin cutting out the things that bring you happiness, you're talking yourself into failure. Remember those gold stars on your elementary school wall? What did they (and the rewards) make you want to do? If you're anything like me, they made you want to work harder!

Further, people who don't take time off dumbfound me. Going on holiday is standard practice in European countries for maintaining health, quality family life, and productivity. By law, workers there get at least twenty days of vacation per year; some receive as many as thirty. Americans consider vacation a luxury. In fact, America is the only advanced country that doesn't guarantee vacation time. According to a study by Oxford Economics, more than 40 percent of American workers who did get paid time off didn't take it. Four out of ten of American workers said they had too much of a workload to take time off.

The result is bad news. A study by the National Institutes of Health found that of thirteen thousand middle-aged men at risk for heart disease, those who skipped vacations for five consecutive years were 30 percent more likely to suffer heart attacks than those who took at least a week off each year. Not taking vacation time is not just bad for your health; it's also bad for productivity and the economy. If employees would take one extra day of paid leave each year, the result would mean positive impact on life quality, on business productivity, and $73 billion in output for the US economy.

Besides that, don't you know success is supposed to be sweet? I simply need little indulgences in order to help me stay motivated. Don't deny yourself pleasure; instead give yourself more! Trust me. Life enhancers help you make more money. You've heard of a bucket list, right? That's an inventory of the things you want to do before you die. Keeping that list is fine. I hope you get to climb

Machu Picchu and run that marathon, but there are things you can do *this week*, *today*, *right now* to make your success sweeter.

Let's call it our Freddy's Fun Bucket. These are the things for which you say, "Screw saving money for a day that might never come; I'm doing this for myself!"

Freddy's Fun Bucket: A List of Life-Enriching Treats to Savor Your Success

1. **Fabulous dinner.** One of my favorite things to do is take Derek and my friends out for a delicious gourmet experience. Yum! I might save money by eating a salad for lunch, but dinner is on me, baby!

2. **Massage.** You need some relaxing me time. Your successful life is stressful! Get yourself a weekly or monthly massage. It's something on the books to look forward to, and studies continue to uncover the physical and emotional benefits of massage therapy. Or perhaps your insurance pays for acupuncture. Take advantage of it for both the health reasons and the nice little escape.

3. **Fancy-hotel night.** Want to feel rich? Book yourself the nicest room in your town and enjoy hotel amenities and then settle in for room service and a night of romantic fun away from home, and you will save on the expensive flights.

4. **Box seats at a concert.** Beyoncé? U2? Rolling Stones? J. Lo? Pick your favorite and pick the best seat in the house! The

two hours of dancing and singing along will be good for your soul and inspire you to work even harder.

5. **Take a lesson.** What's your passion? What have you always wanted to know how to do? Cooking? Painting? Singing? Playing the guitar? Sign up to learn how! Your mind will expand, as will your business.

6. **Get a housekeeper.** Want to feel spoiled? Come home to a clean house. There's nothing like having someone else change your sheets, scrub your toilets, and do your laundry. It comforts me to know someone is taking care of me!

7. **Spa day.** Pick your favorite flavor: manicure, pedicure, facial, scrub. Doing this regularly not only makes you look good; it makes you feel good. And what do you do when you look and feel good? You make more money!

8. **Buy something fabulous.** A shopping spree is satisfying both during and after the experience. Walk down the street in a new fantastic coat or chic sunglasses and see just how special you feel. The extra spring in your step makes you more attractive.

9. **Fresh flowers.** Fresh flowers instantly improve your mood. I have at least one bouquet in the house at all times. It's a simple, relatively inexpensive way to brighten my day, and studies have shown that people with fresh flowers in their home are less anxious and feel less worried about the future.

10. **Throw a party.** Be the one to host a party, and you're the star. Don't do it all by yourself. Book a space and a caterer to help you out. Oh, and nine times out of ten, you'll get a client or a buyer out of the experience. That is, after all, how I built my business.

Come on, high-kicker! Let's fill your Fun Bucket! I want you to really up the ante on your daily experience with nice little gifts for yourself. Improve the *quality* of your life and you'll improve the *quantity* of your business. I promise.

PAY IT FORWARD

I've spent most of this book talking all about you. How you can be the best and most successful. Does that feel selfish? Do you not like feeling selfish? Then share your success!

I have been supported and encouraged by many people over the years. Who is that person who has made a difference for you? First off, write him or her a letter and tell him or her so. Tell as many people as you can! There's no limit on being thankful for kindness. Next, knowing what the good people in your life have done for you, how they affected your life positively, make it your mission to pay it forward, to do something kind, encouraging, life inspiring, for someone else. Start with one and see how you feel.

I always love hearing the stories of the people who buy coffee for the person behind them at Starbucks, and it starts a chain of kindness. Such a simple thing to do. Recently, one such good deed—a woman paying for the caramel macchiato ordered for the driver behind her—continued being passed on for ten hours! It makes me smile to realize the happiness that manifested. That coffee was more than a little pick-me-up. That's success defined.

I certainly wouldn't want to be the one to break that goodness chain. Nor would I have any intention of doing that in life either! I feel more successful when I'm able to do something positive for someone else. And guess what? It makes me want to be more successful so that I can do more.

There are two types of people in this world: givers and takers. If you really want to make The Sell, you know that the more you give, the more you receive. In fact, you need to give *more* than you will receive. Let me be clear. It doesn't have to be money or a big deal either. Give your time, your attention, or your encouragement to another person. Take a batch of cookies to that elderly neighbor living alone. Volunteer to walk a few dogs from the local animal shelter. Offer to mentor someone.

Have some money to spare? What's a cause close to your heart? Want to find a charity organization that helps the challenged in an area specific to your interests? Charity Navigator—CharityNavigator.org—is a super way to help you figure out where to give your money, time, and efforts. The organization explains the goals and success of a wide array of charities, whether your interest is the arts, the environment, humanitarianism, children, animals, or something else.

One of the most rewarding things about my success has been my ability to give to charities close to my heart. I find such satisfaction helping abused animals and animal shelters, and aiding the sick and homeless children of Africa through Zimbabwe's Forgotten Children Organization. This year alone I was able to help build schools and give a borehole to several villages, which is a well that provides fresh water for a whole community without the risk of cross contamination from waterborne diseases and livestock. I find being able to give back makes me work happier,

and the letters that Derek and I get from the kids brings big smiles to our faces and joy to our hearts. That is, indeed, an investment that pays off.

TRAVEL

This is my favorite luxury. I saved this chapter for last because it's all about enjoying success, and I wanted to compose it in my favorite environment. As I'm writing this I'm sitting on a white-sand beach in the Caribbean sipping a rum cocktail. My palm-tree dream has come true many times over.

I covered the walls of my childhood bedroom in posters of the Maldives. In the dark, cold winters of Sweden, I loved staring at those gorgeous palm trees hanging out over the white-sand beaches and dreaming. I was obsessed. The view was the anti-winter belt, very nonspruce. Those posters became my shrine, my heaven. When I was thirteen years old, inspired by those images, I even wrote an extensive paper on palm trees. (Did you know there are about 2,600 different species of palms in the world?) Knowing my parents had no plans of taking me there, my young self decided it would take hard work and dedication on my part if I was going to be able to live that dream. I got a job in a restaurant cutting onions (same job that helped me buy that coat in Venice) and began saving my money. If the world was a big smorgasbord, I wanted to taste it all.

Life is short! That's not just a saying; it's a way of life. Even if I live to be a hundred, there won't be enough time for me to see and do everything I want to. So I collect coffee-table books of travels and rip fantasy trips and locales from magazines, and I love to sit and lose myself in those dreams. There's a little sadness knowing there's no way I can go to all those places, even if I tried, but I love working hard so I can get to as many as I can.

I've never been the kind of person who believes in working really hard so that *eventually* I can spend that money in retirement and *finally* live the good life. Stop living life in the future. What if the future doesn't come? I try to take a vacation every month, even if it's just a weekend getaway, and I always have a big vacation on the books. That's something to look forward to, a mini-retirement. Of course you want to be responsible and save for changing times, but what I've realized is that all we really have is today.

As stressful and demanding as my job and my life are, I now have the freedom to go wherever I want in the world, really whenever I want. Because I make my own schedule, I don't have a boss, and now I can afford to enjoy it. My hard work has paid off. I am that citizen of the world that I dreamed of when I was a kid in Sweden. I now get to take adventures around the world. My favorite thing to do is plan, execute, and enjoy trips to colorful destinations with my loved ones, and I'm not scared to spend money to do it.

For my wedding, I rented an island for $500,000. The joy it brought to our lives and the amazing time our guests had was worth every dime.

Derek and I both agreed we wanted to be married on the beach, so we started traveling around to potential spots on weekend getaways looking for the perfect one. I saw it almost as a mathematical formula, an equation. We wanted the greatest chance for perfect weather, a resort or hotel we didn't have to share with anyone else, great food, and a place that was accessible for guests from all different parts of the world. The moment we got on Little Palm Island, a secluded island in Key West, Florida, I knew it was the spot.

There were palm trees, white sand, and thirty chic bungalows that could accommodate sixty people. It was super private (except for the production team and all the cameras!). We figured we would have had it photographed and videotaped anyway, so why not let it be a part of my story on *Million Dollar Listing*?

Yes, I know that sounds a bit crazy and that it was a lot of money, but guess what? I knew I was only going to do it once, and now, not only do we have the most spectacular memories, but also that episode of the show, our wedding, earned an Emmy nomination.

That's success on many levels.

Call me obsessive. But travel and adventure is, for me, life's greatest reward. It makes me happier than anything else. That makes me want to say, "I do!"

FUN = (MORE) MONEY

What do you do that makes *you* the happiest, that makes you feel alive? I want you to do that as often as possible. Never get so busy making money that you forget to enjoy it. Make a deposit in the account called *you*. You must revel in the fruits of your labor. I've always found that when I'm enjoying myself I'm making more money anyway. I met big clients while sipping cocktails by the pool in Miami, flying first class to Los Angeles, and sitting at a restaurant on the beach in Saint Bart's.

The last, and perhaps most important, thing I'll tell you about making The Sell is this: *Your business expands in direct proportion to the fun you have and the adventures you take.* The hardest part of success is learning when to start enjoying it, but you must start. Knowing how to enjoy success is actually the secret to becoming even more successful. Trust me on this: Whether it's nice dinners out, exotic travel, or giving back to others, these are the moments you'll meet someone, hear something, learn something, or your mind will expand in a way that your career will be given new flight, like a kite finding a sudden puff of air.

So, go forth, high-kicker. Live your dream, make The Sell, and shine like the bright star I know you are.

EPILOGUE

From Me to You

Dear reader, my new confidant, soldier, top seller, and friend . . .

It's a cold, dark, predawn morning in New York City. I think I'm the only one awake. I sit in this metropolis, alone. The sun has yet to rise, and even the yellow cabs are sleeping. It's deadline day, and I'm up working on this pile of papers sitting on my desk. I'm ready to let the manuscript go, to turn it in, hoping it will find its way to you.

There's something I haven't told you, a ritual I did every summer of my childhood. On the last day of my family's beach vacation I'd write a letter, curl it up, and put it in an empty wine bottle my grandmother would save for me. Shoving the cork in tight was the last ritual, like writing this final page. I would gently push the bottle out into the sea, hoping it wouldn't leak or sink, with the wish that it would miraculously make its way to a distant shore and into someone's hands. In the letters, I'd always write a magical blessing that the finder's dreams would come true.

I've made wishes and thrown a lot of bottles into the water in my lifetime. Where are they all now, I wonder. Are they at the bottom of the ocean, or displayed on someone's bookshelf on the other side? I've come to think of this book like that letter in a glass bottle floating in the ocean. This morning, I'm sending it off, letting it go. And it seems it has already found its way to you.

It's odd. Isn't it? We don't really know each other, yet we do. We are similar, you and I. And now you know that I will always be cheering for you. I want you to be the best *you* can be, and my hope is that the words here have inspired you and you've realized that with these secrets and some commitment, you can and will reach your highest dreams.

I'm not big on good-byes, so let me go now. The sun is beginning its rise in New York, and the pillars of fog are starting to reach for the sky. Thank you, yes, thank you for listening to me a little while. Thanks for picking up my letter. It means so much to me.

—Fredrik Eklund
New York City

ACKNOWLEDGMENTS

Thanks to Bruce Littlefield, who helped me figure out how to make this book come to life. I have never given birth to a child, but if *The Sell* is my child, you, Bruce, are the genius—and the oh-so-kind—midwife who helped me deliver it. You made this experience so much fun and became one of my best friends, holding my hand while I pushed this book out.

To Barbara Corcoran, for being an honest and colorful icon and role model.

To my business partner, John Gomes, for lighting up my world every day.

To Douglas Elliman, for believing in my career and dealing with my big personality and a lot of high-kicks.

To my mom and dad, Jannike Wenke and Klas Eklund, for always supporting me.

To Derek, for your endless love, soft skin, perfect beard, kindest, greenest eyes, and for putting a ring on that finger on the beach . . .

To Mousey and Fritzy, for licking my salty tears when I cry.

To Sigge, my brother, for telling me to write this book.

To everyone at Avery and Penguin Random House, especially Lauren Marino, Brooke Carey, and Lindsay Gordon—the three sisters I never had.

To Bravo, for being a mirror where I have seen both the ugly and the beautiful in myself and grown from it all.

To my team members both in New York and Europe, for believing in the Eklund brand philosophy long before you had this guide in your hand.

To all my clients: There are a lot of you, and I love you all equally.

To my social media followers, you helped me write this book.

Special thanks to all the people who have a dream that we can always be better and specifically to these people who've helped me be better:

John Albino

Josh Altman

Eva and Efva Attling

Fenton Bailey

Randy Barbato

Niklas Berntzon

Frances Berwick

Anna Bohlin

Theo Burkhardt

Tom Campbell

Jordan Carlyle

Jan Carlzon

Cassandra Carpio and
    Candice Bruder

The Cayre Family

Andy Cohen

Jack DeNiro

Urban Edenstrom

Justin Ehrlich and Zach Vella

Bengt Eklund

Bror Eklund

Malin Eklund

Viggo, Truls, and Belle
Eklund

Gustaf Enblad

Oscar Engelbert

Megan Estrada

Bethenny Frankel

Nico Fredell

Bruce Friedberg and Edan
Pinkas

Dodde, Kalle, Johan, and
Christian

Ken Gillett and the Target
Marketing Team

Caroline Grane and Robert
Andersson

Josefine Grane

Ken Haber and Bryan Cohen

Dottie Herman

Hans Houeland

Dave Howe and John Sherratt

Henrik Huldschiner and Jan
Gradvall

Humany

Kevin Huvane

Jantelagen

Tobias Kagelind

Barbara and Merv Kaplan

Jay Kidd and Ken Lustbader

Danielle King

Hunie Kwon

April LaValley

Shari Levine

Jen Levy

Adam Lippes

Jennifer Lopez

Howard Lorber

Michael Lorber

Eric Lucrezia

Karen Mansour and Susan
DeFrança

Christopher Mathieson

Ryan McCormick

Donald and Mary Catherine
Mikula

Mona Örjansdotter

Clayton Orrigo

Ryan Orser

Luis D. Ortiz

Shaun Osher

Brandon Panaligan

Sarah Jessica Parker

Chris Peters

Jonas Saeed and Pia Sjöberg

Ari Schwebel and Jona
Rechnitz

Ryan Serhant

Jordan Shea

Todd Shuster

Robert Stalebrandt

Scott Stewart

Sharon Thompson

Jessica Toomer

Gunilla von Platen

Gun-Inger Wenke

Bill White and Bryan Eure

Ben Widdicombe

David Williams

Josh Wood and amfAR

Fylgia Zadig

Everyone at Douglas Elliman

Everyone at Eklund Stockholm New York and Eklund Oslo New York

Everyone at World of Wonder and the entire crew of *Million Dollar Listing New York*

A big kiss to my grandmother

And finally, thank *you* for reading this book. You are now my ambassador. Go out and live The Sell. I hope it inspires your life and that you will share it with others. There's plenty of room in this world for all of us to have great success.